Purity, Power, and Pentecostal Light

Purity, Power, and Pentecostal Light
*The Revivalist Doctrine and Means of
Aaron Merritt Hills*

C. J. BRANSTETTER

☙PICKWICK *Publications* • Eugene, Oregon

PURITY, POWER, AND PENTECOSTAL LIGHT
The Revivalist Doctrine and Means of Aaron Merritt Hills

Copyright © 2012 C. J. Branstetter. All rights reserved. Except for brief quotations in critical publications or reviews, no part of this book may be reproduced in any manner without prior written permission from the publisher. Write: Permissions, Wipf and Stock Publishers, 199 W. 8th Ave., Suite 3, Eugene, OR 97401.

Pickwick Publications
An Imprint of Wipf and Stock Publishers
199 W. 8th Ave., Suite 3
Eugene, OR 97401

www.wipfandstock.com

ISBN 13: 978-1-61097-391-5

Cataloging-in-Publication data:

Branstetter, C. J.

    Purity, power, and Pentecostal light : the revivalist doctrine and means of Aaron Merritt Hills / C. J. Branstetter.

    x + 272 p. ; 23 cm. Includes bibliographical references and index.

    ISBN 13: 978-1-61097-391-5

    1. Hills, A. M. 2. Holiness movement. 3. Holiness movement—United States. 3. Holiness churches—Doctrines. I. Title.

BT767 B76 2012

Manufactured in the U.S.A.

*To my friend and mentor, Dr. Curtis Lewis,
my parents, Russell and Gail Branstetter,
and my wife, Julie*

Contents

Acknowledgments / ix

1 Introduction / 1
2 Hills' Life and Accomplishments / 6
3 The Revivalist Doctrine and Spirit of Post-Bellum Oberlin and Yale / 52
4 The Early Development of A. M. Hills' Revivalist Identity / 101
5 The Tightening of A. M. Hills' Revivalist Canon / 156
6 The Hills Controversies, or Where Does Hills Fit? / 198
7 Conclusion / 253

Bibliography / 259
Index / 265

Acknowledgments

THE RESEARCH FOR THIS project surprised me several times through the years, requiring more archeology than I first imagined. For this reason, there are many persons to thank.

I am grateful to Marilyn at the Public Library in Vista, California and Judy at the Genealogical Library in Carlsbad, California for helping track down 150 year-old newspapers with forgotten A. M. Hills' sermons in them.

Thank you to Marion Snowbarger at the Southern Nazarene University and Sue Whitehead at Biola University for offering their help and advice every time I called.

Thank you Stan Ingersol, Meri Jannsen, and Kara Lyons at the Nazarene Archives in Kansas City. Thanks for stacks of great A. M. Hills' sermons and for very pleasant company.

I am grateful to Tina Simmons at Olivet Nazarene University Library Archives, for digging around boxes in the archives to find several of my best sources.

Thank you, Little Rock First Church of the Nazarene, for an office.

Thank you, Roger Hahn, Kevin, Adam, Neil, and Richard for encouragement on the hardest days.

I would like to express special thanks to my Drew University dissertation committee: Donald Dayton, Chuck Yrigoyen, and Harold Raser. Thank you for your patience, your years of hard work on this project, and your commitments to making the original dissertation the best it could be.

Finally, thank you, Julie, for your hard work and patience, without which this dream never would have been realized.

1

Introduction

IN 1994, PARAMOUNT PICTURES and Robert Zemeckis presented an academy award-winning movie entitled *Forrest Gump*,[1] the adventure of a mildly handicapped, soft-spoken Alabaman who makes regular, significant contributions to history without once being noticed by the history-makers around him. As the story unfolds, the main character, Forrest Gump, meets, interacts with, and even influences persons like Elvis Presley, Paul "Bear" Bryant, John Lennon, Rosa Parks, and three U.S. presidents. He inadvertently contributes to pop culture in at least three different ways, even helping Elvis Presley develop one of his signature dance moves.

An intriguing symbol, Gump can be thought of as a kind of interstitial figure of history, who influences the persons and culture around him without receiving any credit or even notice from the historians. Thus, the movie's central protagonist is an icon representing the "little guy," whose contributions are great, but whose name is overshadowed by the larger figures of history.[2]

It is very likely that American history is full of "Forrest Gumps," figures who are typically not in the history books, but whose stories, when discovered, offer insights into the worlds around them often previously overlooked. The same can be said about American *Christian* history.

---

1. *Forrest Gump*, dir. Zemeckis, 1994.

2. It is for this reason that Gump can be considered a great *American* icon. He represents the democratization of greatness—the possibility that the "little guy" can make a significant mark on history. He is the great, influential "no-name" of history.

Mostly overlooked by historians and historical theologians thus far, Aaron Merritt Hills is one such "Forrest Gump" of American Christian history. Like Gump, Hills was often in key places in American Christian history, surrounded by key individuals, and he frequently made significant contributions. Also like Gump, however, Hills for the most part has been overlooked by historians, who are often focused more on the "giants" of American Christianity than on the interstitial characters whose single or collective accomplishments are of equal or greater significance in the storyline.

Of course, to say that Hills has been *mostly* overlooked in present scholarship is not to say that he has been *completely* overlooked. In fact, his story and certain aspects of his theology have appeared in a few works of holiness scholarship. Two scholars in the Church of the Nazarene have studied the last few years of Hills' life for his significance in understanding the history of the doctrine of holiness.[3] Likewise, Hills is *briefly* mentioned in four different works on the interrelationship between the holiness and fundamentalist movements.[4] Two biographies have been penned, outlining his life and accomplishments, although only one is published.[5] While his life and parts of his theology have been considered in each of these, however, the present scholarship on Hills is still lacking.

There are three particular oversights in the present literature on A. M. Hills. The first is that research into his thought has relied much too heavily upon his systematic work, *Fundamental Christian Theology*. This is not surprising, of course. Indeed, in his autobiography, Hills states that he hopes the work will be remembered as his greatest. Likewise, it hardly requires apology to cite a theologian's systematic theology as if it were the distillation of her or his whole life's work and doctrine. The problem is that a concentration on Hills' systematic treatise neglects a very large percentage of his works. His corpus includes hundreds of articles, thirty-five published and unpublished books, and dozens of manuscript sermons that, when studied, offer a significantly different angle on Hills

---

3. Bassett, "Study in Theology"; Quanstrom, *Century of Holiness Theology*.

4. Bassett, "Fundamentalist Leavening"; Marsden, *Fundamentalism and American Culture*, 95; Lodahl, *All Things Necessary*; and Ingersol, "Strange Bedfellows," 124–27. While Hills is recognized in each of these works, it should be noted clearly that he is always only one of several theologians being considered.

5. McWilliams, "Hills: A Life Sketch"; Gresham, *Waves Against Gibraltar*.

than is possible when looking only at *Fundamental Christian Theology*. As we will see, fixation upon his systematic treatise, published in 1931 when he was eighty-three, has unnecessarily brought about too quick an interpretation of Hills as a fundamentalist, a caricature that is difficult to allow when reading this work in continuity with the first sixty years of his writings.

A second major oversight is that Hills has rarely been considered outside of his contributions to the Holiness Movement. Indeed, other than a single-page reference to him by George Marsden in *Fundamentalism and American Culture*, neither Hills' story nor his theology have ever been considered by anyone outside of Holiness and Methodist scholarship. Ironically, even though he lived nearly fifty years prior to his experience of sanctification, Hills is remembered as *only* a Holiness thinker; and although he was retirement age before he joined the Pentecostal Church of the Nazarene, George Marsden is the only scholar outside of Holiness and Methodists circles to have noticed Hills.[6]

A third major oversight is the non-comprehensive way in which Hills' thought has been treated. To put it simply, not only are the majority of his works neglected when studying Hills, but so also are the majority of his organically interrelated doctrines.[7] Often, a doctrine is excised from his larger system of thought and treated as an island; and more often than not, it is his doctrine of holiness that is the subject being treated out of context.

There are two major consequences to these oversights. The first consequence is that Hills is either misrepresented or only partially understood. As one might expect, these misrepresentations and partial pictures differ greatly, sometimes even offering caricatures that are mutually exclusive.[8]

A consequence of reading Hills as *only* a holiness figure is that his significance as a complex interstitial figure *between* various movements in larger American Christianity has been overlooked. If, as we will see,

6. Marsden, *Fundamentalism and American Culture*, 95.

7. Paul M. Bassett and Michael Lodahl begin to transcend this. Cf. Bassett, "Christology and Ecclesiology" and Lodahl, *All Things Necessary*.

8. For instance, he has been characterized as the "backbone" of the Wesleyan-holiness tradition and as a "non-Wesleyan-Calvinist," by Nazarene General Superintendent J. B. Chapman and Paul M. Bassett, respectively. He has also been called a "fundamentalist," a "liberal," and a "non-fundamentalist" by Bassett, some who knew Hills personally, and Lodahl and Ingersol, respectively.

Hills' identity, doctrine, and means[9] are more complex than those of a simple early twentieth-century Holiness figure, then his broader significance becomes more obvious. Because, even as a Holiness figure, Hills drew from so many sources at once, study of his thought begins to unravel the complex interrelationships between the movements that burgeoned and warred with each other at the turn of the twentieth century.

This book seeks to remedy these oversights by considering A. M. Hills' doctrine and means comprehensively. From the perspective of the whole of his corpus, we will see that all of the present categories used to describe Hills either misrepresent him entirely or are not sufficiently broad. As we will see throughout the book, Hills is best summed up under the broad heading of "revivalist." He was a revivalist all of his life. As a youth, he embraced the Finneyite religion of his family; as a student at post-bellum Oberlin College and Yale Seminary, he systematized a revivalist way of thinking and practiced revivalist means; as a man, he purposefully chose a revivalistic identity for his ministerial paradigm. Indeed, his conviction that revivalism is the truest representation of Christianity was so strong that he forged for himself a tight canon of revivalist doctrines and means against which he contrasted all else.

Because Hills is not a well-known figure, chapter 2 will consider his life, accomplishments, and personal relationships. Since L. Paul Gresham has provided a commendable biography of him, chapter 2 will be as brief as possible. It will particularly highlight those events and relationships that are the most central in understanding Hills' revivalist identity and his significance in American Christian history.

Chapter 3 will review the revivalist context of the nineteenth century from which Hills drew. Specifically, it will outline several of the doctrines of post-bellum Oberlin College and Yale Seminary, the two schools Hills attended from 1867–71 and 1871–74, respectively. The works of Charles Finney, Asa Mahan, Henry Cowles, and James Fairchild of Oberlin and Noah Porter of Yale will be given special treatment.

Chapter 4 will outline the revivalist theology and means of Hills' early ministry. Between the years 1874 and 1895, he pastored four Congregational churches and served as an itinerant evangelist twice. Chapter 4 will be built upon hundreds of pages of manuscripts sermons

---

9. The revivalists' word "means" is similar to the word "methods." A comprehensive definition of "means" will be provided in chapter 3.

that lie mostly un-mined in the archives of several institutions and in the newspapers of the cities in which Hills ministered.

Chapter 5 will begin with the story of Hills' experience of Spirit baptism and the theological shifts necessary for him to come into this experience. Next, the chapter will address the changes in his soteriology, epistemology, ecclesiology, and eschatology after his sanctification and the development of his mature holiness soteriology. The chapter will conclude with the narrowing of his holiness theology into a Holiness-eradicationist position.

Having outlined Hills' revivalist doctrine and means in chapters 4 and 5, we will next apply the study to explain Hills' complex relationship with several movements of the early twentieth century. Specifically, chapter 6 will address the relationship, the similarities, and the differences Hills had with the Keswick-holiness, Pentecostal, and Fundamentalist movements and his own church, the Congregational Churches of America.

Drawing from the comprehensive study of A. M. Hills' life and accomplishments, his revivalist doctrine and means, and his complex relationship with several movements, we will, in chapter 7, make some brief concluding remarks concerning the interrelationship of movements at the turn of the twentieth century. We will see that a study of Hills in fact serves a greater purpose than simply understanding the man himself better. Apprehending the revivalist vision, doctrine, and means of this "Forrest Gump" of American religious history also illumines at least one of the key issues that caused the splintering of American Protestantism at the turn of the twentieth century.

2

Hills' Life and Accomplishments

While some of the accomplishments of A. M. Hills are familiar to many in the Holiness Movement, most of the details of his life remain largely unknown in broader scholarship. For this reason, this chapter will consider the life and accomplishments of A. M. Hills and provide the historical context in which to interpret the development of his revivalist theology and means.

Fortunately, Hills penned an autobiography. An unpublished work completed in the ninth decade of his life, "Autobiography" will provide the basis for much of this chapter.

Alongside this work, two other biographies also exist. In 1936, just one year after Hills' death, H. E. McWilliams wrote "Rev. A. M. Hills, D.D. LL.D.: A Life Sketch." Then, in 1992, L. Paul Gresham contributed what could be considered the definitive biography of this figure, *Waves against Gibraltar*.

THE FAMILY HERITAGE OF A. M. HILLS

The story of the development of A. M. Hills' revivalist identity begins before he was born with the shaping of the spirituality of his extended family. L. Paul Gresham begins his biography of Hills with Henry Ford's words, "'Blood is the strongest thing in the world.' What [Ford] implied about the importance of heredity in determining human character and achievement is true in the case of Aaron Merritt Hills. Judging from the evidence, A. M. Hills' ancestors possessed the same combination of piety, dependability, and intellect that characterized him."[1]

Hills provides a clear picture into this combination of Christian virtues in his unpublished autobiography. Offering many examples from his family history, Hills recalls as far back as 1632 when William Hills immigrated to Massachusetts from Kent, England.

For the purposes of this study, we will not consider everyone that Hills includes in his account. One of the most important parts of the prequel of A. M. Hills' theological development, however, is the story of his grandfather, Hezekiah Hills. His grandson writes, "My grandfather was a godly old Congregational deacon who lived a beautiful and useful life."[2] Of this man, Gresham states that he was "a typical Puritan colonial . . . a devout Congregational deacon."[3]

Born in Windsor Locks, Connecticut, in 1794, Hezekiah would have been a boy when in 1801 the Plan of Union was forged between the Congregationalists and the Presbyterians. Thus, for the larger percentage of his life Hezekiah knew only Congregationalism under the Plan.

In 1812, Hezekiah moved to Bristol, New York, where he met Olive Warren and married her two years later. Bristol remained the home of Hezekiah and his new bride for a short time before they moved east. Hezekiah and Olive had seven children, all of whom lived to adulthood.

What is most significant about Hezekiah Hills' establishment in Bristol is the time period. As Congregationalists living within twenty miles of Rochester, New York, in the decades of the 1810s and 20s, the Hills were in the right place at the right time to be influenced by the revivals of Charles G. Finney. The Rochester revivals, as with all of Finney's meetings, reached far beyond the boundaries of the city. Of the breadth of the Finney revivals in western New York, historian Robert S. Fletcher writes, "Developments at Rochester had attracted so much attention by this time [February 1831] that hundreds came from a considerable distance and the church buildings were taxed to capacity."[4]

---

1. Gresham, *Waves Against Gibraltar*, 15.

2. Hills, "Autobiography," 3 (1). The first page number designates the original handwritten version of "Autobiography" on file at the Nazarene Archives, while the parenthetical number gives the page number for the type-written version on the shelf at Point Loma Nazarene University.

3. Gresham, *Waves Against Gibraltar*, 15.

4. Fletcher, *History of Oberlin*, vol. 1, 20.

While it is only indirectly related in "Autobiography," it would appear that the Hills family was swept up into the revival. Evidence to this fact is seen in that three of Hezekiah's children, two daughters and a son, went to Oberlin College to study for missionary service. Unfortunately, both girls died before reaching the mission field. The third, however, Amos B. Hills "spent years as a missionary on the field until his health broke. Then he settled in Minnesota, and helped to build up Christian institutions in that New [sic] state."[5]

It was another of Hezekiah's sons, Henry Cleveland Hills, who became the father of the subject of this study. Born in 1816, Henry was as deeply stamped by revivalism as the rest of his family. Henry was a lifelong supporter of the Congregational Church, especially in its revivalist form.

At some point in his young adulthood, Hezekiah moved the family east to Pekin, New York, approximately thirty miles northwest of Rome. In Pekin, Hezekiah served the community as the chairman of the school board. It was in this town that a young Methodist woman, Julie Ann Chesbrough, came to work for the school. She lived with the Hills for a while and was thus introduced to the man who would later become her husband, Henry.

Julie was an intelligent young woman from a family that had been in America since 1630. Of his mother's family, Hills writes, "From a human standpoint . . . the Chesbrough family was more intellectual and socially prominent than the Hills family."[6] A family of shrewd business minds, the Chesbroughs were often among the most wealthy and influential members of the various cities in which they lived.

Somewhere around the turn of the nineteenth century, the Chesbrough family became Methodists and remained so for at least four generations. Julie's father Abram and his two brothers, Isaac and Jacob, were prominent leaders in the church. Jacob and one of Isaac's sons became Free Methodist ministers. Isaac also apparently shared deeply in the Methodist vision, for he used some of his wealth to send his niece,

---

5. Hills, "Autobiography," 4 (2).
6. Ibid., 6–7 (4–5).

Julie, to a Methodist academy.[7] There she studied languages and art and, as her son puts it, "got the Methodist stamp upon her inmost soul."[8]

It was immediately after her training that Julie moved to Pekin. She and Henry married in 1840 and wanted to move west. Chicago was too far for Hezekiah's blessing, so Henry and his new bride chose Dowagiac, Michigan, instead. A settlement of only four log cabins, Dowagiac increased considerably in population when the Hills arrived in 1842 and started a family. The Hills lived in Dowagiac for the next twenty years and were instrumental in its development into a more established community. Henry assisted in the erection of the first church building in the city, a Baptist church. Later, he helped build the second, a Congregationalist church that the family subsequently joined.

A. M. HILLS' EARLY YEARS

It was in Dowagiac, in 1848, that Aaron Merritt Hills was born. He was the second son and the fourth out of five children born to Henry and Julie Hills. The settlement of Dowagiac was being transformed into a town in the year of his arrival. Hills writes, "The day I was six weeks old my father drove through the first street of Dowagiac, the day it was opened, with the baby lying in his lap."[9]

Hills' childhood was filled with the realities of frontier life. His son, James, recalls stories of what had already become a vanishing frontier by the 1870s and 80s. James recalls:

> We never tired of Father telling of his pioneer boyhood days. Many times he came down from his attic bedroom in the log cabin to find Indians sitting about the fireplace warming themselves. Grandfather was friendly toward them and they often made his cabin their stopping place. When Father and his brother worked in the hay meadows, they bound hay around their legs to keep the rattle snakes [sic] from biting them, and often snakes ran down their pitchfork handles as they loaded hay on the wagon. The skies were often darkened by flights of wild pigeons, they

---

7. Ibid., 9 (6). Hills is uncertain, but he thinks his mother went to the Troy Conference Academy.

8. Ibid.

9. Ibid., 14 (9).

often roosted around their farm in such numbers as to break off the limbs from the trees.[10]

Frontier life was, of course, much less romantic than James Hills could have understood as a child at his father's feet. It was in A. M. Hills' fourth year of life that the harsh realities of sickness hit the family twice. While no one in the family was ever bitten by a rattlesnake, the diseases of the area had almost as deadly a bite; Julie contracted malaria. Hills recalls that his mother was in bed for six months and that there was a period of six weeks when the family assumed she would die.

His mother in bed and his father busy in the fields, the three-year-old Aaron was left with a young girl who took very poor care of him. Of his first major illness, Hills writes, "It was soon found that from lack of proper care and diet my system was cankered through and through. The glottis was eaten out of my throat, and it was feared I never could talk plain again. My digestive organs were greatly injured. My bowels came out, and they would hold me up by my feet, head-downward, for my bowels to go back into my poor little body."[11]

Nearly dead from malaria and assuming that she would not live to see her son grow into a man, Julie wrote a letter for Aaron to read at age ten. She sealed it and placed it in her Bible. In it she wrote that she had given her son to Jesus Christ to be a preacher of his gospel. She also added a prayer to the letter that he would accept the calling. To everyone's surprise, however, the matriarch of the family recovered and even lived to see the son of her dedication and prayer serve as a minister for sixteen years before she died at seventy-eight.

While this illness stunted Hills' growth for more than a decade, his spiritual and intellectual development came so early as to earn him the label "precocious." At ten, he experienced conversion. From Congregationalist and Methodist stock, Hills' family frequented revival meetings whenever and wherever they were held. This particular time it was held at the Baptist church that Henry Hills had helped erect. Over seventy years later, Hills recalls that a "good gospel was preached and three of us children were converted." Young Aaron was moved to go down to the front pew for prayer. "God did the talking. He told the little

---

10. McWilliams, "Hills: A Life Sketch," 84.
11. Hills, "Autobiography," 15 (10).

fellow ... to just believe that as he did his part, God did His part. The boy believed and, praise God! <u>in a moment, the burden was</u> gone!"[12]

After his conversion, Hills did not have to wait long to experience various challenges to his Christian identity. He recollects, "The boys discovered that I was a Christian and they began to call me 'Little Jesus.'"[13] This was, of course, earned to some extent. Taking his mother's tutelage very seriously, he began to live a life that would be recognized as different from the other children. He writes: "I do not pretend ... that I lived as much like Jesus as I ought to have done. I wish now I had lived more like Him; but I did live at least so that they could see a difference between their conduct and mine. I was carefully taught by my mother not to play marbles or even pins for keeps, as that led to gambling; to keep the Sabbath day holy; to abstain from vulgarity and profanity; to speak the truth and be scrupulously honest."[14]

As already stated, Hills was a precocious child. While still very young, he was pleased to earn a dollar from his mother for reading the entire Bible through before his eighth birthday. Of course, later in life, he was more pleased that he had filled his mind at an early age with "moral ideas and principles of righteousness and the great fundamentals and essentials of our Divine religion."[15]

Hills, of course, excelled at more than just reading. By age twelve, he was studying Latin, higher arithmetic, and algebra. Referring to himself in the third person, he writes, "The stunted little runt pushed right on ... At the age of fourteen he weighed 90 lbs. and was reciting geometry with men that were twenty years old. He had a college course in sight as the goal of his ambition, while his schoolmates were sneering at piety and industriously cultivating evil habits that would make scholarship forever impossible."[16]

As mentioned above, Hills' mother came from a family of gifted businessmen. Her brothers exemplify the fact that it had not skipped their generation. It was in Hills' teenage years that talk of apprenticeships in business began. Two of Julie's brothers were A. M. Hills' namesakes. One brother, Aaron Chesbrough, was a wholesaler on Wall Street

---

12. Ibid., 19 (12). Underlining, Hills'.
13. Ibid., 20 (13).
14. Ibid., 21 (13).
15. Ibid., 18 (11).
16. Ibid., 23–24 (14–15).

and had no children of his own. He talked of adopting his nephew and making him his heir. Consumption, however, ended his career and life in his thirties.

A. M. Hills' other namesake, Merritt Chesbrough, also had no children. A generous man and a committed Free Methodist, Merritt endowed a college in Chili, New York, that as a result of the endowment bore his name, A. M. Chesbrough Seminary.[17]

Hills went to work for this uncle the next two summers. His aunt, however, was never pleased when her husband talked of adopting heirs. She made it very difficult on any apprentice that came to live with them. Near the end of the second summer with Merritt, Julie visited Niagara Falls. When she found her sister-in-law so "hard, unloving, unmotherly, chilling, [and] repelling" she took her son back to Michigan. Probably not leaving under the best of terms, Hills recalls that the parting left Merritt hurt and disappointed. Julie told her brother that the Hills family was not so poor that they would allow their son to be snubbed and crushed. She also stated that somehow they would get him educated for the ministry.[18]

At sixteen, Hills was still very small for his age, a meager one hundred pounds.[19] It was the summer after he turned sixteen, however, that this finally began to change. His father traded the farm for a house in Mount Vernon, Ohio, three plots of land, and $6,000. Henry Hills managed a store for Julie's third brother, Alonzo, reportedly the richest man in Toledo. The Hills left their son in Dowagiac for the rest of the summer to help bring in the harvest and plow for the next season before joining them in Ohio. After a summer of raking, binding, plowing, milking, and playing baseball every evening for exercise, Hills finally overcame the physical retardation he received from his sickness at three.

The move to Ohio opened the door for Hills to go to college in two ways. First, his father's new job provided the financial means.[20] Secondly, the pastor of the Congregational Church in Mount Vernon, T. E. Monroe, provided a positive role model.

Hills writes that Monroe and his wife were "both graduates of Oberlin College and had the Finney revival stamp upon them. We could

17. The school exists today as Roberts Wesleyan College.
18. Ibid., 26–27 (19).
19. He writes that his brother at the same age weighed 165.
20. Ibid., 30 (20).

scarcely have fallen into a more helpful church."[21] Already deeply influenced by revivalism from both sides of the extended family, the Hills fit right in with a pastor who "as much expected to have a revival every year as he expected to preach." Of Monroe, Hills continues, "I doubt if that good man ever failed to have an outpouring of Spirit annually during his entire ministerial life."[22] Thus, Monroe seems to have provided a good example for Hills of how an evangelistic, Oberlin pastor conducted religion.

Of course, Monroe provided more than just a positive role model. He also wrote Hills a commendation for application to Oberlin College when he graduated high school.

What is significant in each of these examples from Hills' childhood and adolescence is the degree to which he was influenced by revivalism, especially the revivalism of Charles G. Finney and of Oberlin College. His family's commitment to revivalistic religion kept them in churches and circles where their values could be instilled in their children. Of course, revivalism was not hard to find in the 1850s. Indeed, Perry Miller, when speaking of the "terrific universality of the Revival" writes, "The dominant theme in America from 1800 to 1860 is the invincible persistence of the revival technique."[23]

At the heart of this religious revivalism was Charles Finney. In Miller's estimation, the force and breadth of Finney's ministry was exemplified in his book, *Lectures on Religion*. "Overnight it sold 12,000 copies in America . . . No religious leader in America since Edwards had commanded such attention; no one was to do it again until Dwight Moody. Hence Finney's book stands . . . as the key exposition of the movement, and so a major work in the history of the mind in America."[24]

Given the heritage and context of Hills' early life, it is of little surprise that he chose Oberlin College for his intellectual preparation. Indeed, if he even considered any other college he offers no evidence of it in "Autobiography." He simply states, "Oberlin was born great. It had so many things that insured its future, it almost might be called finished before it started."[25]

21. Ibid.
22. Ibid., 31 (20).
23. Miller, *Life of the Mind*, 7.
24. Ibid., 9.
25. Hills, "Autobiography," 32 (21).

OBERLIN COLLEGE

While for his first years at Oberlin, Hills was ambivalent about his mother's wishes for his career, he nevertheless received his first formal theological training there. He arrived at Oberlin just two years after the close of the Civil War, entering as a student in the preparatory school. By his second year he was ready to join the college as a sophomore.[26] Concerning the theological department at Oberlin the year Hills arrived, Robert Fletcher writes that it had "declined again almost to the point of extinction in 1867 when it contained only eleven students."[27]

If such statistics bothered Hills, he never mentioned it. There were many reasons he chose the college, not the least of which was the faculty. Indeed, it probably thrilled him to have such a low teacher to student ratio. While Asa Mahan had already been gone seventeen years, the halls were still graced by Charles Finney, John Morgan, and President James Fairchild.

Hills writes of other figures as well, each outstanding in his estimation. "The all around genius of the faculty was Professor Charles Henry Churchill whom every body [sic] loved . . . Dr. Dascomb taught Botany and Chemistry . . . My favorite professor was Judson Smith the finished scholar who required the most of his Latin pupils . . . John M. Ellis taught us Evidences of Christianity, Logic, [and] Mental Philosophy. Professor Penfield taught us Greek."[28] While already retired from Oberlin, Henry Cowles was still often on campus.

By 1867, a large percentage of Finney's duties at the school had already been dropped. Nevertheless, he still taught "Pastoral Theology," and it thrilled Hills to take it under him. As well, Finney continued as pastor of the college's church until 1872, the year after Hills graduated.[29]

Right up until his last year of service Finney remained the primary reason students chose Oberlin over others colleges. Hills was no exception to this general rule. Over twenty-five years after he left Oberlin, Hills still stood in awe of Finney. In 1898 Hills wrote of him as "the mighty Finney, 'full of faith and of the Holy Ghost,' by far the mightiest

---

26. Hills File, Oberlin College Archives.
27. Fletcher, *Oberlin College*, vol. 2, 710.
28. Hills, "Autobiography," 34 (22).
29. Fletcher, *Oberlin College*, vol. 2, 899.

preacher I ever saw stand before an audience."[30] Finney's preaching left an indelible stamp upon both Hills' memory and his personal style of delivery.

Besides its key icon, Finney, Hills also recollects fondly the extraordinary spiritual and prayerful atmosphere of the school. There was an abundance of daily and weekly times when the students and faculty of Oberlin joined together in corporate prayer. Hills remembers that the largest prayer room was capable of seating one hundred and was often overflowing.[31]

Scholastically, it did not take long for Hills' abilities to become apparent. Indeed, he perhaps distinguished himself a little too much his first year. Hills writes that he had been working on a written oration in hopes of presenting it to an 800-member forum, chaired by Professor John Ellis. Ellis would read the submissions and choose a monthly speaker for this particular forum. Apparently, Ellis considered Hills' written oration too fine in quality to be the original work of a freshman. When he was consulted, Judson Smith agreed. They insisted that Hills write another oration, which he did. It was only years later that Hills found out that, after submitting the second oration, the two professors were amazed by the level of his work and were embarrassed at having "done him a wrong."[32]

Noting his oratorical abilities, Hills' parents suggested two career fields, law and preaching. His father wanted him to be a lawyer, while his mother had long since dedicated him to the Lord. Vacillating between these two options for most of his time at Oberlin, he did not decide until his senior year. Eventually, however, he chose the ministry, although not without internal conflict. He dramatically recalls, "The burden grew in weight until it became unendurable . . . I shall never forget how . . . I knelt down solemnly and told the Lord that I would resist His Spirit no longer but would consent to be poor and preach the Gospel. O what a burden was lifted from my soul! A great problem was settled once for all."[33]

Determined from that point on to become a minister, Hills turned his intellectual training fully in that direction. So it was at Oberlin that

30. *Pentecostal Messengers*, 34.
31. Hills, "Autobiography," 35 (23–24).
32. Ibid., 39 (26).
33. Ibid., 44 (29).

Hills received his first formal training in the doctrinal, philosophical, and ethical themes that shaped his thinking for rest of his life.[34] As a result of the confluence of the minds and personalities at Oberlin during Hills' attendance, several key ideas were taken with him upon graduation.

First is the movement of Academic Orthodoxy. Academic Orthodoxy was a movement of like-minded university presidents and academicians devoted to teaching Common Sense philosophy and to disseminating it to every level of society. In the era just prior to the full development of university specialization, the college president embraced a much more active role in the community, especially in teaching. The presidents of Academic Orthodoxy were typically ministers and taught the capstone class of moral philosophy at their respective universities, combining theology, science, and ethics with variations on Thomas Reid's Common Sense philosophy.

Of course, Academic Orthodoxy was broader than this. In his article "Academic Orthodoxy and the Arminianizing of American Theology," James E. Hamilton defines the movement. "It is not sufficient to identify Academic Orthodoxy solely in terms of Scottish realism in this country. Rather, it is the union of Scottish philosophy with freewill, revivalistic Evangelicalism in the above designated old and new institutions in this country that all the Academic Orthodoxy had in common."[35]

Thus, many of the schools led by the Academic Orthodoxy were revivalistic in nature or at least had a history related to revivalism. Oberlin was among the foremost of the revivalistic Academic Orthodoxy. Under the presidencies of Mahan and Finney, the school was committed radically to both revivalism and Academic Orthodoxy. Even under Fairchild's much less radical leadership, the school was still committed to revivalism and Common Sense. He led and taught as a president of the Academic Orthodoxy.

Perhaps one of the most important attributes of Oberlin's Academic Orthodoxy was its scholastic nature. Quoting D. H. Meyer, Hamilton makes the connection between Academic Orthodoxy and the whole structure and vision of higher education in the nineteenth century. Hamilton writes:

---

34. It should be noted that all of these themes had already been mediated to Hills *via* the revivalistic and Oberlin-saturated religious affiliations of his youth. Nevertheless, his first *formal* education in these themes was at Oberlin.

35. Hamilton, "Academic Orthodoxy," 56.

Meyer points out that the American system of higher education in the nineteenth century has been aptly described as "Protestant Scholasticism" because of its ambitious effort "to organize all knowledge, including knowledge of the cosmos, of men, and of society, into a consistent and intelligible whole," establishing a correspondence between secular knowledge and basic Christian principles.[36]

All of the above characteristics of this movement deeply influenced A. M. Hills. Academic Orthodoxy, its scholastic vision, and its significance will be considered in greater depth in the next chapters.

The second major idea that made a deep impact upon Hills at Oberlin was its eschatology, which can be summed up in one word, postmillennialism. A natural (and perhaps even necessary) corollary to the scholastic vision of Oberlin was the goal of a thoroughly reformed world. Finney's particular articulation of the relationship between revivalism and world reform was the vision that captured Hills. According to Finney, with the continual and exponentially growing effects of revivalism, the world could be converted in a matter of a few decades or even years. With the conversion of more and more individuals, Finney taught that social reform would become easier to accomplish, eventually climaxing in the global peace of a substantially Christianized world. This new Christian world characterized by peace would last one thousand years, the Christian millennium. Thus, for Finney and therefore for Hills, the first priority in world reform was mass conversion through revivalism.

Oberlin's bedfellow doctrines of moral ability and moral necessity in personal and social ethics were also foundational truths taught during Hills' time there. Between these two doctrines Oberlinites like Hills allowed no room for vice and even frivolous amusements. Avoiding not only sin and vice, but even the doorway or the slippery slopes leading downward, A. M. Hills' lifelong theology and ethics were permeated with the code of ethics he received while at Oberlin.

It was also at Oberlin that Hills received his first systematic training in the doctrine of the moral government of God. Embracing Finney's teachings, Hills maintained this cosmology and its implications for the present and eternal realms for the rest of his life.

---

36. Ibid., 53.

These four streams of thought intersected Hills' life again and again. They provided a foundation for his theological development that did not change from the 1870s to the 1930s.

Interestingly, although Hills' mature theology includes a doctrine of perfection, he did not acquire it from Oberlin.[37] Oberlin perfectionism was in disrepute at the school long before Hills arrived.[38] The only introduction to this doctrine he recollects is reading Asa Mahan's *Baptism of the Holy Spirit* in his senior year. He writes that the book "deepened all former impressions and filled me with longings for the great blessing."[39] To Hills' mind, however, the book had not been clear enough on the conditions for the blessing. He writes, "Its directions were meager and indefinite where they should have been full and plain, and I missed the way."[40] Still, the central hope of the book intrigued him enough to seek the advice of Finney. Hills recalls: "I went to President Finney's home and asked for light. The old saint knelt and prayed with me, putting his dear hands on my head; but he gave me no instruction, and left me in darkness as dense as ever. I marvelled [sic] at it then, but understand it now. His own philosophy, erroneous in two or three particulars . . .

---

37. Here a humble correction of two interpreters of Hill is in order. Both are built upon the false assumption that Hills studied holiness at Oberlin. First, in recounting the battle between Hills and R. A. Torrey over the doctrine of baptism with the Holy Spirit, George Marsden writes, "Hills had studied holiness doctrine at Oberlin." Marsden, *Fundamentalism and American Culture*, 95. The second correction is of Paul Bassett's comments in a 1981 article. He writes, "[Hills'] deep and sincere commitment to Christian perfection comes by way of Charles G. Finney, not by way of Wesley." Bassett, "Christology and Ecclesiology," 81. As we will see in chapter 4, Hills' early sermons contain no evidence of a *systematic* doctrine of sanctification or holiness. Hills did not, in fact, "study" holiness doctrine until the 1890s. Again, the unquestioned assumption that because Hills' later theology is permeated with holiness and perfectionist language, he must have gotten it from Oberlin is fundamentally incorrect. Robert S. Fletcher is clear that from 1850 to 1865, the several events culminating in the decline of the original radicalness sufficiently killed the earlier perfectionist tendencies of Oberlin's "founding" and "peculiar" years. Long before Hills' arrival in 1867, "Sanctification was seldom mentioned, and then apologetically. Oberlin was too successful and too respectable now to be heretical." Fletcher, *Oberlin College*, vol. 2, 920.

38. Fletcher, *Oberlin College*, vol. 1, 886–922, esp. 920.

39. *Pentecostal Messengers*, 34. Interestingly, Hills does not mention that he read Mahan's book at Oberlin in "Autobiography."

40. Ibid., 34.

unfitted him to lead others into that blessing of which he himself was such a marvelous example."[41]

The disappointed Hills continues that as he moved on from Oberlin College to Yale Seminary he found the spiritual atmosphere of the latter too "depressing," and soon thereafter "the longing for the blessing subsided. The baptism with the Holy Ghost was never mentioned, and nothing definite and tangible about sanctification, that I can recall, was ever spoken in my hearing by any professor or minister during all those important three years when I was being trained to preach the Gospel of Christ. I am amazed at this now."[42]

Thus, although Hills' later theology would be deeply committed to a doctrine holiness and sanctification, its roots in his system of thought cannot be attributed to his Oberlin training.

In 1871, Hills graduated from Oberlin with a Bachelor of Arts degree.[43] The next fall, after having considered several options for graduate school, he entered Yale Divinity School.

YALE SEMINARY

The next major step for Hills was graduate school. Having excelled at Oberlin, he felt compelled to take his own theological development to the next level. Yale Seminary was his choice.

While Oberlin had been Hills' one and only choice for college, he writes that several graduate schools courted him, including Harvard and Yale. Indicative of his immersion in and acceptance of the central concerns of Academic Orthodoxy and Common Sense philosophy, Hills chose Yale over Harvard. He writes, "The current of unbelief was altogether too strong at Harvard. If I had given up the practice of law to preach, I wanted to have something to preach worth while."[44]

This is not say, however, that Hills was entirely happy with Yale. In fact, this serious Oberlin graduate was not pleased with the irreverence

---

41. Ibid.

42. Ibid., 35–36. Hills continues, "Rev. R. A. Torrey, of Chicago, says the same, and declares that in all his years at Yale, he never heard the baptism with the Holy Ghost mentioned, save once by a student, and then he did not know what the man was talking about." Ibid., 36.

43. Hills File, Oberlin College Archives.

44. Hills, "Autobiography," 46 (31).

and coarseness of the average fellow-student at Yale; at least, he was fairly impressed with the faculty. Noah Porter was inaugurated president only two weeks after Hills' arrival. Hills was already familiar with Porter as his *Human Intellect* had been a text at Oberlin. In *A Hundred Years of British Philosophy*, Rudolf Metz notes that this book was a major American contribution to Common Sense philosophy. Indeed Porter's contributions to this philosophical stream were so significant that he is one of only two names Metz's lists as significant *American* contributors.[45]

While the transcripts of individual seminarians from the 1870s are no longer on file at Yale there is sufficient evidence to suggest that Hills had the opportunity to sit under lectures with Porter. Although the Yale catalogs from 1871–74 confirm that Porter did not teach any required classes in the seminary during this period, each of the three catalogs for these academic years offered seminarians the opportunity to sit in on Porter's "lectures in the Academical Department . . . free of charge, provided that they do not interfere with the regular studies of the Seminary." For the 1871–72 academic year, President Porter lectured on "Mental and Moral Philosophy"[46] and the next two years "Natural Theology and Moral Philosophy."[47] Again, it is uncertain how many of these lectures Hills might have attended. It is highly unlikely, however, that he would have missed the opportunity to study with the man whose *Human Intellect* had been a key text at Oberlin.

Although Porter's lectures were not required at Yale Seminary during Hills' years, the opposite is true concerning Samuel Harris' classes. Another recent addition to Yale, Harris had just arrived from Bowdoin College and was installed in the chair of Systematic Theology during the inaugural ceremony of Porter. From his time under Harris' tutelage, Hills recalls that there "was no trimming or trifling with the great foundation and essential doctrines of Christianity."[48] Of this mentor who helped him deepen the doctrines he learned at Oberlin, Hills writes, "[Harris] taught us day by day for three blessed years practical truths of the gospel

---

45. Metz, *British Philosophy*, 30. Metz refers to only J. M'Cosh and Noah Porter by name as American proponents.

46. *Catalogue of Yale College, 1871–72*, 53.

47. *Catalogue of Yale College, 1872–73*, 73; *Catalogue of Yale College, 1873–74*, 75.

48. Hills, "Autobiography," 50 (33).

that we could incorporate into our lives and preach to others with the hope of extending the kingdom of God and winning souls."[49]

Hills also studied Greek under Timothy Dwight and remembers the tedious classroom exercises that helped shape his later linguistic and exegetical skills. George P. Fisher was Hills professor of church history, although Hills believed that his "literary productions are his true monument."[50]

Another relationship that Hills developed at Yale was with Reuben A. Torrey. Two very serious Congregationalists about the same age, these classmates had enough in common to build a strong friendship. Torrey esteemed Hills highly, asking him to preach his ordination sermon. It is unfortunate, however, that a significant doctrinal rift formed between them in the first decade of the twentieth century. So significant was this rift that by the 1930s, when Hills sat down to pen "Autobiography," he wrote virtually nothing concerning this relationship.

During his three years at Yale, Hills spent summers in practical ministry. The summer after his first year, he preached at a Congregational home mission station in East Madison, Maine. He states that while he and the church faced "satanic opposition" from the Universalist Church with which they had to share a building, the Lord nevertheless gave them a revival. Twelve were converted that summer and joined the church.[51]

The next summer, he preached at a Congregationalist church in Ravenna, Ohio, upon a recommendation from his former pastor, T. E. Monroe. Hills impressed the church so much that they asked him to become their pastor and even waited a year for him to graduate.

In 1874, Hills completed a B.D. at Yale and moved to Ravenna to begin pastoral ministry. Shortly after graduation, he married Altha Alamanda Ford, an 1870 Oberlin graduate with whom he had been engaged for three years. They were married May 26, 1874.[52]

---

49. Ibid., 50 (33).

50. Ibid., 52 (34). Hills speaks specifically of Fisher, *History of the Christian Church, The Reformation*, and a later volume of essays defending miracles and other evangelical doctrines. Likely, Hills means Fisher, *Manual of Christian Evidences*.

51. Hills, "Autobiography," 54 (35).

52. *Alumnus Report*, 1904, Hills File, Oberlin College Archives, 2.

HILLS' FIRST PASTORATE, RAVENNA, OHIO

A week after the Hills' marriage, an installation service was convened at the church in Ravenna. Hiram Mead of Oberlin was elected moderator and was so pleased with his former student that after two hours of questioning he slapped him on the back and affirmed, "Well! my boy, Yale hasn't spoiled you." Decades later, Hills seems to smile as he recalls, "I was glad to feel that I was still in the old Oberlin faith that had already brought such blessing to the world."[53]

Many of the characteristics of Hills' mature pastoral theology and ecclesiology were apparent immediately after his installation at Ravenna. One was his lifelong commitment to and development of the underprivileged. Hills was disturbed by alleged reports that the previous pastor had neglected everyone in the church except the leading families. He writes, "I determined that I would be the pastor of all but especially of the poor, the humble, the lowly, the nobodies; and if any body [sic] just had to be neglected it must be the well-off somebodies. In process of time it revolutionized the whole church and its standing in the community."[54]

Another clear characteristic of Hills' mature pastoral theology and ecclesiology was his use of the revivalistic, soul-winning techniques he had learned at Oberlin. Hills writes of this passion, fanned into flame after reading Mahan's *Baptism of the Holy Spirit*. While he admits that the book did not do for him what he had hoped while at Oberlin, (that is, find the blessing of Spirit baptism), he remembers that "the book quickened in me a great desire to be a soul-winner, and I began my first pastorate at Ravenna, Ohio, with that purpose burning like a flame in my soul."[55]

Also Hills' reformist ecclesiology played itself out in several practical ways while at Ravenna, but nowhere as much as in his support of the Woman's Christian Temperance Union. A rising leader in the movement, Mrs. Mary A. Woodbridge, was a member of his church. She was so impressed with her pastor's persuasive oratorical ability that she asked him to speak regularly for the Ohio Union. One year, Hills recalls, he delivered forty-two addresses from the northern tip of Ohio to its southern

---

53. Hills, "Autobiography," 56–57 (37).

54. Ibid., 57–58 (38).

55. *Pentecostal Messengers*, 36. Hills continues, "During my ten years' pastorate, God gave me in that and neighboring churches with whom I labored in revivals, five hundred souls."

border in favor of a Constitutional amendment for temperance. During his ten-year pastorate in Ravenna, there were only two townships in his own county he had not visited for speaking engagements.

Beyond his work for temperance, Hills also led revivals for churches in the area. His straightforward approach did much to facilitate the conversion of many and stir a desire for social reform everywhere he went. In his own church, he regularly preached clear messages on social and personal ethics, often speaking against the evils of card-playing, dancing, theater-going, and intemperance.

Three children were born into the Hills family while in Ravenna. Nellie Ford was born September 11, 1875. Henry Merritt came December 13, 1876 and Anna Althea January 26, 1882.[56]

In his autobiography, Hills offers no reason for his resignation from the Ravenna church, but simply states directly that he bundled up his wife, children, "a car-load of household goods, and a train load of regrets that [he] had not been a more faithful preacher, a better pastor and a more Christ-like man."[57] After a pastorate of ten years, Hills moved on in 1884.

HILLS' SECOND PASTORATE, ALLEGHENY, PENNSYLVANIA

Hills' next pastorate was in Allegheny, Pennsylvania, just across the river from Pittsburgh. The large twin-city area offered many challenges and new avenues for ministerial development. As he had before, Hills applied his usual vigor and was recognized for his community leadership. His oratorical gift caught the attention of area newspapers and many of his sermons were published. The papers were not the only ones who noticed his oratorical abilities, however. The labor unions of the city also chose Hills to preach their annual sermon.

Recognized as a strong leader, Hills was also asked to serve as the Congregational representative for "The Committee of Seventeen," an interdenominational group composed of community leaders from every "orthodox" denomination in the county. Hills recalls that they organized

---

56. *Alumnus Report*, 1904, Hills File, Oberlin College Archives, 2.

57. Hills, "Autobiography," 63 (41). One wishes that Hills had offered an example of what disappointed him in his own leadership during his first ten years of pastoral ministry. Concerning specific regrets, however, Hills is completely silent.

many events during his six years in Allegheny, but the most memorable was a revival with Dwight Moody. Of Moody, Hills' only comment in "Autobiography" is that this great man dodged the subjects of holiness and sanctification and thus "no minister ever reported any special increase of power as a result."[58]

As in Ohio, Hills maintained a willingness to hold revival meetings in his second pastorate. He writes, "No pastor asked for help who asked in vain. God's Spirit was graciously poured out in every protracted effort."[59]

Hills found the Allegheny church building was in poor condition when he arrived. Unable to overcome the financial burdens of renovation or relocation, Hills and his congregation put together a plan to raise outside support. The plan involved Hills traveling and raising money for several months. In August 1886, however, just six weeks before he was scheduled to leave, Hills' wife was stricken with a gall stone attack and died.

Hills, however, kept his appointment for raising money. His former pastor while at Yale, John E. Todd, asked him to speak at The Church of the Redeemer. William M. Taylor of the Broadway Tabernacle also offered Hills his pulpit. His tour took him as far north as Portland, Maine, and as far west as Chicago. Upon his return, Hills had almost ten thousand dollars, with which the church built a house of worship that could seat eight hundred.

A widower for only six weeks before his fundraising trip began, Hills always considered it providential that he found someone to care for his children while he was away. Hulda Jane Freischkorn was an impressive twenty-one year old, who would later became his second wife. As one of thirteen siblings, Hills mused, she knew children, and as a Methodist, she knew God. Hills asked her to marry him within a few months of his return to Allegheny. They were married almost exactly one year after the passing of Altha.[60]

Among his many stances, Hills always held a strong posture against secret orders. From his Allegheny years, he relates a story concerning some pastoral advice he once gave on the subject. Apparently, a deacon's son asked him if he should join a Masonic lodge. Anti-Masonic since

---

58. Ibid., 82 (53).
59. Ibid., 70 (46).
60. Ibid., 76 (50).

his days at Oberlin, and as blunt and boisterous as ever, Hills quickly retorted, "If I wanted to be a crooked and dishonest and dishonorable man and wanted protection in wickedness, I would join the Masons."[61] Hills' suspicion about the man's question were confirmed when later this same young man, while embezzling funds for, among other things, church furniture, was able to avoid court because his Masonic brothers settled the bill between them.[62]

It was during the Allegheny pastorate that Hills began to perceive dissonance between his views and changes within the Congregational Churches of America. While he refused to leave the church of his youth for more than another twenty years, Hills relates a story that marks the beginning of the split, an encounter with Washington Gladden.

Near the end of his time in Allegheny, Hills was asked to serve in the ordination and installation of a pastor in Stubenville, Ohio. Typical of Congregational polity, the oldest minister present was appointed moderator of the examination of the candidate. Among others, Dr. Washington Gladden was on the committee and was the obvious choice for moderator, both in age and stature.

Gladden is remembered today for his contributions to the then burgeoning movement of the Social Gospel. From Hills' perspective, however, Gladden was simply one who "coveted above all else a reputation for scholarship."[63] Of course, Hills' stated contention with such covetousness was that it often went hand in hand with "the viper of 'Higher Criticism.'"[64]

When in the interview, neither Gladden nor any other elder asked the candidate his thoughts on higher criticism, Hills, who was the youngest minister present, asked several questions.[65] To his disappoint-

---

61. Ibid., 83 (54).
62. Ibid., 83–84 (54).
63. Ibid., 85 (55). Underlining Hills'.
64. Ibid.
65. In a 1922 article in the *Herald of Holiness*, Hills recalls his questions. He writes that he asked, "1. Do you believe in the Bible as the book of God specifically and peculiarly inspired as no other book is inspired? and do you believe its account of creation? 2. Do you believe in Abraham as a historic character, or was he a myth? 3. Do you believe that Moses led the children of Israel out of Egypt and wrote the Pentateuch? 4. Do you believe in the Psalms as largely a work of David? 5. Do you believe in one Isaiah or many? 6. Do you believe in Daniel as a historic character? 7. Do you believe in the real Deity of Christ? 8. Do you believe in the sacrificial death of Christ as the divinely

ment, one of the members on the board blurted out, "O Hills! You are progressing backwards!"[66] The young minister was appointed with only a single vote against him.

While in Allegheny, Hills and his new bride had a son, the first of four children with his second wife. James Aaron Hills was born October 13, 1888.[67]

Much to his disappointment, Hills' pastorate in Allegheny ended abruptly in his seventh year. In a regular business meeting, a member made an unexpected motion to vote on the pastor for the coming year; Hills was stunned. Since fewer than 15 percent of those voting wanted a new pastor, many expected Hills to stay for life. Shocked and hurt by the unexpected motion, however, Hills took it as a sign for him to leave. He resigned within a few days.

HILLS' THIRD PASTORATE, OLIVET, MICHIGAN

In 1890 Hills moved to Olivet, Michigan, where he served as pastor of Olivet College Church. Olivet College was founded by John J. Shipherd on the pattern of Oberlin. Since his oldest children were almost college age, Hills was delighted at the opportunity, thinking the move would facilitate their education.

The summer of that year, Hills' parents, Henry and Julie Ann, died. Occurring within three weeks of each other, the deaths hit the Hills family hard. It was at his mother's coffin that he recalls thinking, "There is the one that made me all I am for the service of God and Christ!"[68]

Hills' time at Olivet College Church began and ended mostly in disappointment. Until the arrival of Hills, the church had always been led by various faculty members of the college taking turns preaching alongside their regular teaching duties. Under the leadership of Joseph

---

appointed atonement for the world's sin? 9. Do you believe in the necessity of the new birth by faith in Christ? 10. Do you believe in the eternal punishment of the wicked who knowingly and wilfully reject Christ?" Hills, "Progressing Backwards," 4–5.

66. "Autobiography," 87 (56). While attacked in this setting, Hills seems to take some comfort in the vindication that the minister who shouted out against him eventually "progressed out of the ministry to a Jersey-cow ranch." "Autobiography," 88 (57).

67. *Alumnus Report*, 1904, Hills File, Oberlin College Archives, 2.

68. Hills, "Autobiography," 93 (60).

Estabrook, the college and church decided that after half a century, it was time to call a full-time pastor. A. M. Hills was their choice.

With his usual vigor and straightforwardness, he poured himself into the task before him. While the church grew numerically and financially, however, Hills' leadership at Olivet lasted only two years. It would appear between the lines of Hills' "Autobiography" that there was some opposition to the idea of a full-time pastor even before Hills arrived. While it is partially a matter of speculation, both Hills and his biographer agree that the opposition to change probably had much to do with the fact that the pastoral office had been used as a steppingstone to the college presidency for many decades. So when the president of Olivet College resigned during Hills' second year, there may have been some behind-the-scenes maneuvering over who would be the president's successor.

As was the case at the previous church, a surprise motion was made at a regular business meeting for a pastoral vote. Again, even after an overwhelmingly positive vote, the motion itself was enough for Hills to resign. Such similarities stir Gresham to ponder whether or not Olivet Church was using Hills' own Allegheny resignation story against him.[69] Whether it was a carefully laid plan or not, however, the interweaving of church and college politics was more than Hills was ready to engage. He left Olivet after only two years of service.

In 1891 Hills and his second wife had their second child. Charles Finney Hills was born June 5, 1891. An interesting namesake, Charles Finney would be the first of three children named after revivalist leaders. Mary Woodbridge Hills was born in 1894 and Dwight Moody Hills was the last child, born in 1897.[70]

HILLS' FIRST TERM AS AN EVANGELIST

For the next year, Hills turned his attention to another calling in which he had already proven himself, evangelism. Offered a position by the Michigan Congregational Home Missionary Society to be their state

---

69. Gresham, *Waves Against Gibraltar*, 68. Hills also states that his next year of ministry was so rewarding that it was far better than "staying in Olivet and contending with Prof. ____ for a position!" Hills, "Autobiography," 102 (66). Blank underlining, Hills'.

70. *Alumnus Report*, 1904, Hills File, Oberlin College Archives, 2.

evangelist, Hills busied himself with itinerant preaching for a year. A great success in many ways, Hills enjoyed the year of service.[71] While his ministry bore obvious fruit, however, an unnamed preacher persuaded the Home Missionary Society to drop Hills from service the next year as he "was doing great harm to Olivet College!"[72]

HILLS' FOURTH PASTORATE, SPRINGFIELD, MISSOURI

In the summer of 1893, Hills was offered a church in Springfield, Missouri, which he promptly accepted. Missouri was far from New England and Hills muses that many people would, in all innocence, say that they had never heard of the "Congressional Church."

The shortest of Hills' pastorates, his Springfield ministry was largely spent in relief to the poor. The "Panic of 1893" left the city struggling. Although he had been in the city for only a few weeks, Hills' gifts of leadership were recognized and "he was appointed to a committee for solicitation of food to relieve the destitute of Springfield."[73] Unfortunately, beyond this Hills offers nothing in "Autobiography" concerning this year-long pastorate, leaving one wondering why it was cut so short.

HILLS' SECOND TERM AS AN EVANGELIST

Frustrated by his experiences and early resignations at the Olivet and Springfield churches, Hills began to consider evangelistic ministry again. In 1894, he moved to Oberlin, Ohio, enrolled two of his children in college, and began itinerant revival preaching.

In this same year, Hills began a voluminous writing career.[74] His former parishioner and fellow temperance reformer, Mary Woodbridge,

---

71. Hills, "Autobiography," 106–7 (68). Hills measured his success according to the eight new churches he organized and the 852 new Congregational members that were added in that year as a direct result of his ministry.

72. Ibid., 107 (69).

73. Gresham, *Waves Against Gibraltar*, 71.

74. Hills, "Autobiography," 117–18 (75). Hills mentions that the librarian at Oberlin wrote him that he "had written and contributed more books to the College library than any other one of the forty thousand students who had ever been connected with that institution." 75, 118.

"was stricken with paralysis and went home."[75] Remembering the eloquence of their former pastor, the family asked Hills to write her biography. The 401-page book was finished by the summer of 1895, *Life and Labors of Mrs. Mary A. Woodbridge.*

That winter Hills held what John Barnard, in his history of Oberlin from 1866–1917, called "the last important" revival at Oberlin.[76] While Barnard calls it an "important" revival, he couches it within the story of the decline of revivalism at Oberlin. He writes, "The accounts stressed the 'entire absence of all gush and mere sentiment,' but, regardless of the preacher's restraint, the college students were mostly indifferent. The revival did not result in many conversions, although it was claimed it had contributed to a deepening of student spirituality."[77]

Hills' recollection of the event is strikingly different. "God gave us a great outpouring of the Spirit and the most successful revival the Church had ever had since that great man's [Finney's] translation. I remember I spoke fifteen times a week in that meeting and Rev. A. N. Currier of the theological department . . . expressed surprise that any preacher could do it. There were about two hundred conversions."[78] Hills goes on to cite very warm and unsolicited testimonials from Profs. E. J. Bosworth and A. N. Currier and Congregational pastors Henry M. Tenney and James Brand.[79]

Hills' glowing commentary in "Autobiography" is not the only positive report, however. *The Oberlin Review* also published an article concerning the revival services of 1895 that seems to echo the evangelist's recollections. "Mr. Hills began work without any attempt at union with other churches, and absolutely none of the advantages of combination and organization of the community. . . . In spite of these circumstances, however, Mr. Hills' preaching began at once to draw large audiences and converts began to multiply . . . The results have been most gratifying.

---

75. Ibid., 118 (75).
76. Barnard, *Oberlin, 1866–1917*, 104.
77. Ibid.
78. Hills, "Autobiography," 119 (76).
79. They write, "Mr. Hills has preached for nearly three weeks in connection with the Congregational Churches of Oberlin with marked success. His power as a preacher compares favorably with any evangelist we have heard. He is thoroughly educated, is a man of good judgement, and unobjectionable methods, is entirely evangelical, thoroughly consecrated to his work, and profoundly in earnest." Hills, "Autobiography," 119 (76).

More than a hundred persons . . . have signed the cards in the inquiry room, besides large numbers of children in the public schools."[80]

HILLS' BAPTISM WITH THE HOLY SPIRIT AND EARLY LITERARY CAREER

The year of 1895 was the most life-changing year of Hills' life. Not only was it the year of his first published book, but it was also the year he experienced what he usually called his "baptism with the Holy Spirit." While the former took only a few months, the latter required the whole year.

It was a Congregational layman living in Oberlin, L. C. Presler,[81] who first introduced Hills to the Methodist literature on sanctification. As the leader of a "holiness band," Presler had dozens of books on the subject. Hills spent the first three or four months of 1895 reading numerous books from this man's library. "He would loan me a book, and if I did not buy it, he would take it back and loan me another. I soon began to realize that this was the greatest truth that had ever entered my mind. I was especially amazed that I had a library of fifteen hundred volumes and had mingled with Methodist ministers through my entire ministry and had not learned about this distinctive doctrine of Methodism."[82]

Hills continues that after he finished writing the biography of Woodbridge, he read nothing but holiness literature. He was captured by the subject. With a hunger growing inside of him, Hills writes that he desired the blessing of Asa Mahan, A. T. Pierson, and Dwight Moody that would increase his ministry as the blessing had increased theirs.

In May, Hills held revivals throughout Massachusetts. He writes that he was asked providentially to assist Rev. G. S. Butler, "who with his wife had received the baptism with the Spirit and had much literature on the subject in his library."[83] It was on May 29, 1895, that Hills first prayed to receive the blessing of Spirit baptism. He laments, though, that he "retained a lingering doubt."[84]

---

80. Photocopy from *The Oberlin Review*, Hills File, Nazarene Archives.
81. *Pentecostal Messengers*, 37.
82. Hills, "Autobiography," 122 (78).
83. Ibid., 125 (80).
84. Ibid., 126 (80).

It was not until December, after reading Varley's *The Sin of Unbelief*, that Hills "determined not to be shut out of the blessing any more by a wicked unbelief so cruel and dishonoring to Jesus."[85] Ignited by S. A. Keen's *Faith Papers* to confess to God, Satan, and his own heart that the promise of God was for him, Hills sought Spirit baptism vigorously for a day and a half. He prayed and repeated the lines, "I can, I will, I do believe that Jesus saves me now."[86]

On December 7, 1895, Hills rose from bed with the divine suggestion in his mind that he should "thank God for the blessing as a thing received, just as F. B. Meyer advises." He continues, "I began to do it, when speedily the Holy Spirit came to bring the witness that <u>God is true. A tide of joy swept into my soul</u> and I cried out, <u>O bless the Lord! Praise the Lord! He does come and fill my soul!</u>"[87]

Hills notes that, just as the blessing had done for Mahan, Pierson, and Moody, his ministry was enlarged. "My ministry to Christians was enriched and deepened and extended beyond measure. A whole realm of new texts were [sic] opened to me with a new meaning, which I had never thought of preaching on before."[88]

As was stated above, it took Hills a full year to find the blessing. While we will see in chapter 5 the reasons it took so long, Hills always believed that God allowed the process to be extra slow in him so he would be a better teacher on the subject.[89] At one point during the struggle, Hills even slapped his leg in either frustration or excitement and promised that, if he ever found this blessing, he would write a clearer book on the subject than had ever been written. Later, when retelling this promise to a friend, "the brother . . . answered instantly, '<u>If you do write a book on holiness, you must answer the Oberlin philosophy</u>,' and he loaned me a pamphlet written by Pres. James A. Fairchild, on '<u>Perfection in Oberlin Theology</u>.'"[90] Very soon thereafter, Hills began to write and within four months he completed a 386-page book, entitled *Holiness and Power for*

---

85. Ibid.

86. Cf. Keen, *Faith Papers*, 16.

87. Hills, "Autobiography," 127 (81).

88. Ibid., 128 (82).

89. See Hills' comments on the speed of Finney's baptism with the Holy Spirit and the resulting inability to teach correctly on the subject. Hills, "Autobiography," 99–102. Cf. Hills, *Life of Finney*, 218–28.

90. Hills, "Autobiography," 129–30 (83).

the Church and the Ministry. In it Hills cites dozens of writers on the subjects of sanctification and Spirit baptism.

Near the end of the summer of 1896, the excited author began searching for a publisher. Much to his disappointment, however, the Congregational Publishing House was not interested in the work. One more event adding to the dissonance Hills felt between him and his church, their rejection of his book was only a prelude to what he would later consider to be their rejection of revivalism as a whole. Although he states that he was not surprised when they rejected his book for publication, he was "grieved to have [his] own people turn away from such a blessing."[91]

After more failures with holiness publishers, Rev. E. S. Dunham suggested that Hills send the manuscript to Martin Wells Knapp. Knapp decided to publish not only the book, but was actually thrilled with it, writing Hills, "You have struck out on a new line of thought, and it is the best book in the world on the subject."[92]

Once printed, the book immediately propelled its author into repute in the Holiness Movement. It was deemed by many to be an instant holiness classic. In "Autobiography," Hills seems proud as he writes about presiding Methodist elders and bishops who sold or gave away dozens and sometimes even hundreds of copies at their respective districts or at conferences. By the end of Hills' life it had been translated into nine languages. It was, however, only the first holiness book of many for Hills.

Pentecostal Light was written next. In it, we see a glimpse of how Hills' earlier Oberlin and Yale methodologies and doctrines begin to come together with his newfound experience and articulation of Spirit baptism. Epistemological clarity in the sanctified mind and Oberlin ethics concerning prayer, card-playing, dancing, and theater-going form the heart of this book.

The almost instant success of *Holiness and Power* opened many doors for Hills' career in the Holiness Movement. Within even a few short months of its publication, the author received multiple invitations to preach in Methodist and holiness churches and camp meetings. At a meeting in Chicago, four of Hills' sermons were written down by a shorthand reporter and published by Knapp as *The Whosoever Gospel*. Hills always marveled at the speed with which this book was published,

---

91. Ibid., 131 (83).
92. Ibid., 131 (84). See also Hills, *Holiness and Power*, 3–4.

the reporter turning a publish-ready manuscript over to Knapp in just four days. An exposition of four scriptural texts, the book is a defense of the Arminian position on salvation. Tearing away at Calvinism's doctrine of the decrees, Hills, like his Oberlin mentors, laid the locus of salvation wholly in the will of the person. Whosoever will believe, Hills proclaims, will be saved.

Another book came as the result of a question by Rev. Dr. Haydn in a streetcar in Cleveland. When asked by Haydn if he knew a suitable book for training children in church membership, Hills answered that he did not. When the idea immediately came into his head, "Write one yourself," Hills decided to go to work. The result of the conversation was several months of intensive consideration on how to lead children into conversion, sanctification, and church membership. Hills published his conclusions in *Food for Lambs*.

HILLS' EDUCATIONAL AND CONTINUED LITERARY CAREERS

Asbury College

Over the next three years, Hills moved more exclusively into holiness circles. Deeply impressed with Hills, the president of the National Campmeeting Association for the Promotion of Holiness, C. J. Fowler, invited him to speak at multiple campmeetings each summer. It was within these new circles that Hills was eventually asked to become an educator. In the summer of 1898 he led a campmeeting in Wilmore, Kentucky, where his homiletic style and scholarly depth caught the attention of several from Asbury College. He was soon invited to teach theology and began that fall. As would become his regular teaching style, Hills drew sharp distinctions between the several contemporary schools of thought. Of his teaching at Asbury, he writes:

> There was a keen intellectual stimulus about the work, day by day searching for the truth amidst all the conflicting schools of theology, Unitarian and Trinitarian, Calvinistic and Arminian, Atheism, Pantheism, Modernism, Agnosticism, Russelism, Christian Scienceism and all the rest of the cults and fads and isms of the day, and finding at last the gospel "once for all delivered to the saints," which a man can preach without fear or misgiving, without excuse or apology, and have the endorsement

of the Holy Spirit, and even a rich harvest of souls for the heavenly garner.[93]

While he thoroughly enjoyed his time at Asbury, Hills had not even finished his first academic year there when he received a letter informing him that he had been elected a new university's founding president. A holiness group in Texas had a thirty-seven acre plot adjoining a campground near Greenville where they wanted to start a university with Hills' help. Intrigued and excited by the offer, Hills accepted the invitation and moved as soon as the spring semester ended. One student from Asbury, Will Huff, went with him.

Texas Holiness University

In May 1899, Hills arrived in Greenville, Texas. A campmeeting was in progress and as the "shed" was usually packed beyond its capacity of two thousand, Hills promptly sat down in the straw between the front row of benches and the platform. It was there that he first heard Bud Robinson preach. Of the experience, Hills recalls, "I remember sitting on the ground in the straw and looking up into his Spirit-illumined face and weeping as I heard him tell the story of his sinful early-life and his conversion and entrance into the ministry and sanctification. I remember how humble I felt as one utterly outranked and outclassed by this selected saint of God!"[94] The two became instant friends and formed something of a mutual-admiration society, especially after Robinson lived with the Hills for several months in 1900.[95]

Texas Holiness University literally had to be built from the ground up, a fact that seems to have pleased its first president immensely.[96] In Hills' words, "I accepted the presidency of a thirty-seven-acre cow-pasture with a multitude of briars, centipedes, scorpions and blacksnakes thrown in for good measure, and one student, Will Huff!"[97]

---

93. Hills, "Autobiography," 139 (88).
94. Ibid., 142 (90).
95. McWilliams, "Hills: A Life Sketch," 77.
96. As we will see more closely in chapter 6, Hills shaped his presidency after the vision of Academic Orthodoxy and his universities after the model of Oberlin. Thus, the fact that T.H.U. began with such humble beginnings seems to have pleased Hills immensely. It was simply one more characteristic that made it like his beloved Oberlin.
97. Hills, "Autobiography," 141 (90).

While facing a daunting task with virtually no capital up-front, Hills applied his usual ceaseless vigor and inspirational preaching and leadership to secure money and subscriptions for building projects. Often speaking twice a day, he inspired the region with a vision of a holiness university and by the end of the summer there were twenty-eight student enrolled.[98]

That summer Hills also had to write a university catalog and build a faculty. He and the Texans dreamed of a Christian liberal arts college.[99] A baccalaureate curriculum was developed with emphases in theology, religious education, business, and fine arts. Beyond these emphases, the school also required classes in ancient and modern languages, philosophy, literature, mathematics, and science. Dr. and Mrs. D. S. Arnold were chosen to teach music while Hills' son, Henry, taught philosophy and science. All Oberlin graduates, they shared Hills and their alma mater's philosophy of liberal arts education, the education of the "whole man."[100]

While his ability to lead and motivate the surrounding communities was exceptional, Hills notes one setback the first year. One "good brother," who was intending to invest $1,000 in the school, was caught up in the third blessing of fire "heresy" and when he found out that Hills "was going to hold the college back from all the devil's fads, and keep it on safe and scriptural lines he took his money and went elsewhere." After recalling this story, Hills simply comments, "It is a well known trick of Satan, when he cannot suppress holiness, to sidetrack it, or switch it off into some foolish excess of unscriptural absurdity . . . It is only good things that are counterfeited."[101]

Setbacks notwithstanding, Hills was able to build up the school and the community at an amazing speed. By the end of his seventh year, the area boasted "an incorporated town of over eight hundred population, surrounding a live young college of nearly four hundred enrolled students, with a good classical, theological and musical course, a strong faculty, three substantial buildings and only $7,000 of debts."[102]

---

98. Ibid., 148 (94). By the end of the first year, there were 200 enrolled. Gresham, *Waves Against Gibraltar*, 122.

99. Again the specifics of Hills and the Texans' vision for a liberal arts university will be considered in detail in chapter 6.

100. Fletcher, *Oberlin College*, vol. 1, 341–72.

101. Hills, "Autobiography," 148 (94).

102. Ibid., 150 (95).

Of all the accomplishments of Hills' seven years, however, nothing was greater to him than the revivals and those who "prayed through" at the altars of the school. By his estimates, about fourteen hundred people were saved or sanctified at the college altar.

While Hills' schedule of teaching, preaching, and administering was more than most would want to accept, it did not stop him from traveling as well. One particular trip to Chicago marks a significant moment in Hills' theological journey and illustrates the lines that were being drawn more clearly between movements just after the turn of the twentieth century. Not only did Hills feel the need to contend with the above mentioned three-blessings "counterfeiters" in Texas, but also with the "suppressionists"[103] in Illinois.

What would become Hills' lifelong argument against the "suppressionists" began with his trip to Moody Bible Institute, where his friend and Yale classmate, R. A. Torrey, was president. Because the school had already begun to embrace a Keswickian doctrine of holiness, Hills' position that the depraved nature within a person is thoroughly removed in entire sanctification received only a negative hearing. Indeed, when at mealtime the murmurings against his position grew loud enough for Hills to overhear, he assumed that the school and the Keswick movement no longer considered themselves to be a part of the Holiness Movement. When in the next year Moody Bible Institute did not send a single representative to the General Holiness Assembly in Chicago, Hills was disturbed enough to write a book. Going on the apologetic offensive, he wrote three books against what he considered to be the false, Keswickian articulation of holiness.

The first book, *Pentecost Rejected: and the Effect on the Churches*, was published within a year. In it, Hills makes an explicit theological connection between the pentecostal baptism with the Holy Spirit and complete cleansing from sin. Hills' development of an interesting pentecostal primitivism begins to show as he argues that as long as the church

---

103. "Suppressionist" was a term used pejoratively within the Holiness Movement for those who preferred the Keswick Convention's articulation of the doctrine of holiness. The Keswick Convention, typically more Reformed in their conceptualizations, did not teach Hills' "eradicationist" position that the sin nature is thoroughly "eradicated" from a person in sanctification, although they did allow that sin's effects could be sufficiently counteracted or suppressed. As we will see in chapters 5 and 6, from Hills' exegetical and experiential position, this seemed to be an incorrect and anemic holiness doctrine.

of the first centuries renewed their experience of cleansing by Spirit baptism, their expansion remained unchecked. This new paradigm offered Hills an explanation why the church of the latter centuries was not experiencing the same rate of growth. A church that rejects Pentecost is a church without power. Thus, Christian ministers can no longer afford to reject Pentecost, the only sufficient power to make the church effective in its mission to reach the world for Christ and concomitantly usher in the millennium. Of course, what Hills meant specifically is that the church can no longer reject the message of the eradication of the sin nature by the cleansing baptism of the Holy Spirit.

A year later Hills published a second book on the subject, *The Secret of Spiritual Power*. Following exactly the same logic of his previous work, Hills strengthens his argument, stating it more clearly, that God will never offer his spiritual power to a person still harboring sin in the soul. The only soul that can be fully empowered by God for service is the soul that has been emptied completely of sin. Thus, the eradication of sin *is* the secret of spiritual power.

Although Hills did not write another book on this subject for another decade, he continued to spearhead the anti-suppressionist position. In 1912, he published *Scriptural Holiness and Keswick Teaching Compared*, an extensive work, where he attempted to accomplish exactly what the title implies. The first half of the book is devoted to brief expositions of dozens of scriptural texts. In this section he defines the Holiness Movement's differentiation between sin and sins, as well as their twofold soteriology.[104] His terms defined and his exegetical foundation set, Hills then contrasts this with the several writings of R. A. Torrey, F. B. Meyer, A. J. Gordon, and others, showing how their central affirmations concerning holiness are at odds with his plain, scriptural holiness.

Beyond his two books against the Keswick variation of holiness theology, Hills also wrote five other books while in Texas. An apologetic for holiness theology for those of more "traditional" or pre-modernist

---

104. Quoting Adam Clarke, Hills offers some introductory definitions, "'Sin exists in the soul after two modes or forms: (1) in GUILT, which requires *forgiveness* or *pardon*; (2) in POLLUTION, which requires *cleansing*. GUILT, to be forgiven, must be *confessed*; POLLUTION, to be cleansed, must also be *confessed*. In order to find *mercy* a man must know and feel himself to be a sinner, that he may fervently apply to God for pardon; but in order to get *a clean heart* a man must know and feel its depravity, acknowledge and deplore it before God, in order to be fully sanctified." Hills, *Scriptural Holiness and Keswick*, 10.

methodologies, *Holiness: Not a Modern Fad Run by Cranks* was published in 1902. In this short book Hills presents an historical theology of the doctrine of sanctification. As the title implies, the book defends the holiness adherents against the accusation that they are a bunch of cranks, (i.e., "nuts") teaching a brand new doctrine with no precedent in Christian tradition. For rhetorical effect, Hills traces the doctrine of eradication of sin by Spirit baptism backwards from 1902 to show just how old the doctrine is. Each time he moves farther back in time he concludes that the doctrine must at least be as old as the example just cited.

Hills first traces it back to the 1894 statement of the bishops of the Methodist Episcopal Church, South, concluding that "the doctrine then is at least eight years old."[105] He then traces it back through John McClintock of Drew University, Bishop Elijah Hedding, Francis Asbury, Adam Clarke, John Fletcher, and John Wesley. Of course, still needing to prove that holiness is not a *modern* fad, Hills is forced to trace it back even farther. Madame Guyon "received the baptism with the Holy Ghost, Roman Catholic though she was."[106] Likewise, George Fox "was filled with the Holy Ghost, and with that sanctifying baptism he received the enduement of power, the very thing we are preaching today."[107] Further, Philipp Jakob Spener and August Hermann Francke were sanctified and "kept the fires of piety burning in their hearts in dead universities and churches . . . But that, too, is modern."[108]

From Spener and Francke, he leaps directly all the way back to New Testament times. The apostles in Acts received the cleansing blessing of Spirit baptism. This, of course, is still too recent for Hills' apology. He next traces it back to Malachi's preaching, Isaiah's cleansing with a coal of fire, Moses' exhortations for Israel to be holy, and finally to Abraham's physical circumcision.[109] With these he concludes, "Here then is a distinct second blessing, heart cleansing, holiness experience such as we are advocating now, that took place thirty-eight hundred years ago. A

---

105. *Sparks from Seven Hammers*, 74. Unfortunately, I could not locate an original copy of *Holiness: Not a Modern Fad Run by Cranks*.

106. Ibid., 82.

107. Ibid.

108. Ibid., 82–83.

109. Ibid., 84–85.

modern fad! I should say so! . . . The person who talks about it as a modern notion of cranks simply advertises his ignorance."[110]

While in Texas Hills also wrote two biographies, *The Life of Charles G. Finney*, mentioned briefly above, and *A Hero of Faith and Prayer: Life of Rev. M. W. Knapp*, both first published in 1902.

While the years from 1897 through 1902 were an incredibly productive period for Hills' publications, the busy administrator and teacher refused the pen for most of the next three years. From 1902 to 1905 he found time to write only *The Tobacco Vice*, a rather blunt compilation of medical findings, gross descriptions of tobacco habits, and horror stories concerning tobacco usage.

Around 1905, he wrote *Backsliders and Worldly Christians*. In it, Hills allegorizes the fall and restoration of Peter, applying it to the moral and intellectual streams of Christianity in the early twentieth century. Soon thereafter came a collection of ten of Hills' most favored sermons, *Dying to Live*. Then in his last year in Texas he put together two essays in a single volume entitled *Christian Education and Anglo Israel*. In the first half of the book, the college president outlines his philosophy of education. This published address clearly bears the Oberlin emphasis upon education of "the whole man."[111] Hills also outlines and defines his vision of a Christian holiness university. The second half of the book is Hills' exposition of the thesis that the ten lost tribes of Israel migrated to England after their exile and became the Anglo-Saxon people. Drawing from the key literature on the subject, Hills reveals his general adherence to this movement. Useful to some extent in the interpretation of American historical, political, and evangelical identity, it is arguably the most intriguing of Hills' writings.

While Hills built many friendships in Texas, one seems particularly worthy of notice. As was mentioned above, "Uncle Buddy" Robinson and Hills held a mutual respect for each other from the moment they first met. As highly as Hills' thought of Robinson, however, while Hills' reputation was beginning to skyrocket in the Holiness Movement by 1899, Robinson was still mostly unknown. Feeling that Robinson was not half as appreciated as he should be, Hills wrote to *The Standard of Philadelphia*, the *Revivalist* of Cincinnati, *The Herald of Holiness* of St. Louis, and *The Christian Witness* of Chicago. Apparently, the

110. Ibid., 85.
111. Fletcher, *Oberlin College*, vol. 1, 341–72.

recommendations immediately helped establish Robinson outside of the South for within a few weeks he received an invitation for a series of meetings at First Methodist Church, Chicago.

While the meetings were a great success, the twelve weeks of work resulted in a relapse of Robinson's epileptic seizures. He recovered within three months, but after this always required a travel companion. Will Huff agreed to serve in this capacity, which gave his own ministry a new impetus as well. Some months after their original travel agreement, C. J. Fowler wanted to appoint Robinson to a series of conventions across the country, but questioned Hills about Huff. Upon Hills' endorsement Fowler took them both together. Hills writes, "When they got across the country, Will Huff was one of the most sought-after camp-meeting preachers of the entire nation, and so was Buddy. I fondly believe I had something to do with the success of both."[112] Indeed, it is very likely that Hills' recommendations did propel both into broader, nationally recognized careers.

It would be an understatement to say that Hills' seven years in Texas were very productive. Naturally, his abilities began to be noticed by others who had visions for new holiness universities. During his time in Texas, Hills received seven different offers to found, preside over, or teach at various schools or theological departments. The only one that tempted him away from Texas, however, was an offer from the Iowa Holiness Association. The organization had an interdenominational holiness vision, which appealed to Hills' conviction that holiness folks should not be "come-outers."[113] The proposed school was also to be supported by a large and relatively generous constituency. Hills accepted this offer and moved to Oskaloosa in 1906 to found Central Holiness University. Apparently there were no hard feelings in Texas concerning the loss of their president to another school, for that same year Texas Holiness University conferred upon their out-going leader an honorary Doctor of Divinity.

---

112. Hills, "Autobiography," 153–54 (97).

113. A "come-outer" should be contrasted with a "stay-inner." A come-outer holiness person advocated the forming of *new* holiness denominations from those who "come out" of their home denominations. Stay-inners believed the most effective place of ministry for holiness people was in their respective home denominations. During this period, Hills was a staunch stay-inner.

Central Holiness University

As Dr. Hills had hoped, everything about Central Holiness University was on a larger scale than T.H.U. The school started with six times as much acreage and the first year started with over two hundred students. Several students followed Hills from Texas and a sizable number transferred from Taylor University. As the second year boasted just over four hundred students, Hills set a vision for 1,000 within five years. Unfortunately, the faculty was not unified under Hills' leadership, and he was voted out of office at the end of the second year. Still, even in only two years, Hills was able to pool together enough resources and persons to build a strong school.[114]

As he had done at T.H.U., Hills formed a liberal arts curriculum. Seven programs of study were outlined: science, languages, philosophy, history, mathematics, music, and theology.

After his termination from C.H.U. in 1908, Hills went back to preaching. Accepting offers as he always had, as they came in, Hills spoke until November and went home to Oskaloosa when his invitations ran out. Lacking invitations for work, Hills was uncertain what life held next.

When he reached home in Oskaloosa, however, he found two letters and a telegram from England. All were invitations to Star Hall in Manchester. Having never been abroad, the opportunity intrigued him. Deciding to accept the invitation, Hills traveled with Ben Kilbourne, partner and companion of Charles E. Cowman of the Oriental Missionary Society of Japan.

First Term at Star Hall

Star Hall was founded by Francis Crossley, who had passed away several years before Hills' arrival. Purposefully locating his mission in Ancoats, one of the worst parts of Manchester, Crossley had a Salvation Army-like vision to transform the area through the message of holiness and ministry to the poor. After his death, Crossley passed the ministry on to his daughter, Ella D. Crossley, and to Miss Mary A. Hatch. The two were women of exceptional vision and leadership. They led Star Hall's educational, preaching, and development ministries.

---

114. Later it became John Fletcher College.

Already familiar with him from *Holiness and Power*, the "sisters," as they were called, invited Hills to Star Hall because he articulated so well their vision and version of holiness. Upon his arrival, they immediately put him to work preaching and teaching at the mission and also in as many churches in England and Scotland as would accept him.[115]

Besides the regular services and educational venues offered daily and weekly at the mission, there was a special revival, "Four Days with God," that was the spiritual highpoint of every year. Hills was asked to be the primary speaker of the 1908 Four Days.[116]

During his travels throughout England and Scotland, Hills made many significant friends. Two particular contacts are worthy of note. Hills made warm acquaintance with both Reader Harris and George Sharpe. Harris was in his last days; so he and Hills knew each other for only a short time. Sharpe, on the other hand, was the leader of the Pentecostal Church of Scotland and he and Hills maintained a friendship long after both joined the Nazarenes. Sharpe was very impressed with his American colleague and made it his business to promote Hills for revivals at every occasion.

Beyond his duties of preaching and teaching, Hills also wrote for *The Way of Holiness*, Star Hall's periodical. It was started during Hills' first visit to England, and he made numerous occasional contributions to it for the rest of his life.

Near the end of his stay at Star Hall, the sisters insisted that Hills see some of the rest of Europe. Not a man of great means, Hills had never considered visiting Europe. Giving him a generous check, however, the sisters enabled Hills to tour several cities in England, France, Switzerland, Belgium, and the Netherlands.

---

115. Hills, "Autobiography," 183 (116). In point of fact, many churches did allow Hills to come and speak. His own records indicate that he preached in Stockport, Manchester, Oldham, Locksfield, London, Wesleyan Hall-London, Rawtonstall, Parkhead-Glasgow, Motherwell, Paisley, Crieff, Scotland, Perth, Southport, and Watford.

116. Apparently, Hills was in good company, preaching for Star Hall's "Four Days with God." One resource reports that many prominent names preached for this convention including John George Govan, Thomas Cook, Reader Harris, F. D. Sanford, Isabella Leonard, G. D. Watson, Dwight Moody, Samuel Chadwick, G. Campbell Morgan, and C. T. Studd. "Holiness Movement in Great Britain," 4.

Illinois Holiness University

Upon his return to America, Hills was asked to serve again as college president. A group in Illinois desired to transform and relocate their small independent school into an institution of higher education. Hills moved to Olivet, Illinois, in the summer of 1909.

Just prior to the September inauguration, a full salvation campmeeting was held at the new site and the faculty was installed. More than half of the initial faculty had worked for or been students under Hills at other universities. Former students from Central Holiness University, Fred Mesch Jr., Maggie Sloan, and James A. Hills, were invited to serve. Lena and Dana Averill came up from Texas Holiness University to teach piano and stringed instruments, respectively. President Hills, of course, in the style of the old-time college president of Academic Orthodoxy, taught the capstone class "Moral Philosophy," as well as various theological and homiletics classes.[117]

One of the most significant difficulties facing Hills' administration (and later administrations) was the disparity between the high levels of education of the faculty and the equally low levels of the board of trustees. Hills writes that all of the faculty members had at least a college degree, while not a single person on the board "had more than the veriest rudiments of a public school education."[118] Hills, of course, esteemed them highly for their godliness. He seems to remember them fondly as "dear good men . . . [who] could sing, and pray, and shout."[119] He also recalls, however, that "even sanctification does not always insure any one person from making a mistake. Much less does it secure the perfect agreement of ten members of a Board of Trustees and ten teachers of a faculty of a holiness college about college business."[120] In Hills' estimation, the trustees knew too little about the "grave duties" thrust upon them in their university positions. He was nevertheless able to navigate these difficulties for the first few months to put together schools of music, oratory, business, science, the classics, Bible, theology, and philosophy for a school that still exists today.[121]

---

117. *Catalogue of Illinois Holiness University*, 5.
118. Hills, "Autobiography," 187 (119).
119. Ibid., 187 (119).
120. Ibid., 188 (119–20).
121. It was not two years later that Olivet gave up its independent status and transferred to the Pentecostal Church of the Nazarene. The school still exists today as Olivet

Gresham notes that beyond the trustees' lack of schooling and experience in university affairs, two other key issues caused a rift between trustees and the president. The first was the hiring of the president's son, James A. Hills, as an instructor. Apparently as outspoken as his father, but without the wisdom of years, James never impressed the trustees. The second issue Gresham notes was Hills' eschatology. By the end of the first decade of the twentieth century, many in the Holiness Movement staunchly advocated premillennialism. Gresham concludes that apparently the premillennialist trustees did not approve of their postmillennialist president.[122]

While Hills was able to put together a solid course of study, the difficulties of faculty and trustee navigation eventually became too much for the president. By March 1910, the trustees were talking of faculty replacements. Soon thereafter Hills was asked to resign. His career at Olivet thus ended less than one year after it began.

With a five-year contract as president and a brand new $4,000 house, Hills writes that he could have made it difficult for the school to be rid of him. Never one for staying beyond his welcome, however, Hills left with a small severance compromise and a significant personal financial loss in the house. Whether or not he had other feelings on the subject, he wrote twenty years later, "[I] could have held the place under strained relations. But it would probably have done harm to the cause of Holiness which was far-dearer to me than my own reputation."[123]

Southwestern Holiness College

Rarely one with a short list of opportunities, Hills was immediately invited to found another holiness college in Elida, New Mexico. The New Mexico territory was growing steadily at that time and the Southwest Holiness Association was having moderate success throughout the region. While the association was already flirting with the Pentecostal Church of the Nazarene, in 1910 they had not yet made the transfer. Because they still maintained the larger interdenominational vision that many felt was the truest calling of the Holiness Movement, Hills accepted the difficult assignment.

Nazarene University. In the middle of campus stands Hills Hall, a dormitory for men.

122. Gresham, *Waves Against Gibraltar*, 144.

123. Hills, "Autobiography," 189 (120).

Unfortunately, even though Hills worked with great enthusiasm, the school failed. In retrospect, it is clear that the project never had a chance. Too few churches with too few resources made the situation impossible for the president. Although plans were drawn up for campus buildings, nothing more than three foundations was ever erected on the site.

While the "college" was closed within a year, the president was still able to instruct a number of students in his home using books from his own library. Likewise, he used his time productively to write. It was in the desert of New Mexico that he began and completed much of the first volume of his systematic theology. Apparently the demands of the presidency of a small and failing college allowed him a great deal of time for writing. He states that while in New Mexico he wrote the first half of the theology, sometimes turning out "ten pages of foolscap a day, on those great subjects, not rewriting a line."[124] So although the college failed, its founder was always pleased that he had the opportunity to "get away" to the "Land of Enchantment," New Mexico.

When it became apparent that Southwestern Holiness College was not going to continue, Hills was asked to teach at Oklahoma Holiness College. It was as he was preparing to move to Oklahoma, however, that Hills received an urgent request to come back to Star Hall to help the sisters with an emergency situation. Apparently, a teacher had been teaching a class of girls what the sisters considered to be a false understanding of holiness.

Second Term at Star Hall

Long before Hills' arrival, Crossley and Hatch had dismissed the teacher and made the girls destroy all their notes. When Hills arrived, they put him in the class immediately. Sitting in on the class themselves for the first two weeks, they directed Hills to write out everything he taught concerning scriptural holiness. From these manuscripts, Star Hall published three books, *The Way of Holiness*, *Scriptural Holiness and Keswick Teaching Compared*, and *The Tongues Movement*.

While the latter two of these three are the most polemical of Hills' books, *The Tongues Movement* is by far the most scathing of the two. Indeed, as we will see in chapters 5 and 6, Hills' dislike for the Keswickian

---

124. Ibid., 190 (121).

holiness "counterfeiters" is relatively mild compared with his disdain for the Pentecostals. In Hills' estimation, while both dangerously distort the message of the pentecostal blessing, the latter group was by far the worst. Begrudging the Pentecostals even their name, Hills, defending the *true* pentecostal message, merely refers to them as "the tongues movement." And even though Hills nowhere in the book *explicitly* states that there is no such thing as the gift of tongues as the tongues movement is experiencing it, he offers only horror stories about persons who receive the gift. Thus, while Hills seems reluctant to state that his horror stories are *always* the case, the reader is still left with the impression that tongues is a gift of the devil, suitable for only Mormons, witches, and pagan Indians.

As he had done on his previous trip to Star Hall, Hills kept very busy preaching throughout England and Scotland. He renewed old friendships, visiting George Sharpe frequently. He preached again for the "Four Days with God" revival and worked whenever he could on his unfinished systematic theology. Thus his second trip in England passed quickly and he was saying good-bye to the sisters before they were ready.[125]

Oklahoma Holiness University

Upon his return to the U.S., Hills moved to Oklahoma to begin the task for which he had been hired when the Keswick emergency in England arose. Late in the summer of 1911, he moved his family from New Mexico to Bethany, Oklahoma, arriving just before classes began.

The situation could have been a bit awkward for Hills and the school's president. Very much Hills' junior, President Fred Mesch, Jr. had been a student of Hills and was now presiding over his former mentor. If there were any awkwardness in the situation, however, there is no evidence of it on Hills' part. What is apparent, Gresham points out, is that "Hills was recognized as the ranking member of the OHC community" and that the younger president often consulted with and deferred to Hills on many issues.[126]

Hills' duties at O.H.C. included membership on the library, literary society, and catalogue committees. As the Dean of the School of

---

125. Hills recalls that they lamented that with all the holiness preachers on the other side of the Atlantic, the Americans "might spare one to help us here in England." Hills, "Autobiography," 192 (121).

126. Gresham, *Waves Against Gibraltar*, 151.

Theology, he taught theology, homiletics, biblical theology, philosophy, ethics, and logic. Outside of this department, Hills also occasionally taught psychology and several other social science courses.

Not surprisingly, this pastor-evangelist could often be found in the pulpit at local churches, revivals, and campmeetings throughout the region. He taught weekly classes at the Nazarene Rescue Home in Bethany.[127] He was also a regular and a favorite at the university chapel.

It was after one particular chapel service in March of 1912 that Hills first met Phineas F. Bresee, the founder of the Pentecostal Church of the Nazarene. The two had already made acquaintance *via* correspondence, but had never had the opportunity to meet face to face. Hills had just finished preaching in the morning chapel service with nothing in hand but a few notes and the Greek New Testament when Bresee approached him, grasped his hand, and said, "Dr. Hills, we will not ask you to join our body; but if you ever want to join it, we will receive you with open arms."[128] Hills writes, "Still holding his hand, I looked into his noble face and said: 'Dr. Bresee, I thank you for your confidence, and I wish to say that my Congregational denomination is having its last probation. If it does not very soon welcome me, holiness and all, into its ministry in this state, I shall gladly make my home among you.'"[129]

It was not long after this that the "last probation" ended. Hills writes, "Some weeks afterwards, Rev. Charles Jernigan opened the doors of the Bethany College Church and I rose up and joined. I have never regretted it one moment from that day to this."[130] That Sunday was May 26, 1912.[131]

---

127. C. B. Jernigan writes concerning Hills' weekly teaching at the Nazarene Rescue House, "Dr. A. M. Hill [sic], teacher of Theology in the Oklahoma Holiness College, gives the girls a Bible lesson every Friday evening. You ought to see how eagerly they study their Bible." Jernigan, *Pentecostal Advocate*, 6.

128. Hills, "Autobiography," 195 (123).

129. Ibid., 195 (123–24).

130. Ibid., 195–96 (124).

131. Gresham, *Waves Against Gibraltar*, 152. Recently, rumors have spread questioning whether or not Hills membership with the Nazarenes was ever finalized. The nature of these rumors stems from a fire in the Congregational Church in Oklahoma City from which he would have transferred. Ample evidence exists elsewhere, however, that Hills made the transfer. When asked on an Oberlin questionnaire about denominational membership, Hills wrote, "Pentecostal Church of the Nazarene." *Quinquennial Catalogue Questionnaire*, 1915, Oberlin Archives. See also Membership Roll Book, Bethany First Church of the Nazarene Archives.

Always one with a pen in his hand, Hills edited his own philosophy of education in *Christian Education and Anglo Israel* for the 1911–12 O.H.C. catalogue. Addressing the education of "the whole man" and the infidelities of higher criticism, Hills set a precedent and a vision for the school that remained in many ways for decades. That same year, he wrote multiple articles for the *Pentecostal Advocate* and also began what would become an extended relationship with *The Herald of Holiness*.[132]

Oklahoma Holiness University struggled financially during the years that Hills taught there. In the summer of 1912, Mesch resigned and moved to Pasadena, California, to join the faculty of Nazarene University. Hills was the obvious replacement, although he accepted under the conditions that it would be only temporary. Hills' strong leadership helped the school financially almost immediately. Likewise, as the college was now getting two positions, president and professor, for one salary, O.H.C. took an immediate turn for the better under Hills. Unfortunately, it did not prove to be enough to secure fully the school's financial standing. So when in December, 1912, Hills received an urgent call to return to England, he, the O.H.C. faculty, and the college church made an arrangement. The new pastor of the Bethany Nazarene Church, E. J. Lord, assumed the presidency alongside his pastoral duties. This arrangement eased the financial burden on the school, and allowed Hills to leave for Star Hall around Christmas, 1912.

Third Term at Star Hall

Hills' third trip to Star Hall found him arriving just before New Years Day, 1913. As had been the case on previous journeys, Hills was kept very busy. The longest of his visits abroad, Hills' third trip to England did not end until July 1915.

One of his more vivid stories, Hills recalls a Dr. Knight, who had recently read *Holiness and Power* and wanted to talk with its author. Hills agreed to meet with him, and the result of their conversations was Knight's sanctification. Very excited about his newfound experience, Knight promptly began preaching it at his Congregationalist church and soon decided to rent the town hall for a four-day mass meeting. It was during one of the morning services of the mass meeting that Knight uttered the words, "O what will God think of us, after all He has given for

---

132. From 1912 to 1934, Hills wrote 178 articles.

us, if we refuse to give ourselves to God" and immediately thereafter fell down dead from a heart attack.[133]

When cancellation of the mass meeting was proposed, the Star Hall sisters and Hills insisted to the contrary. In their minds, the Lord was at work and the services needed to continue. The sisters appointed Hills to preach and, as had been their tradition, the sisters led the altar calls. In the end, although the death of Dr. Knight did not generate any momentum for a great revival, Hills was always pleased that the decision was made to push the meetings through to completion.

During his third trip, Hills also renewed old friendships. His relationship with George Sharpe only deepened during his third and longest visit. Having just recently joined the Pentecostal Church of the Nazarene, it is very likely that Hills was influential in George Sharpe's church merger with other holiness groups and the Nazarenes in 1915. Gresham asserts the same, stating, "It is readily apparent that, as a new Nazarene, A. M. Hills used his considerable influence to promote the ideas of union of holiness groups in England and Scotland with his own denomination."[134]

As he had always done at Star Hall, Hills busied himself not only with teaching and preaching, but also with writing. The sisters published an abbreviated version of *Holiness and Power* in 1913. Hills also finished his systematic work, *Fundamental Christian Theology*, although it would not be published for almost twenty more years.

After two and a half years of continuous work in England, Hills very much lamented the end of his third visit to Star Hall. His family, however, was in America and World War I was beginning to have an effect on the mission. The student body was decimated numerically by the military draft, and Hills' reasons for staying were dwindling. Of course, the fewer numbers and consequent lighter duties were the very reason he was able to finish his systematic theology. By the summer of 1915, however, even the sisters were admitting that he should return home.

By the time the decision was finally made the pollution of the area had given their beloved evangelist a "serious carbuncle on his face." As generous and grateful to Hills as ever, the sisters paid for its removal and his passage home. Saying good-bye to them and the mission for the third time, Hills never traveled abroad again.

---

133. Hills, "Autobiography," 207 (131).
134. Gresham, *Waves Against Gibraltar*, 158.

Pasadena University

When Hills returned home he was sixty-eight years of age. Having been away from the U.S. for so long, he feared that he might have trouble locating a job. For a time immediately after his return, he teamed up with Will Huff for a campmeeting in Richland, New York. On his way back home, he did some short series and single-event preaching, but nothing substantial opened up for him. Reaching home, he did not find any invitations waiting for him. Likewise, when at the quadrennial Nazarene General Assembly in Kansas City nothing opened up, Hills and his wife decided to move to California to be near children and grandchildren.

It was soon thereafter that President H. Orton Wiley of Pasadena University invited him to begin what became Hills' longest term of service. From 1916–32, he taught religion, theology, and homiletics for the young holiness university and wrote voluminously.

To Hills' surprise, not more than a few days after his invitation from Wiley, the president resigned. It came at the end of what had already been a long embroilment involving the University Church's pastor Seth Cook Rees and the school's trustees. Wiley was succeeded by E. F. Walker, who presided only one year before being elected a Nazarene general superintendent. A. O. Hendricks was elected next.

Hills' writing career during this period revolved mostly around the two major Nazarene organs, *Herald of Holiness* and *Preacher's Magazine*. He wrote dozens of articles for each every year. Besides this, Hills also kept up correspondence with leaders in England and America.

Significant to the final stage of Hills' writing career was his relationship with J. B. Chapman. Chapman, who later became a very influential Nazarene general superintendent, was the editor of the *Herald of Holiness* and was quite impressed with Hills. It was at Chapman's prompting that Hills wrote one of his most substantial works, *Homiletics and Pastoral Theology*. Published by Nazarene Publishing House in 1929, it is nearly 400 pages of Hills' mature insights into the duties of the pastoral office.

As was stated above, Hills finished his systematic theology during his third trip to England, sometime between the years of 1913–15. Ten years in the writing, the book took nearly twenty more to be published.[135]

---

135. Nazarene Publishing House refused to publish it for at least two reasons. First, Hills' postmillennial eschatology was poorly received by both premillennialists and those who did not think eschatology should have so much governance over the larger system of thought. Second, H. Orton Wiley had already been commissioned by the Nazarenes to write their definitive systematic work.

Fundamental Christian Theology was eventually published when J. B. Chapman helped Hills by writing an addition to his chapter on eschatology. With a short disclaimer that he wanted readers to know both positions, Hills allowed Chapman to graft a premillennialist statement onto his chapter defending postmillennialism. An unusual solution, it was enough for C. J. Kinne to publish it under his personal name in 1931. Thus, the treatise, from start to finish, took almost thirty years.

Again at the request of Chapman, Hills wrote a short commentary on Rom 5:1—8:14, 12:1,2, and 15:16. Expanding one of his earlier works, Hills entitled the book *The Establishing Grace or Holiness in the Book of Romans*. It was later republished simply as *Holiness in the Book of Romans*.

Besides the projects in which Chapman had a hand, several other shorter books were published while Hills was in California. In 1927, a series of "full salvation" sermons was written entitled *The Uttermost Salvation*, and three years later a brief biographical sketch of Phineas Bresee went to print.

Beyond these, Hills also drafted a considerable number of manuscripts that were never published. "Autobiography," upon which much of this chapter is built, is over 200 pages in length and was completed in 1933. His commentary on Romans, although undated, is very likely to have been written during his California period. Likewise, on file at the Nazarene Archives is the last manuscript of Hills' hand, *Commentary on John*. It was completed the year he died, 1935.

Pasadena College demonstrated their love for and confidence in Hills in many ways, but perhaps most especially in 1925 when the school conferred upon him his second honorary doctorate. A Doctor of Laws degree was given to him that year. Seven years later, he was made Professor Emeritus.

Hills continued to teach at Pasadena College until his eighty-fifth year. Never tiring from work, he was eventually forced to retired because of the accumulation of health problems. Two minor strokes, increasing deafness, and an apparent growing generational gap between him and his students finally convinced Hills to retire from teaching in 1933.

It was on September 11, 1935, on the kind of brisk, sunny day that is so frequent in Southern California that A. M. Hills died from a cerebral hemorrhage. He was survived by his second wife of many decades, Hulda Jane, who passed away only two months later, and six of his seven children.

The Revivalist Doctrine and Spirit of Post-Bellum Oberlin and Yale

Having considered the life and accomplishments of A. M. Hills, we now turn to the schools he attended, Oberlin and Yale.[1] Because his choice of these schools was neither random nor haphazard, we will begin with Hills' rationale for choosing them.

HILLS' RATIONALE FOR CHOOSING OBERLIN AND YALE

Hills' Upbringing and Choice of Oberlin College

Even in the *brief* biographical sketch provided in chapter 2, we see that A. M. Hills' identity, ministry, and theology completely revolved around revivalism. Indeed, the sketch illustrates that from his birth until his death, through all of the vocational, denominational, and theological changes, revivalism was the only constant.

Early nineteenth-century frontier Christianity was permeated with a matrix of religious, philosophical, and ethical ideas and methods that were particular to the revivalist spirit of the times. A. M. Hills' drew profoundly from and contributed to this matrix for his identity, thought,

---

1. It should be clearly noted up front that this chapter will not be an exhaustive study of either school, but a brief survey of the key figures, doctrines, philosophies, and methods that contributed most directly to the revivalist identity of A. M. Hills.

and ministry. Throughout his life, both accidentally and purposefully, Hills was surrounded by and surrounded himself with revivalism.

Between the Methodists, Presbyterians, Congregationalists, and Baptists, the American West was thoroughly permeated with a revivalist spirit by Hills' birth in 1848. Each of these denominations contributed at least in some way to Hills' earliest spirit and theology. As was mentioned in chapter 2, Hills' mother was a Methodist; his father was a Congregationalist; his childhood churches were Baptist and Congregationalist; and his professors of theology were Presbyterian and Congregationalist.

By the year of his birth, Hills' entire family had already been influenced by revivalism. While there is too little evidence to know whether or not the Hills were infected by revivalism before the move of Hezekiah to western New York, what is certain is that they were in the Rochester area in the 1820s and 30s and several family members chose Oberlin for their education. Thus, A. M. Hills was born into a family where a revivalist identity was already exemplified and constantly nurtured.

Hills' story is not an unusual or unique. In his history of Oberlin College, Robert S. Fletcher writes that years before Hills' birth, "Congregationalism in the Yankee belt from Vermont to Kansas and even in California and Oregon became thoroughly seasoned with Oberlin radicalism."[2]

It is of little surprise, therefore, that Hills chose Oberlin for his preparatory and college education. The college embodied institutionally and in the person of Charles Finney the religion of Hills' youth. His education there confirmed and extended the revivalist identity he had always known and the one he would claim for the rest of his life.

Hills' Choice of Yale Seminary

To a very large extent, Hills' choice of Yale seminary was an extension of the same desire to stay within revivalist circles; at least, it was the school least likely to challenge his Oberlin-forged identity. Yale was no stranger to revivalism, especially the form Hills was raised under and trained in at Oberlin. Only a generation prior to Hills' attendance there, Nathaniel Taylor's powerful presence and doctrine had penetrated the whole divinity school. Of Taylor, Douglas A. Sweeney writes: "Even after

---

2. Fletcher, *History of Oberlin*, vol. 1, 221.

assuming his post at Yale, Taylor maintained an active commitment to revival preaching that made a clarion Edwardsian call for immediate repentance. To be sure, Old Calvinists had a place for revivalism as well. But the Taylorites' radical commitment to 180-degree conversions and immediate repentance distanced them from the more thoroughly covenantal and means-oriented spirituality of Old Calvinism."[3]

Because the two figures often ran parallel tracks, Taylor and Finney's methods for the transformation of society by mass evangelism were often similar. Sweeney writes, "Furthering the trend set by earlier generations of Edwardsians, the Taylorites responded to these changes with a heavily spiritual message of individual conversion. Less interested than even their forebears in Christianizing the social order from the top down . . . Taylor and his followers worked to ameliorate American society one soul at a time."[4] Beyond these similarities between Taylor and Finney, Sweeney also notes, "Even Taylor himself could at times espouse a Christian republicanism, arguing that the health of the nation rested on the level of genuine piety among its citizens."[5]

All this being the case, Sweeney goes on to point out the obvious priority of Taylor's ministry. "First and foremost, the Taylorites—Lyman Beecher not excepted—saved souls."[6]

Late in life, Hills writes that these similarities to Oberlin attracted him to Yale. In the foreword to *Fundamental Christian Theology*, he states as much very clearly.

> Some things we are impelled to do by a power above our own. A Divine hand guides us in our meditation and study. Providence co-operates. Men impress us with an abiding influence. Sixty-four years ago I met the mighty Finney, a king among men, and sat four college years under his ministry . . . Associated with him was a faculty of strong independent thinkers, President James A. Fairchild, Dr. John Morgan, . . . Dr. Henry Cowles, . . . and Dr. Judson Smith . . . I then went to Yale sixty years ago, and met President Woolsey, just retiring, and President Noah Porter, and Timothy Dwight, . . . and Dr. George P. Fisher, . . . and Dr. Samuel Harris . . . These men were nobly endowed intellectually,

---

3. Sweeney, *Taylor, New Haven, and Edwards*, 58.
4. Ibid., 61.
5. Ibid., 61–62.
6. Ibid., 62.

and ranked high in scholarship, and were inspiring to a youth who was *ambitious to be a soul-winner*.[7]

Thus, to a very large extent, Hills chose Yale over other schools because he knew he could further his education along the lines he had already developed at Oberlin. At least in A. M. Hills' mind, Yale and Oberlin were very much of the same ilk. From his perspective, both embraced or were compatible with some form of revivalism.

Hills' Own Estimate of Oberlin and Yale

Before beginning an in-depth look into Hills' training at Oberlin and Yale Seminary, a word is in order on the relative value he placed upon these two schools. That is, lest we think Hills' estimation of his graduate education at Yale was greater than, or even equal to, the value he placed on his training at Oberlin, a word of perspective is needed.

As we have seen, the Hills family was an Oberlin family. They were followers of Finney, and three were graduates of Oberlin before A. M. Hills was born. Thus, he came into the world through a family that was already dyed-in-the-wool Finneyite revivalists. The pastor and spouse of his youth, Rev. T. E. and Mrs. Monroe, were both Oberlin graduates. Every indication from Hills' "Autobiography" is that there was never any question where he would attend college. Oberlin was the only choice for Hills.

At Oberlin, Hills was confirmed in the revivalist identity of his upbringing. The values of revivalism and its system of doctrines and means were a part of his class work and extracurricular activities. There is no indication that Hills ever regretted his choice of Oberlin.

Hills' choice of Yale was very different. In "Autobiography," he speaks of weighing several options and finally deciding upon Yale. What is most significant in his account of choosing a seminary is how grounded and dogmatic he was after his time at Oberlin. He writes:

> In September of 1871 I left . . . to enter Yale Theological Seminary. I had been solicited to be a student in several seminaries; but I felt drawn to Yale. The distractions at New York were too many. The current of unbelief was altogether too strong at Harvard. If I had given up the practice of law to preach, I wanted to have something to preach worth while. I couldn't leave the ministry

---

7. Hills, *Fundamental Christian Theology*, vol. 2, 5, italics mine.

of the mighty Finney with its sharp, keen, incisive doctrines, and try to feed my soul on the windy surmises and speculations and delusions of Carnal men. I believed in an inspired Bible and an Omnipotent Savior and an omnipotent salvation. Consequently the "happy-go-lucky"—"think-as-you-please," "believe what you will," "do-as you like," "we-are all going to heaven together," style of religion made no appeal to me what-soever. But I did want to meet new minds, new methods, new manners, new environments. I chose Yale and never regretted it.[8]

Implied in these statements is an affirmation of just how deeply Hills had come to embrace the spirit and thinking of Oberlin. While on the one hand he desired new minds, methods, manners, and environments, on the other hand he still chose the graduate school closest to the sharp, keen, incisiveness of the mighty Finney. It would not be too much to say, therefore, that he chose Yale over other seminaries because it was the closest to the identity he had already come to embrace deeply at Oberlin.

This fact is even more clearly illustrated by Hills' recollections of his pastoral installation only a few days after his graduation from Yale. Still a very young man, fresh out of seminary, it might be true that Hills was slightly insecure at his installation questioning. Having been outside of Oberlin circles for three years, he may have felt particularly self-conscious in the presence of his old mentors. Nevertheless, the questioning and his sermon went very well, exemplified by the fact that he was ordained and appointed the same day without any problems.[9]

What is the most telling out of an entire day of events, though, is what Hills chooses to write in "Autobiography." From the whole day, he only retells the moment when Hiram Mead slapped him on the back and said, "Well! my boy, Yale hasn't spoiled you." Still beaming with delight at the statement decades later, the unspoiled Yale B.D. recollects, "I was glad to feel that I was still in the old Oberlin faith that had already brought such blessing to the world."[10]

This story reveals the profound imprint that Oberlin had already made upon Hills. Nowhere in any of Hills' published and unpublished sermons, books, pamphlets, or articles does he speak of concern about

---

8. Hills, "Autobiography," 46–47 (31).
9. *The Portage County Democrat*, 3 June 1874.
10. Hills, "Autobiography," 56–57 (37).

being outside the "old Yale faith." This is not to say that Hills did not very much appreciate his training at Yale; on the contrary, he did. It does reveal, however, that his Oberlin training was the defining influence on his theological and ministerial identity. Hills was an *Oberlin* revivalist, molded into what could be characterized as an Oberlin College "poster child." He appreciated Yale, but took from there only what was in line with his already-developed Oberlin paradigm.

The considerable sway that Hills' Oberlin training held over his Yale education must be kept in perspective as we consider the development of his thought. As we will see, very little in Hills' theology can be traced back to Yale that is not first traceable to Oberlin.[11] Yale allowed Hills to reexamine and deepen much of his thought, but it did not redirect any aspect of his doctrine or means.[12] Indeed, it was not until Hills' introduction to the Holiness Movement in 1895 that we see a significant shift in his thinking.

Inasmuch as Hills' theology and methods are sufficiently definable within the boundaries of revivalism and both of the schools he attended had revivalistic leanings, this chapter will consider the major Oberlin and Yale mentors that contributed to his revivalist identity. Because there is virtually no evidence in the whole of Hills' corpus that he ever took anything out of his schooling years incompatible with a revivalistic identity, the remainder of this chapter will consider only the revivalistic

---

11. My research into all of Hills' doctrinal training at Oberlin and Yale reveals that only his thesis of Anglo-Israel is unique to Yale. Samuel Harris was likely the first to teach it to Hills. Cf. Gresham, *Waves Against Gibraltar*, 46.

12. Gresham makes the point of how little Yale influenced Hills even stronger. He compares Hills' systematic work with Harris' *Self Revelation of God* to conclude, "[It] contrasts greatly in both the approach used and the organization of the content. The topical headings and arrangement of materials differ in the two works." Indeed, Gresham seems even to stretch to find similarities by saying, "Only in the profuse use of quotations from literature does Hills show the influence of his Yale mentor." Gresham, *Waves Against Gibraltar*, 45. While he continues, noting similarities between Hills' and Harris' eschatologies and Anglo-Israel, Gresham finally concludes, "All this points to the conclusion that the theology of Hills' mature years resulted predominantly from his *private* pursuit of the Calvinist and, later, Wesleyan literature. Yale helped Hills know how to study and to think independently. He never ceased to give credit to his college and seminary professors. Through the rest of his life, he read assiduously. He collected a large personal library and was a frequent patron of libraries across America and in Britain. Still, he often credited his skill in his use of sources, *not to Yale, but to reading the Bible through before the age of eight as a result of his mother's promptings*." Gresham, *Waves Against Gibraltar*, 47, italics mine.

characteristics of Oberlin and Yale. The methods, tenets, and aspirations of revivalism so formed Hills' identity that collectively they served as the hermeneutical lens for his entire canon of thought and practice.

Both Hills and his interpreters agree that the persons or writings of Charles G. Finney, James Fairchild, Henry Cowles, and Asa Mahan at Oberlin and Noah Porter at Yale were the most notable in shaping his revivalistic identity.

REVIVALIST THEOLOGICAL METHOD

Defining the exact parameters of A. M. Hills' theological method is more complicated than simply comparing his doctrines with a cross section of his commonly used sources. A second generation Oberlin revivalist and an advocate of Academic Orthodoxy, Hills espoused the same orienting principles as his mentors. His theological method was shaped by many of the key figures associated with Academic Orthodoxy, theologians and philosophers who merged Common Sense philosophy, scientific language, and biblical texts to produce a revivalist theology. This theology was thought to be sufficient both to save souls and reform the social order through the vehicle of revivalism. Thus, a study of the theological method of a revivalist like Hills is a look at the confluence of three orienting principles, Academic Orthodoxy's scholastic and postmillennial visions, its doctrine of the will, and its Common Sense epistemology, all systematized according to Baconian logic and rhetoric.

For the purposes of this study on a single figure, we will not outline the teachings of all the names on Hamilton's list; we will consider only those associated with the movement itself and the mentors of A. M. Hills.[13]

---

13. As was reviewed in chapter 2, James E. Hamilton writes of the complexity of Academic Orthodoxy's identity. "It is not sufficient to identify Academic Orthodoxy solely in terms of Scottish realism in this country [the United States]. Rather, it is the union of Scottish philosophy with freewill, revivalistic Evangelicalism in the above designated old and new institutions in this country that all the Academic Orthodoxy had in common." Hamilton, "Academic Orthodoxy," 56. Hamilton lists many of the presidents of Academic Orthodoxy. He writes, "In addition to Wayland [of Brown, and] Mahan, Finney, and Fairchild, [the first three presidents of Oberlin,] the following names, at least, would have to be included in any representative roster: Jeremiah Day (Yale), Henry P. Tappan (New York University), Laurens Perseus Hickok (Union), Thomas C. Upham (Bowdoin), Noah Porter (Yale), Francis Bowen (Harvard), James

Of course, narrowing the fifteen names of Hamilton's muster to those directly affiliated with Oberlin and Yale during the late 1860s and early 70s respectively does not delimit the list to obscure or even lesser names. Hills' mentors were among the most influential in the movement. He studied with Porter at Yale and was expected to be well versed in Porter and Mahan's key writings at Oberlin. It is arguable that these figures alone were two of the three most influential *American* Common Sense philosophers and among the most influential of the Academic Orthodoxy.[14]

The theological methods of these like-minded college presidents and professors were tightly interwoven fabrics of source materials agreeable with Common Sense philosophy and an Arminian-like doctrine of the will, systematized scientifically. The nature of the interrelationship between Common Sense philosophy, an alleged "Baconian" scientific paradigm, and ethics with biblical and theological sources made their methodology complicated, to say the least. There are, however, no more apt examples of this methodology than the mentors with whom A. M. Hills studied while at Oberlin and Yale.

In consideration of the revivalist theological method that Hills would have absorbed,[15] three orienting principles must be considered: the related visions of Academic Orthodoxy and postmillennialism, the Oberlin doctrine of the will, and the interrelationship between natural and revealed theology, all systematized according to Baconian categories.

The Scholastic Vision of Academic Orthodoxy and Postmillennialism

There were two highly interrelated visions of Oberlin College (and to some degree Yale as well), that relate specifically to theological method.

McCosh (Princeton), Mark Hopkins (Williams), Andrew Preston Peabody (Harvard), Taylor Lewis (New York University), and Leicester A. Sawyer (Central College, Ohio)." Ibid., 58.

14. Metz, *British Philosophy*, 30. In his history of *British* philosophy, Metz offers a few pages on the American Common Sense philosophers. Of note, he considers only J. M'Cosh and Noah Porter as significant enough American Common Sense philosophers to name. Of Asa Mahan, James Hamilton writes that he was "the man who was perhaps the most complete single representative of this movement." Hamilton, "Academic Orthodoxy," 52.

15. It should be noted that the phrase "the revivalist theological method" is used as a single entity for simplicity's sake. Obviously there was a proliferation of subtle differences among the figures addressed. For the sake of space, they will referred to as a unified whole.

The scholastic aim of Academic Orthodoxy and the postmillennial dream provided what could best be characterized as an underlying attitude or an overarching vision for all other doctrines and means.[16] The first of a trinity of orienting principles, these sibling visions shaped revivalist doctrine and praxis alike. These visions provided the parameters within which revivalism and reform were accomplished and the aim toward which they hoped to move.

The Scholastic Vision of Academic Orthodoxy in the Age of Science

While it is generally true that A. M. Hills maintained an *ad populam* style of communication and that his written sermons and works are considerably more "down-to-earth" than his Oberlin texts, this is not to say that he did not have any scientific or philosophical aspects in his overall theology. One of the chief similarities between Oberlin and Yale was their adherence to and application of Common Sense philosophy and its basic scientific and philosophical perspective.

At the heart of Scottish Common Sense Realism was a basic epistemological goal to organize and articulate a religious body of philosophy and ethics with the precision of a science. While both Oberlin and Yale philosophers differed slightly from him, Thomas Reid's basic methodological relationship between common sense, induction, and categorization, summed up in his *Essays on the Intellectual Powers of Man*, was maintained by his American "children" and "grandchildren." Reid writes:

> Natural philosophy must be built upon the phenomena of the material system, discovered by observation and experiment . . . [If] all the length men can go in accounting for phenomena is to discover the laws of nature, according to which they are produced; [then] the true method of philosophizing is this: from real facts ascertained by observation and experiment, to collect by just induction the laws of nature, and to apply the laws so discovered, to account for the phenomena of nature . . . Thus the natural philosopher has the rules of his art fixed with no less precision than the mathematician.[17]

---

16. By "means," I intend what Finney means when using the word. For Finney, the word is fairly synonymous with the dictionary definition of the word: a vehicle or method for achieving a result. Finney uses the word most often in reference to his pragmatic, anti-traditional, and controversial programs for bringing about revival *via* stirring, rousing methods. The revivalists' "means" are discussed more in depth below.

17. Quoted by Bozeman, *Protestants in Age of Science*, 14.

Among those of the Academic Orthodoxy, this method was stretched to draw in every aspect of every science. Their goal to collect, organize, and master enough philosophical, psychological, historical, moral, ethical, doctrinal, and biblical data to describe the laws according to which the whole universe worked was no small task. Of course, Hills was not interested in the study of the natural universe for its own sake *per se* or the application of these principles to the natural sciences alone. He and many other evangelicals were interested in the application of this methodology to moral philosophy, theology, and ethics. The gathering of psychological, philosophical, biblical, ethical, and practical data to induce the laws of the divine-human relationship became the task of many theologians in the nineteenth century. Hills was one such theologian.

As the above quotation reveals, the goal of Reid's method was the articulation of the "laws" of nature. Of course, the apprehension and articulation of a law was no easy goal. In Reid's method, it required "adequate mastery of a body of facts sufficiently large and complex to establish a law of nature."[18] The process of mastery was long and slow. Through an arduous, inductive method, the scientist gathered facts over a long period of time until the mind was shaped by the data and began to apprehend meaningful and regular patterns. Theodore Bozeman summarizes, "The aim of scientific inquiry, on the model, was nothing less than a patient and precise fitting of the mind to the concrete pace and contour of nature."[19] Laws were not ascertained quickly, but slowly, through an inductive method.

As we will see below, the theological applications of this methodology were numerous, and the formal and populist responses to such theologies were profound. It was, after all, the age of science. Bozeman points out, "Realism and Baconism by 1843 had come to seem inextricably mutual."[20] Of Bacon, he writes: "It is difficult to recapture the grateful urgency with which many Americans now turned to Bacon [in the wake of Locke's decline]. By 1860, his name had been invoked to bless and harmonize nearly every cause in the republic. Poetry, science, philosophy, religion, psychology, medicine, law, agriculture—all found plenteous use for the quickly formalized magic of the name 'Lord Bacon.'"[21]

18. Ibid., 15.
19. Ibid., 16.
20. Ibid., 30.
21. Ibid., 24.

Bozeman does not speculate as to the influence of Oberlin in the dissemination of science or Common Sense philosophy. It is clear, however, that whether or not Finney and the revivalists introduced Realism and Baconism to the masses or merely reflected it back to them with a degree of practical sophistication, revivalism of the early and mid-nineteenth century was permeated with the language, concepts, and illustrations of this new science. Large numbers responded positively to this kind of presentation like those who were hearing the gospel in their "heart language."[22]

The Postmillennial Vision

Closely related to the scholastic vision of Academic Orthodoxy was the revivalist vision of the biblical millennium. To a large extent, the postmillennial vision could be considered the practical or reform side of Academic Orthodoxy's aim. The hope of the millennium was the concrete picture of how the world would look, think, and function when all of the sciences were effectively merged, broadcasted, and disseminated to the utter ends of the earth through revivalism and reform.

While most of Hills' mentors at Oberlin and Yale adhered to some version of this eschatology, the best systematic presentation of the vision is offered by Henry Cowles. Among other things, Cowles was professor of Literature of the Old Testament.[23] In his 1841 series of articles for *Oberlin Evangelist*, he offers as clear a presentation of the Oberlin vision as is recorded.

Desiring to draw a distinction between what most people *think* or *want* the millennium to be and what is actually revealed in the Scriptures, Cowles asserts:

> We think that certain things ought to exist in a perfect state of society, and therefore infer that they *will* exist in the Millennium. Now our ideas of a perfect state of society may be nearly correct,

---

22. "Heart language" is a missiological term of unknown origin used to describe the one language of a people group that is dearest to the heart, and therefore, the language to which they are most likely to respond favorably.

23. Fletcher, *Oberlin College*, vol. 2, 689. Fletcher points out that at various periods Cowles taught "Ecclesiastical History" and "Pastoral Theology" in the Theological Department and for a while languages in the college. Unfortunately, Fletcher continues, while "'a studious, mild, careful, kind and lovely' man," he was considered "generally a poor teacher and 'not much a preacher,' his greatest work being done as an author and as editor of the *Evangelist*." Ibid.

or it may be wide enough from the truth. Deductions as to what the Millennium will be which are made in this way, will be more or less correct according to the justness of the ideal before our mind. The one chief, and vital point therefore to which we turn our inquiries shall be—what has God said? 1. Respecting the political and social state of the world, and 2. Respecting its religious state during the Millennium.[24]

Regarding the first, Cowles lists several things that the Scriptures are clear will not be a part of the millennium. There will be no "mighty conquerors . . . whose fundamental principle [is] conquest and supreme power—which [exist] only to reign and conquer. That entire system of things will pass away."[25] War will be a thing of the past. Oppressive rule over the weak and poor will be abolished. Along a similar vain, Cowles continues that slavery will be no more, an institution that in 1841 in America was in no danger of collapsing.

Having stated what will *not* be a part of the millennium, Cowles next writes that while many think or believe there will not or should not be any form of civil government at that time, "Yet, laws may be needed then, (1.) On account of human ignorance to determine what [is] right in many departments of social action, [and] (2.) On account of remaining selfishness and depravity which may sometimes need to be repressed by precisely these instrumentalities."[26]

Having defined briefly the political side of the coming millennium, Cowles next turns to what the religious state of affairs will be. Quoting dozens of scriptural passages, he articulates what he considers to be the biblical eschatological hope in seven numbered statements.

First, with the Lord putting his law directly upon humanity's inward parts, "right knowledge of God will be exceedingly prevalent." While at present there is much lack for knowledge and many do not know God or his goodness,

> in the later day Christ shall open those eyes and unstop those ears. God will be known.—Let us look a moment at this great and precious truth. All shall know God rightly. The right knowledge of God is that which fills Heaven with joy and holiness. This it is which pours fourth tides of blessedness over all holy beings

24. Henry Cowles, "The Millennium."
25. Ibid.
26. Ibid.

> in the universe. O, how happy are they to know God. That the Maker of the universe is such a Being, so great, so worthy, so ineffably and immensely good—this is the joy and the peace of their souls forever. This knowledge of God puts forth the only influence which can make rational beings happy.[27]

Cowles next laments at how little as of yet has been understood about God. So much error is mixed with too little true knowledge.

> But in that later day the knowledge of God shall abound exceedingly. And it shall be the true knowledge of the true God. Then men will study God's word as they never yet have done. And his works too will be objects of rational and most intense investigation. Little else will men then care to know except what relates to God and their relations to Him and to the whole circle of duty. Education will then be as it should, the training of mind to know God. The great central science will be Theology. The grand result of these pursuits will be human well-begin.[28]

One can hear echoes of Finney's means of the proclamation of the truth in Cowles' statements. The proclaimed truth will be heard, understood, and accepted on a global scale. The truth, having brought about the millennium, will then nourish it.

Second, Cowles continues, "God will manifest his presence most remarkably and gloriously among his people. He will be with them as He never has been in former times."[29] Concluding that on that day Zion's mourning will be past, he simply asks, who could mourn while God's radiating "ineffable glory," the "brilliant sun-light of his truth," and the "sun-beams of his love" pour down constantly? "Who could mourn, when the people shall be all righteous? O come, that happy day!"[30]

Third, Cowles writes, "The Spirit will then be given in glorious and immense effusions." Ezekiel describes its subduing and transforming effect. The promises in Ezekiel 36, that God will cleanse his people with clean water and send his Spirit to cause his people to walk in his statutes, form the basis for Cowles' fourth statement concerning the coming millennium. "There will be a high degree of holiness and a flourishing state of piety." The "broad road" that leads to destruction will be replaced by

27. Ibid.
28. Ibid.
29. Ibid.
30. Ibid.

The Revivalist Doctrine and Spirit of Post-Bellum Oberlin and Yale 65

Isaiah's "highway of holiness." "So greatly will piety prevail that it shall seem spontaneous like nature's vegetation."[31]

All of this implies Cowles' fifth point—"The great mass of the people on earth will be Christians"; or prophetically, "all nations shall serve him."[32] Drawing from two different prophecies, Cowles points out, "(1.) That the Jews shall all be restored, converted, and immensely increased in number" and "(2.) That numerous throngs of Gentiles shall be proselyted, and be united to her."[33]

Having said this, however, Cowles immediately qualifies this point. Just because most of the world will belong to the people of God, "It does not seem by any means that absolutely *all* the inhabitants of the earth at that time shall be real Christians."[34] Nevertheless, Cowles is clear that a very large percentage of the world will be Christian.

Of course, Cowles' use of the adjective "real" in the above statement qualifies the kind of Christians that will be. His sixth point is, "There will then be no hypocrites in the church ... Religion will then stand for what it is. Its real character can then be known. And then, too, the progress of the church in revivals and in holiness will not be hindered by the dead weight of a mass which have no religion."[35]

The seventh and final assertion that Cowles makes concerning the millennium is that "dissension and division shall utterly cease."[36] According to the prophetic vision, the prince of peace shall reign and even the wolf and the lamb will dwell together as God extends peace like a river.

Unfortunately, Cowles concludes, while all of these great blessings will reign upon the earth, persons will still be born with and under the same parental and social constitutions that have marked the race since Adam's fall. Thus, children born even during the time of the millennium will still be in need of conversion. "Parents, then, and the Church, will have work to do in those days. Their children must be taught, prayed for, and with most earnest efforts, through grace plucked from eternal

---

31. Ibid.
32. Ibid.
33. Ibid.
34. Ibid.
35. Ibid.
36. Ibid.

ruin."[37] The only difference will be that during the millennium the manifestation of divine agency will be greatly increased.

Also unfortunate, Cowles continues, the saints will still be tempted, although to a lesser degree than now. Likewise, the Christian life will remain, at least in some sense, a warfare. "The grand difference between Christian experience, then and now, stands thus: now, unbelief—then, faith; now, a little effort without expectation of success—then, much effort, invigorated by rational expectation: now of course much defeat—then, much and glorious victory."[38]

Cowles concludes his reflections on the millennium at the personal level that entire consecration will be the common experience of the church. "Men shall be holy. Every thing shall be 'HOLINESS UNTO THE LORD.'" In dress, equipage, diet, regimen, and every other aspect of daily life, all Christians will do all things to the glory of God. "Men will be willing to know and do what is right, and what, in all these things God would have them do. The opposition made by prejudice, and selfish passions having subsided, it will not be difficult to arrive at the truth. Of one thing I am quite sure, benevolence, good-willing, and good doing towards our fellow beings, will be the grand law of social action."[39]

Summary of the Postmillennial Vision

While in his definition of the millennium, Cowles does not attempt to depict absolute utopian perfection, one can still perceive the hopefulness of Oberlin's vision for a substantially better world. The goal of a world where truth and the Spirit permeate most of the political, social, and personal realms, where peace reigns because truth is known and followed, and where entire consecration and holiness is the norm for the majority of earth's inhabitants did not fail to thrill and empower even the most noncommital Oberlin student. Indeed, this vision was so powerful that it influenced every level of Oberlin religious and reform identity.

Having considered the above systematic definition, it should be noted, however, that the postmillennialist doctrine of Oberlin was much less a systematic doctrine than an underlying attitude or an overarching vision. As such, it was much more dynamic and engulfing than a simple creedal affirmation often is. The millennial vision functioned as

37. Ibid.
38. Ibid.
39. Ibid.

an orienting principle, shaping all philosophical, doctrinal, and reform efforts. The living aspiration of an entire community, postmillennialism took on a life of its own, dynamic enough to re-invent itself, at least in A. M. Hills' imagination, for six more decades. Thus, while Henry Cowles' definition is the best *systematic* presentation on the subject, to see how it functioned as an overarching vision, one needs only to read any of the writings of Oberlin in the early period. The vision is used generously, although more often than not unsystematically, throughout Finney's sermons and lectures on revivalism, in various treatises by Mahan, and in multiple other published works from the early Oberlin period. In such places, used as an overarching vision, we find the idea in its most natural habitat. This will be illustrated in the sermons and books of A. M. Hills' in the next two chapters.

Summary of the Two Overarching Visions

Although some might characterize the visions of Academic Orthodoxy and postmillennialism to be unrelated, from the perspective of Oberlin, they are better understood as two manifestations of a single vision. Oberlinites desired to unify every field of knowledge and to disseminate their teachings and reforms to every nation of the earth. Simply, postmillennialism was the practical application of Academic Orthodoxy's scholastic endeavor. More living and evolving visions than rote doctrinal affirmations, these two related visions together are the first of three orienting principles in the revivalists' theological methodology.

Doctrine of the Will

The second orienting principle in the revivalists' theological methodology is their doctrine of the will. As above, while many examples from both Oberlin and Yale could be called upon to represent the subject, its clearest articulation is located in a single treatise, Asa Mahan's *Doctrine of the Will*. The culmination of Mahan's thoughts on the subjects of obligation, moral philosophy, and the volitional powers of human persons, *Doctrine of the Will* remained a central text at Oberlin decades after its author's departure.

In his autobiography, Mahan retells the story of how he came to his mature doctrine of the will and why he considers it to be the litmus test for the legitimacy of all theological and moral systems. Unlike other Oberlin figures, who adopted doctrines of the freedom of the will for various other reasons, Mahan's path tended to be more straightforwardly intellectual. Simply, Mahan was troubled by the intellectual implication of high Calvinism's system of divine decrees as it related to justice. A God who would condemn sinners to everlasting perdition for sins that they were obligated to commit, either because of their natures or because of a divine decree, did not seem just. For Mahan, the notion represented a God who would be very difficult to love.

From his early studies, Mahan recalls the only options from which to choose: the Old School System, Hopkinsianism, and the Exercise Scheme of Dr. Emmons. None of these, however, satisfied his intuitive sense of justice. Of these three, Mahan writes: "In contemplating the systems, it became at once perfectly evident to my mind that one and the same difficulty was strictly common to them all; namely, *the absolute necessity* of all creature volitions, choices, determinations, acts, and states, whether denominated sinful or holy; and that this necessity originated first in the eternal and unchangeable decree, and secondly in the agency, direct or indirect, of God Himself."[40]

While such inconsistencies were frustrating his logical mind, another central question bothered him. "How can the doctrine of eternal decrees and election, and the consequent necessity of all creature volitions and acts, be reconciled with the fact of creature responsibility for the same? has ever been the vexed question of the Calvinistic faith in all its forms."[41]

Mahan continues that when questions were asked concerning these apparent contradictions, "Very commonly the question has been set aside as mysterious."[42] Such a dismissal was too nebulous for Mahan, who felt there were too many certainties within the parameters of the subject for there to be a glaring mystery at the center. "When all the elements of a given judgment are distinctly known and apprehended, as I then clearly saw, the element of mystery can have no place in that judgment."[43]

---

40. Asa Mahan, *Autobiography*. On the internet page from which this was quoted, editor and copyist Richard M. Friedrich states that it is "republished from the edition of 1882, London, without altering anything but format and page numbers."

41. Ibid.

42. Ibid.

43. Ibid.

Of course, the questions were only exacerbated by multiple biblical passages, the seeming plain meaning of which stood in contradiction to Calvinist dogma. Mahan questioned what the Bible meant when it said, "As I live, saith the Lord, I have no pleasure in the death of the wicked; but that the wicked turn from his way and live" if not that "'He has NO pleasure in the death of the wicked,' and has no desire or will in respect to him, but that he should turn and live."[44]

After considerable reflection, such verses began to suggest to Mahan that God does not and, therefore, did not at any time desire, will, or decree the damnation or even rebellion of any person. In fact, he eventually concluded that the Bible did not teach any doctrine of the bondage of the will at all and that the atoning work of Christ was efficacious for all of humanity. This being the case, human persons had no acceptable excuse for their sinful actions and the realities of moral obligation and liability became obvious.

Mahan's mature conclusions were, thus, that human persons are free and not necessary agents. Mahan continues that not only is this scriptural, but all persons intuitively know it as well.

> Another all-valid reason why I repudiated the doctrine of necessity and adopted that of liberty, is the absolute testimony of the inner consciousness. Whenever we put forth an act of choice, we are as conscious of a power to choose differently from what we do, as we are that we exist at all. The remembrance of all past acts of choice is attended with the same absolute consciousness, that we *might* have chosen differently from what we did. Hence the remorse, and conscious desert of retribution, which attend the consciousness of sin.[45]

This mature conclusion, (and another reason he came to the doctrine of volitional freedom), Mahan calls here the "intuitive convictions

---

44. Ibid. Mahan also noticed the verse "Hear, O heavens, and give ear, O earth: for the Lord hath spoken, I have nourished and brought up children and they have rebelled against Me." Mahan thought it unnatural that God should predestine many persons to be rebels and then in the Scriptures call "heaven and earth to unite with Him in astonishment at the fact, that those children had done what He had thus rendered it impossible that they should not do; as if He had placed a mass of water on an inclined plane, and then called upon the universe to unite with Him in amazement, that that water should run down instead of up that plane." Ibid.

45. Ibid.

of the race."⁴⁶ He believed that any person on the planet, when asked concerning the choice of good and evil, will answer that the good should always be chosen. This fact proved, in Mahan's mind, that the intuitive understanding of human persons, unless trained in a high-Calvinist school, naturally affirms volitional freedom and consequent obligation and culpability.

In retelling his own intellectual development on this subject, Mahan next appeals again to biblical texts and reason. In agreement with the intuitions of the race, there are all of the "express and implied revelations of Scripture in respect to the subject. In the sacred Word, God appeals to the reason, conscience, and moral nature of man in verification of the integrity and rectitude of His moral administration . . . In view of such facts, the deduction is self-evident that God's retributive administration is not, and cannot be, based upon a principle which renders it absolutely impossible for the reason and conscience of all rationals, good and bad in common, not to condemn and reprobate that principle."⁴⁷

In conclusion to his reflections upon his mature thought, Mahan writes: "In absolutely affirming the accordance of the moral administration of God with the necessary intuitions of the reason, conscience, and moral nature of man, the Scriptures have, in the most absolute form conceivable, affirmed the freedom of the will, and denied the doctrine of necessity. All the commands and prohibitions, promises and threatenings, invitations and admonitions of Scripture imply the same great truth."⁴⁸

All this is not to say, however, that Mahan's conclusions were based solely upon the Scriptures and intuitive reflections. His final reflection on his mature thought recognizes also the testimony of the early church. He notes that it is readily understood, "The unanimous testimony of learned men who have fully acquainted themselves with all the facts of the case, is that the primitive Church universally held and taught the doctrine of liberty, as opposed to that of necessity."⁴⁹ Mahan quotes Justin Martyr, Tertullian, Irenaeus, Basil, Chrysostom, Jerome, Epiphanius, Origen, Theoderet, Clement of Alexandria, Eusebius, Didymus, and even Augustine to illustrate the fact that the

46. Ibid.
47. Ibid.
48. Ibid.
49. Ibid.

major theologians of the early church believed and taught some form or another of volitional freedom.[50]

All these evidences led Mahan to his overarching conclusion. "I . . . reached a very far-sweeping conclusion, one which required me fundamentally to reconstruct my entire system of theology, and to 'read with new eyes' the Word of God."[51]

From his conclusions, Mahan eventually developed a system of thought that conformed to what his own intuitive introspections and the early fathers told him about the biblical record. He reasoned that if his own intuitive, common sense of justice and perceived volitional freedom agreed with the early church fathers to answer all of his theological dilemmas and bring greater meaning to the Bible, then his new conclusions must be correct. The system that Mahan eventually articulated, therefore, was one that maintained a high view of volitional freedom and also appealed to the common sense intuitions of individual persons. He published his new system in *Doctrine of the Will*.

Doctrine of the Will undoubtedly strikes some as an unusual title for a hermeneutical text. Indeed, as with postmillennialism, it sounds more like an actual doctrine than a method. The title, however, reveals just how central Mahan and Oberlin's statements of the volitional powers of humans were. Because the book itself was written explicitly as a hermeneutical text, Mahan's doctrine of the will is the second orienting principle of the revivalists' system of thought.

Mahan opens the first chapter: "The doctrine of the Will is a cardinal doctrine of theology, as well as of mental philosophy. This doctrine, to say the least, is one of the great central points, from which the various different and conflicting systems of theological, mental, and moral science, take their departure. To determine a man's sentiments in respect to the Will, is to determine his position, in most important respects, as a theologian, and mental and moral philosopher."[52]

Without stopping to consider the degree to which every other theologian or philosopher of the world might agree with the author's final statement, these opening lines at least reveal just how central volition is for Mahan. It is both the governing principle and also a lens through which one views the moral self and God. Mahan writes that in

50. Ibid.
51. Ibid.
52. Mahan, *Doctrine of the Will*, 14.

our contemplations concerning the character of God and the nature of his government over humanity...

> all our apprehensions here, all our notions in respect to the nature and desert of sin and holiness, will, in many fundamental particulars, be determined by our notions in respect to the Will. In other words, our apprehensions of the nature and character of the Divine government, must be determined, in most important respects, by our conception of the nature and powers of the subjects of that government ... I wish [the reader] distinctly to understand, that in fixing his notions in respect to the doctrine of the Will, he is determining a point of observation from which, and a medium through which, he will contemplate his own character and deserts as a moral agent, and the nature and character of that Divine government, under which he must ever "live, and move, and have his being."[53]

His thesis stated, Mahan next dives into the particulars of his method of introspection. Criticizing other philosophers and theologians for developing doctrines of the will from external sources alone, Mahan posits his definitions for appropriate internal sources. Every person has a natural ability of introspection available to the mind whereby he can study his own volitional nature. Mahan writes, "The mind has but one eye by which it can see itself, and that is the eye of Consciousness. This then, is the organ of vision to be exclusively employed in all our inquiries in every department of mental science, and in none more exclusively than in that of the Will."[54] The consciousness for Mahan, therefore, is the mind's eye peering into itself, revealing the inner workings of the mind, emotions, and will to the self.

That such an inward sense exists and can be used efficiently is self-evident to Mahan. Believing the consciousness to be a powerful tool that can lead any person to the realizations of his own volitional freedom and consequent moral responsibility, Mahan rejected any doctrine of the will built by external reflections, that is, syllogistic logic framed from traditional dogmas or seeming biblical ideas.[55] Drawing an analogy, Mahan asserts that no philosopher would form a theory of optics by looking at the stars. While the eyes are certainly used to view the stars,

---

53. Ibid., 14.
54. Ibid., 15.
55. Ibid., 17.

one must look into the eye itself to understand the eye. Analogously, one does not form a doctrine of the will by looking into the philosophical or theological textbooks on the subject. A proper doctrine of the will is best founded upon the consciousness looking inwardly. It is for this reason that Mahan entreats:

> That he pursue his investigations with *implicit confidence in the distinct affirmations of his own consciousness in respect to this subject*... [Regarding human voluntary powers] it is imperiously called for; so long have philosophers and divines been accustomed to look without, to determine the characteristics of phenomena which appear exclusively within, and which are revealed to the eye of consciousness only. Having been so long under the influence of this pernicious habit, it will require somewhat of an effort for the mind to turn its organ of self-vision in upon itself ... Especially will it require an effort to do this, with a fixed determination to abandon all theories formed from external observation, and to follow impliedly the results of observations made internally.[56]

On the surface, Mahan's statements seem to set up a false dichotomy between natural and revealed knowledge and psychological and biblical sources. Mahan's contention, however, is simply that too often what is passed off as "biblical" is in fact neither in line with what the Bible teaches nor what psychology intuits. In Mahan's estimation, the psychological and the biblical are in perfect harmony concerning the volitional powers of humans. That a few recent theologians teach a doctrine of necessity does not change the reality of the volitional freedom of persons and their consequent moral culpability and responsibility.

Of course, it is not only the biblical and the psychological that are in agreement in Mahan's doctrine of the will, but also, as we saw above, the testimony of the primitive church. In *Doctrine of the Will*, Mahan points out that no theologian of the primitive church until Augustine taught the innovative idea of the doctrine of necessity. Listing the same early church fathers as above, Mahan concludes: "The doctrine of Necessity is a dark innovation upon the universal faith, as published by inspired apostles and prophets, and as received and proclaimed by the universal church, founded by such men, during the first five centuries of her existence, an innovation introduced by the great enemy . . . for no other

---

56. Ibid., 16–17.

purpose than the corruption of that faith, by sapping the foundation of morality and moral government both."[57]

Grounded in psychological and, to a lesser degree, patristic sources, Mahan felt confident that he had found the truth of the Scriptures. Indeed, he was convinced that moral obligation based upon volitional freedom was *the* biblical system. While he understood and affirmed that the Scriptures do not directly reveal any explicit system of mental philosophy, Mahan nevertheless asserted that psychological introspection reveals a doctrine of the will that opens up the implied biblical view. Thus, in Mahan's estimation, the objective and subjective forms of knowledge from revealed and natural sources agree without contradiction.

The juxtaposition and agreement of the internal consciousness with the external biblical revelation was common in revivalist theology of the nineteenth century. An aspect of the scholastic vision of Academic Orthodoxy, it was simply assumed that sure scientific, theological, ethical, and biblical knowledge would all fit harmoniously into one system.

It becomes obvious in only a few pages just how powerfully governing over Mahan's system his doctrine of the will is. It is the key to his moral philosophy. His sentences ring with the gravest admonitions for human persons to apprehend their place of personal culpability with regard to sin and responsibility with regard to salvation and moral reform. Thus, in the few pages of *Doctrine of the Will*, Mahan lays the foundation for the interrelationship of soteriology, eschatology, ecclesiology, and personal and social ethics, all arising from his orienting principle of the doctrine of the will.

Mahan's placement of the volitional category as the hermeneutical key for his philosophical, theological, and ethical systems was not, of course, unique to him. Nor could Mahan even claim to be the first. Mahan's book was, however, the key text in the Oberlin curriculum on the subject; and as an Oberlin student, A. M. Hills was required to study, digest, and reproduce, at least in some fashion, its contents.

Natural and Revealed Theology: Common Sense and the Bible

In consideration of the revivalists' third orienting principle, three names are of greatest importance to the study of A. M. Hills: Charles Finney, Noah Porter, and James Fairchild.

---

57. Ibid., 55.

Finney's Natural Theology

Finney's system of Common Sense is best understood as a pyramid of logic, three layers of knowledge built upon one another in a geometry of theological ethics. At the lowest level are his axiomatic truths, or as he more often called them, the "first truths" or "self-evident truths" of reason. Built upon these are the "truths of demonstration," and at the top are the "truths of revelation."

In his *Lectures on Systematic Theology*, Finney defines terms and makes distinctions.

> By self-evident truths of reason, then, I mean that class of truths that are directly intuited and affirmed by that faculty in the light of their own evidence, and by virtue of its own laws, whenever they are so stated that the terms of the proposition in which they are conveyed are understood. They are not arrived at by reasoning, or by evidence of any kind except what they have in themselves. As soon as the terms of the propositions in which they are stated are understood, the reason instantly and positively affirms their truth ... The mathematical axioms belong to this class.[58]

Finney goes on to assert that the self-evident truths of reason are truths of certain knowledge. The mind of a person perceives such axiomatic formulation to be true as soon as they are made explicit to the mind. Conceptualizing ethical and theological equivalents to geometric axioms, Finney often makes the comparison.

While Finney rarely uses the term "common sense," his explication on the mind's ability to intuit first truths as truth without outside proof is clearly his variation on Reid's philosophy. Of the mind's abilities in relation to self-evident truths, Finney writes, "The mind only knows them by virtue of its own laws, and directly assumes and intuits them whenever they are suggested."[59]

Throughout his *Lectures on Systematic Theology*, Finney reminds the reader of several obvious first truths that he insists no one would question: the presence of space, the assumptions of causation, and the obligation of right and wrong.

Finney's system of logic worked much like geometric mathematics. Just as in geometry there were certain postulates and axioms that do not need to be proven, but are regarded as self-evident, so also in

---

58. Finney, *Systematic Theology*, 5.
59. Ibid., 6.

moral philosophy. Just as in geometry more complicated mathematical understandings are built by reason upon the foundational postulates, so also with moral philosophy.

Throughout his systematic lectures, Finney offers lists of what he considers to be first truths. While many such lists exist, three particularly deft representations stand out. In lecture ten of his 1851 lectures, Finney writes:

> In every affirmation of obligation, we do, without noticing it, assume the first truths of reason—our own liberty or ability; that every event must have a cause; that the good of universal being ought to be chosen and promoted because of its intrinsic value; that whatever sustains to that good the relation of a necessary means, ought to be chosen for the sake of the good; that God's revealed will always discloses the best ways and means of securing the highest good, and therefore reveals universal law. These first truths are at the bottom of the mind in all affirmations of obligation, and are, universally, conditions of the affirmation of obligation.[60]

The second statement, from lecture forty-one, offers a similar list, with only minor variations. Finney writes: "Most of the first truths are developed in idea, long before the language in which they are expressed is or can be understood. Thus, the ideas of space, of time, of causality, of liberty of will, or ability, of the good, of oughtness, or obligation of right and wrong, of praise or blameworthiness, and many others, are developed before the meaning of these words is at all understood."[61]

The third statement, taken from lecture fifty-four, adds a new idea to his list. "That selfishness is sin, and that it is right and duty to consecrate the whole being to God and his service, are first truths of reason."[62]

Among these three statements is a representative whole of the moral ideas that Finney held to be first truths. Other levels of truth could be

---

60. Finney, *Lectures on Systematic Theology*. On the home page of this work, editor and copyist Richard M. Friedrich states, "The only source for these lectures came from the printed 1851 English edition of Systematic Theology by Charles Finney. This is 100% Finney with no deletions or additions. This version has been out of print for over 150 years." As this version of Finney's systematic work is prior to Hills' attendance at Oberlin by only a few years, and is not a later version abridged by Finney and Fairchild, I have chosen it to represent the most likely form in which Hills received Finney's teachings. Thus, when available, I have preferred the 1851 version.

61. Ibid.

62. Ibid.

found by virtue of reason or revelation, but only these are considered first truths. All of his other affirmations, no matter how strongly he asserted them, were understood to be *demonstrated* truths, built by logic upon axiomatic foundations, or revealed truths.

Because it will relate to the development of Hills' thought in the next chapter, it should be noted here that Finney *never* referred to the knowledge of the unending punishment of sinners as a first truth, a self-evident axiom, requiring no proof for moral agents to intuit inherently. He does, however, everywhere in his systematic lectures, treat it as one of his "truths of demonstration," a logical deduction built upon axiomatic first truths.

Of course, even while a truth of demonstration was not a self-intuitive truth, in Finney's estimation, it was still regarded as the single, self-evident conclusion of the axioms and reason upon which it was built. Thus, Finney could state that while demonstration was required, nevertheless, "This class when truly demonstrated, are known to be true with no less certainty than self-evident truths."[63] His doctrine of divine sanctions, which are discussed below, are best understood under this head.

Fairchild's Dynamic Relationship between Natural and Revealed Knowledge

At Oberlin, James H. Fairchild, like all of the other presidents of Academic Orthodox, taught the capstone class of university studies, "Moral Philosophy." While his actual lectures from the late 1860s are not available for comparison, the culmination of his decades of teaching is systematized in his *Elements of Theology Natural and Revealed*.

In *Elements of Theology*, Fairchild sets forward what had already become the standard definition of and sources for a revivalist theology. Beginning with natural theology, he opens:

> Theology . . . is the science of religion; that is, a scientific presentation of the facts and doctrines of religion . . . Theology, in its generic sense, receives . . . different designations, according to the sources from which the facts are derived. We may go directly to the works of God, guided by principles of our own reason and intelligence; and the truths we thus gather in reference to God, his attributes and government, and pertaining to man as related

---

63. Finney, *Systematic Theology*, 9.

to God, are called *Natural Theology*. Natural theology, therefore, embraces those facts pertaining to God, and to man as related to God, which might be gained from nature, without what is strictly called revelation."[64]

Common Sense inherently implied a natural theology of some kind or another. A belief in humanity's sharing of certain *a priori* intuitions was a basic assumption of all proponents of Reid's philosophy. Common Sense philosophy assumed common access to certain knowledge that pointed toward a deity which governed the universe justly, rewarding the righteous and punishing the wicked.

Of course, no revivalist theologian maintained that the knowledge obtained from natural sources was exhaustive. Knowledge also given by revelation was required for one to know in the fullest sense. Fairchild writes, "Revelation comes in to supplement this [natural] knowledge of God, his providence and government, and of ourselves as related to God, giving us a better view of facts of natural theology, and adding truths which lie beyond the scope of reason. Theology thus extended and sustained is called *Revealed Theology*."[65]

While Fairchild's definitions are fairly standard for nineteenth-century revivalist theology, what is unique to him among Hills' mentors is his next phrase on the possibility of a dynamic relationship between natural and revealed theology. He writes:

> [The knowledge based upon natural theology] is not limited to what men do actually learn, but includes what may be established from nature *when once the truth has been suggested*. To illustrate—the truths of geometry are truths of reason, can be established on rational grounds. They might have been given by revelation; but when once we had the truths, we should not depend on revelation for their validity. So the facts of natural theology might be first suggested by revelation, but they can be established and sustained apart from revelation.[66]

An interesting addition to the typical revivalist relationship between the spheres of natural and revealed theology, Fairchild's definitions propose a semi-permeable boundary between the two. The implications of this addition are, of course, that conceivably one could extend the

---

64. Fairchild, *Elements of Theology*, 1–2.
65. Ibid., 2.
66. Ibid. Italics mine.

boundaries of common knowledge, pulling down at least some of revealed theology into the realm of natural theology.

There are two factors that account for Fairchild's openness to the extension of the boundaries of natural theology. First, such a possibility could be taken as a natural consequence of Fairchild's own definitions. For him, there was only a slight difference between natural and revealed theology. "[They] differ, primarily, in the sources from which their materials are derived, as well as in the extent and minuteness of their facts and doctrines. Revealed theology presents more minutely the facts of the divine government, the special dispensations of God's providence, the historical facts of the origin of sin in the world, the history of redemption, and the doctrine of the future life."[67] With only a slight difference in degree of detail between the two, the boundaries of natural theology's realm were open to subjective interpretation.

While the first reason is obviously partially true, what is much more likely is that Fairchild's position is the consequence of his and Oberlin's vision of progress. After considering the interrelationship among the theological, philosophical, metaphysical, ethical, historical, and natural fields of knowledge, Fairchild concludes, "A glance at this wide field makes it obvious that theology is a progressive science. Every advance in philosophy, in natural science, in philology, or in history, may lead to a corresponding improvement in the expression of theological doctrine."[68]

Fairchild's logic was simple. Given the Oberlin assumptions of the continuous and exponentially growing expansion of revealed religion through mass evangelization, the spread of Christianity would result naturally over time in a broader base of common knowledge with regard to revealed ideas. As more and more persons encountered revealed religion, and as these were taught the minute facts of revelation, eventually many revealed ideas would take on a common or natural status. Indeed, although Fairchild does not articulate it in so many words, his and Oberlin's vision of a soon-coming millennium implies an entire world where the revealed ideas of Christianity would already have become common knowledge.

---

67. Ibid., 3.
68. Ibid., 4–5.

Porter's Psychological-Oriented Common Sense

Noah Porter's *The Human Intellect* was a text at Oberlin for many years including those of Hills' attendance.[69] This methodological treatise on his version of Reid's philosophy makes use of psychological categories and language to undergird his articulation of Common Sense intuitions and reasoning.

To a large extent, Porter's underlying assumptions are the same as Finney and the other Common Sense philosophers' in the section. For this reason, we will consider only his choice of language and categories and his unique contribution to Hills' education.

Building upon axiomatic foundations much as Finney did, Porter insists that the phenomena of the soul are apprehended by "consciousness." "Psychology proceeds on the assumption that certain facts or phenomena may be known by the soul concerning itself. The power of the soul to know itself and its own states is termed *consciousness*."[70]

For Porter, consciousness is the inward eye of investigation, offering the observer foundational principles for all the sciences. The inward gaze of consciousness, accomplished habitually and organized scientifically, provides content not only for psychology, but for every other science relating to humanity. Of its epistemological implications, Porter writes, "Psychology either furnishes or makes known *the first principles* for all those sciences which either directly or remotely relate to man—which concern his being, his aspirations and wants, the products of his genius, his institutions, his studies, or his destiny."[71]

Porter next offers five different "sciences" for which psychology's consciousness provides first principles: ethics, political and social sciences, aesthetics, theology, and logic and metaphysics.[72]

While Porter appropriates slightly different language in his psychological conceptualization of Common Sense, to this point he has not differed substantially from Finney and Fairchild's methodologies. Where

---

69. An abridged form of this work appeared later under the title *The Elements of Intellectual Science*. Because the similarities between the two are not greatly significant, the latter being simply an abridgment of the former, and as Hills was aware of both versions, I have opted to make reference to the more succinct latter of the two.

70. Porter, *Elements of Intellectual Science*, 3.

71. Ibid., 7.

72. Ibid., 7, 8, and 9.

he adds something unique to the training of A. M. Hills is in his usage of psychological introspection for interpersonal understanding.

In Porter's scientific use of the consciousness, inward self-study teaches more than doctrinal, philosophical, or ethical knowledge. For Porter, it provides a window into knowledge of the depths and hidden places in human persons themselves. Articulating something of the potential for psychological discernment, he writes:

> The self-knowledge which psychology fosters, and to which it insensibly trains, is the one instrumentality by which we learn to understand our fellow-men. The sharp and searching look by which one man sees through another, and reads the secret which he is unwilling to confess, is attained only by the fine and subtle analysis of one's self . . . The only thoughts and feelings which the interpreter can know directly, are his own; and it is by a close and habitual study of these that he is able to connect them with the signs through which the thoughts and feelings of other men are revealed.[73]

In knowing oneself, one knows human persons better.[74] A form of natural discernment based upon the insights of introspection, the addition to Hills' training of a psychologically-oriented version of Common Sense broadened his understanding of the usefulness of this philosophy. Not only did the application of Common Sense offer a window into every form of knowledge and ethics, but it also gave Hills at least perceived access into the hidden parts of the human intellect, sensibilities, heart, and will. Not only could the Common Sense philosopher access the heights of human knowledge, but also the depths of the human soul. A. M. Hills found multiple uses for this perceived access into the shared psyche of all human persons.

As was stated above, Hills' Yale and Oberlin sources do not differ conceptually much from each other. Both schools worked with Reid's

---

73. Ibid., 6.

74. Porter illustrates that the great writers of the past "may not have learned the technical names which are given to his capacities, or the theories which have been formed of the essence and powers of the soul; but they have studied its thought and feelings to the most effectual purpose, and have exhibited the results of their studies in characters of surpassing interest, and by words of wondrous power. From their works the student of psychology may find most valuable aid, and, to enjoy and appreciate them, there is no study which is so useful as the systematic study of the human soul, with the habits and tastes which this study engenders." Ibid., 7.

basic anxieties, values, assumptions, and framework. Nevertheless, Porter's psychologically-oriented Common Sense certainly extended at least Hills' formal training in Reid's philosophy, allowing him one more field to weave into his complex of unified knowledge. While Hills' later language never betrayed direct reliance upon the language of Porter, the practical extensions of this Yale president's ideas will be seen in the next chapters.

Summary: Revivalist Theological Method

Whatever other adjectives might be used to describe the above revivalist trinity of methodologies perhaps "scholastic" is the most descriptive.[75] The method was both rigorous and assumed to be universally applicable. Academic Orthodoxy's goal to systematize all the worlds of philosophy, science, theology, ethics, and reform was no small thing. Their method, therefore, called for a complex and arduously long process.

The above characteristics of Oberlin and Yale methodologies formed the background against which A. M. Hills' theology, life, and ministry must be considered. As we will see in the next two chapters, the revivalist trinity of orienting principles, systematized in the scientific framework of Baconism, operated and directed the development of Hills' thought, offering him a clear canon against which to judge doctrine, philosophy, and ethics for the rest of his life. Hills' works are permeated with and shaped by the scientific and philosophical concepts and language of Academic Orthodoxy and postmillennialism, the revivalist doctrine of the will, and the epistemology of Common Sense.

As was stated above, it was the goal of the Academic Orthodoxy to combine all fields of knowledge, ethics, and practice into a workable social and personal revivalism that could be applied on a global scale. Hills embraced this vision fully and advocated it well into the fourth decade of the twentieth century, even long after other philosophical and scientific paradigms had pushed it to the intellectual periphery.

Hills applied the above methodology conscientiously throughout the entirety of his life. He arduously collected data as a proper theological, ethical, and psychological scientist should, painstakingly exegeting the Scriptures from the original and collecting stories and illustration from literature, history, and the sciences. A lifelong student and vora-

---

75. The use of the term "scholastic" here is not intended to imply any of the negative connotations that the word sometimes carries.

cious reader, Hills seemed never to tire of the vision instilled in him at Oberlin and Yale. Well into the twentieth century, he worked to wed an adequate biblical understanding with psychology and philosophy to define the "laws" of religion, ethics, revivalism, and reform.

Of course, it is important to note here that revivalism's task of global evangelism and universal education and reform would not be accomplished by any one person, but only by an exponentially growing army of thinkers and reformers. Thus, the revivalists relied upon each other's work as much as possible. The most significant reliance that took place was, of course, that they worked with the systems and conclusions of the former generation. Since much of the arduous work of developing the laws of the universe had already been accomplished by the 1860s when he began his formal education, Hills simply started with the systems, conclusions, and laws of the earlier revivalists.

One of the clearest examples of the shared nature of the work can be found in a story Hills offers of a class with Timothy Dwight, the professor of Greek at Yale. Hills recalls that Dwight once spent nine class sessions in the Greek New Testament on a single verse, Rom 9:5. "When we got through, any real student had a solemn sense of the importance of scripture doctrines, and of the sacredness of the greek [sic] texts of Scripture."[76] Of course, although he does not articulate it, after those class sessions, Hills also had a significant amount of *content* from that verse. An education from multiple mentors like this gave Hills not only a rigorous method for his enormous task, but also a doctrinal and philosophical content with which to start. Further, the revivalist schools, especially Oberlin, also provided students with a network of like-minded peers with whom to work out the laws of the universe and the reformation of the world. Intellectually stimulated and empowered by their goal, students like A. M. Hills burst into the world ready to rid it of all its evils, inducing new laws and applications from the revivalist philosophical method and applying these to global reform.

REVIVALIST THEOLOGICAL CONTENT

Having considered above the revivalist method, a word is now in order concerning the actual doctrines of the revivalists' systems that made a

---

76. Hills, "Autobiography," 51 (33).

significant impact on A. M. Hills. Two particular doctrines are of the greatest significance for understanding Hills, the doctrine of the moral governance of God and the unity or simplicity of moral action. The two spokespersons we will consider here for these doctrines are Charles Finney and James Fairchild.[77]

Finney's doctrine of the moral governance of God, with the related theme of moral sanctions, is one of the most important theological affirmations of Hills' system. Likewise, although Hills would eventually reject the doctrine, Fairchild's idea of the unity or simplicity of moral action is key to understanding the revivalist mind as well as some of the issues that later produced tensions within revivalism.

Finney's Moral Government and the Necessity of Moral Sanctions

In order to fully appreciate his doctrine of moral government and the necessity of moral sanctions, a brief account of Charles G. Finney's spiritual and intellectual journey is required.

Christianity of the first three decades of the nineteenth century in America was, in Finney's estimation, a declining religion in need of revival. The opinion that early nineteenth-century American Christianity was in a general state of dilapidation was, of course, not uniquely held by Finney. Many others recognized what he did. Indeed, even Finney's greatest opponent, Benjamin B. Warfield, in his monumental attack on Finney and all other perfectionists, *Studies in Perfectionism*, writes, "The churches were in a depressed state and this meant both an abnormally low condition of Christian life within them, and an abnormally large mass of indifference or worse without them."[78]

While he agrees with Finney that the church of those decades was in something of a slump, Warfield's agreement with Finney ends there. Finney's revivalist (and eventually perfectionist) response was the worst possible answer to the problem, Warfield firmly asserted. Finney's solution was to stir the church out of its complacency with the strongest possible exhortations concerning human culpability and responsibility. This

---

77. It should be noted here that another *earlier* voice at Oberlin is often considered more significant than Fairchild's for the doctrine of the unity or simplicity of moral action, William Cochran. Cf. Cochran, *Simplicity of Moral Actions*. Because Hills studied directly under Fairchild and never knew Cochran, however, the former's work has been chosen to represent the teaching that Hills would have received on the subject.

78. Warfield, *Studies in Perfectionism*, 22–23.

message was combined with the use of "means," a set of practical and controversial psychological and spiritual devices with greater persuasive and conversional abilities than the standard "means" of grace. Since individual responsibility for sin was at the heart of Finney's message, the power of human choice was particularly emphasized.

Finney laid the axe at Calvinism's root, undermining the foundation of every major doctrine. Having no use for the Calvinist doctrine of divine decrees, Finney and the revivalists placed all of the responsibility of salvation upon the human person's decision in favor of Christ.

The Calvinist doctrines of predestination and bondage of the will had been losing sway in America, especially on the frontier, for decades. Optimism and progress and limitless possibility were the spirit of the early nineteenth century. By the second decade, Methodism was making its presence and ethos felt, challenging virtually every traditional church structure, doctrine, and method. Then came Charles G. Finney, the perfecter of early nineteenth-century revivalism.

Converted and converting others in a matter of only a few hours, Finney was, to say the least, an extraordinary personality. Charismatic, persuasive, strong-willed, and at the same time open and closed-minded, Finney made the other leading revivalists of his age look like amateurs at their own game. He could out-preach the best and emotionally stir even the most respectable to a point of frenzy. At the heart of it all was his message of personal responsibility based upon his own version of the doctrine of volitional freedom.

Of course, Finney was not the first evangelical in nineteenth-century America to offer a more positive estimate of human volitional ability. The foundational doctrine of the bondage of the will had already been eroded in New England theology when Finney began systematizing his thoughts. The name most famous with challenging high-Calvinism in the first decades of the nineteenth century is Nathaniel Taylor. An Arminian-like alternative to high-Calvinism, Taylor's New Divinity was becoming "in vogue" by the second decade of the nineteenth century.[79]

While the two often ran parallel tracks with regard to content and conclusions, Taylor and Finney began at vastly different starting points. Taylor's theology arose out of his pastoral concern for parishioners being crushed under the psychological weight of high Calvinism. Thus, his first message was one of comfort. God's governance is one of fair-

79. Ibid., 19.

ness and justice. Cognizant of Taylor's more pastoral concerns, Sweeney points out:

> Taylor believed with all his heart that "God is a God of sincerity and truth." To sinners racked with anguish and self-doubt, he declared continually that God's offer of salvation was genuine, reliable, and open to all. Despite what they might have heard from some *hyper*-Calvinist clergymen, the Lord's governance was just and fair. God did not withhold grace from any who earnestly sought it and only those who willfully persisted in the error of their ways would be abandoned ultimately to perdition ... Taylor exhorted his fellow ministers to drive this fact home to troubled parishioners, freeing them from the debilitating psychology of high Calvinism and reassuring them with the infallible promises of the gospel.[80]

Finney's own version of modified Calvinism often brought him to similar doctrinal conclusions and content as Taylor. Whether or not he drew directly from Taylor or not, Finney's theological development must at least be interpreted in light of the context of waxing Arminianism in the early half of the nineteenth century.

Unlike Taylor, however, Finney's system is best understood from the starting point of his frustrations with an overly passive church than with a pastoral concern for psychologically overburdened souls. Everywhere Finney looked he saw (and sometimes perhaps projected) a volitionally weak, excuse-making Christianity. Falling far short of his vision of pro-activity, Finney regularly charged Christians with complacency toward their own salvation and in their mission of evangelism and community renewal.

Thus, Finney's greatest contentions with the church, as he perceived it, revolved around the volitional powers of humanity. He considered the church on the whole in a state of decline and, therefore, in need of "revival." Subtle spiritual, psychological, and doctrinal forces worked together to hold Christians in a state of passivity. Finney's greatest strength lay in his ability to strip away logically the ideas that fed and strengthened complacency while embodying before a congregation and community volitional strength and active service. This combination was powerful and catalytic. Many thousands placed faith in Christ for the first time and

---

80. Sweeney, *Taylor, New Haven, and Edwards*, 91.

were added to the church while thousands of others confessed never to have known Christ during their years or decades of church attendance.

Finney's preaching and embodiment attacked quietism and passivity anywhere he perceived it. In some settings, Finney contended against the use of the sacraments, while in other places he would lay the blame at the feet of a doctrine misused to excuse spiritual self-satisfaction. Doctrinally, Finney perceived the problem of quietism in the Reformed teachings of bondage of the will and in the Methodist doctrine of gracious ability.

Finney's personal story is significant in understanding his doctrine of the moral government of God. In this cosmology, Finney's two main concerns were addressed. Not only is the justness of God emphasized, but it is actually strengthened by emphasis upon the responsibility of the human person.

In his doctrine of the moral government of God, Finney attempts to systematize and articulate the moral laws by which the whole universe runs or at least should run. Because his whole system of thought is the wedding of demonstrated truths and biblical insights, it is not surprising that the doctrine is grounded in several self-evident first principles. Finney writes that we may infer from our very nature that God is a moral governor. Likewise, he also asserts, "From the very laws of our being, we naturally affirm our responsibility to him for our conduct."[81] Finney reasserts this self-evident moral axiom in another place. "The idea of obligation, or of oughtness, is an idea of the pure reason . . . Obligation is a term by which we express a conception or idea which all men have, as is manifest from the universal language of men."[82]

Just as all humans recognize from inward intuition and even the very language they speak that they are obligated to do good and shun evil, the other first principle upon which the moral governance of God is built is that of free will. As we saw above, "our own liberty or ability" is one of Finney's self-evident first principles. "Moral agency implies the possession of *free will*. By free will is intended the power of choosing, or refusing to choose, in every instance, in compliance with moral obligation. Free will implies the power of originating and deciding our own choices, and of exercising our own sovereignty."[83]

81. Finney, *Systematic Theology*, 26.
82. Ibid., 30.
83. Ibid., 32–33.

For Finney, it was absurd to believe that God expects the good to be accomplished by persons if their wills are bound by evil. Any doctrine of bondage of the will necessarily negates moral obligation. A person whose will is bound to evil, and is thereby incapable of doing the good, is neither under obligation nor responsibility for the evil she or he is bound to do. Because he believed the doctrine of volitional bondage tended only toward increased spiritual complacency, Finney rejected it in favor of a free-will system of moral government and obligation. In his system, God is just in his governance because every person has the power to choose or reject the good that is before her or him.

It is, of course, but a small step of logic from here to infer that the God who set up such moral laws is a good, just, and moral governor. As such, Finney reasoned that God indeed expects the good to be accomplished and evil to be shunned by all persons, and that God will reward and punish as a just governor should.

As it relates to A. M. Hills, what is most important in Finney's doctrine of moral government is the absolute necessity of sanctions, (i.e., rewards and punishments). For Finney, a sanction is the only suasion God has to entreat human persons to choose the good and shun evil. "The sanctions of law are the motives to obedience, the natural and the governmental consequences or results of obedience and of disobedience . . . They are remuneratory, that is, they promise reward to obedience . . . They are vindicatory, that is, they threaten the disobedient with punishment."[84]

Unwilling to coerce persons to do the good, God has to put these rewards and punishments into place. "Moral government includes the dispensation of rewards and punishments; and is administered by means as complicated and vast as the whole of the works, and providence, and ways, and grace of God . . . Therefore that God's law has natural sanctions, both remuneratory and vindicatory, is a matter of fact."[85]

For Finney, both positive and negative sanctions were absolutely integral to a moral government. Humans, in his estimation being free to choose or reject good and evil, were profoundly culpable for their actions or inactions in this system. In this life, persons can expect natural and governmental occurrences of pleasure or discomfort for their right and wrong decisions. Likewise, Finney maintained that in the next life

84. Ibid., 202.
85. Ibid., 25.

these same principles will apply as well. The sanctions of God's moral government include a blissful heaven for the righteous and an unending hell for the unrighteous.

Fairchild's Simplicity of Moral Action

Oberlinites were often characterized as overly simplistic, black-or-white kinds of thinkers. To a large extent, this was and is a general characteristic of revivalism. Finney's preaching was intentionally designed to leave the listener with a clear understanding of her or his present religious stance and duty before God. Because this stance was based entirely upon the listener's own choices and actions, one was given a fairly simple, black or white, choice—"opt in" or remain out. Revivalists' volitionally-centered form of religion brought simplicity to Christian ethics as well. The converted Christian, having heard the proclamation of the truth, had but two alternatives. A person was either fully consecrated to the truth proclaimed, living up to all known obligations, or she or he was not. Revivalism by its very nature offered only "in" or "out" kinds of choices.

The doctrinally systematized form of this revivalist straightforwardness was given the name of the unity or simplicity of moral action. Among A. M. Hills' mentors, James H. Fairchild is the best representative of this doctrine. He recorded his mature thoughts in *Moral Philosophy, or the Science of Obligation*. In the ninth chapter of this book, he expounds upon the questions, "Can virtue and sin co-exist in the same heart?" and "Can the same man be both [virtuous and sinful] at the same time?"[86]

Of course, as was illustrated above in the story of Charles Finney, brewing in the background of all Oberlin doctrines and means was the shadow of a perceived dysfunctional Calvinism. In this case, fearing that variations on the Reformed doctrine of *simil justus et peccator* led only to complacent religion, Oberlinites cast moral philosophy in such a way as to allow for no excuses.

In answer to these two questions Fairchild states, "With few exceptions, writers on morals and theology answer this question in the affirmative; but if the foregoing views of the nature of moral action, of sin and virtue, be correct, the question must be answered in the negative."[87]

---

86. Fairchild, *Moral Philosophy*, 85.

87. Ibid., 85. Again, one hears the Reformed theologian in the affirmative, and the Oberlinite rejection in Fairchild's negation.

In Fairchild's "foregoing views," he argues that the nature of moral obligation is in the possession of intellect, sensibility, and free will. Under the terms of his definitions, in order for a being to be morally obliged, it must possess all three of these capacities. In the intellect is the general capacity to know and perceive. It is also the intellect that possesses the faculties of sense, memory, imagination, judgment, and reason. All of these capacities and faculties working together offer the human person the unique possession of knowledge. Knowledge, however, is only the first part of moral obligation.

Next, in order for an agent to be a morally-obliged agent, it must possess sensibility. For Fairchild, sensibility is the connection between natural revelation (or common sense) and moral philosophy. "Sensibility is the susceptibility of pleasure and pain, of natural good and evil."[88] The person's ability to experience pleasure for doing good and pain for doing evil provides an intuitive foundation for moral obligation, without which the intellect alone would not suffice. With sensibility, however, the intellect will perceive and judge clearly right from wrong.

The third necessary ingredient for moral obligation is free will, the actual ability to do the good. Fairchild writes: "Free-will, or the voluntary faculty, is the power of choosing or refusing the true end of life, as presented by the intelligence. The possession of the faculty is implied in the very idea of obligation. To affirm obligation of a being destitute of the faculty of free action, is impossible in the nature of the case. Power for any act, in the sense of ability to do or not to do, is a self-evident condition of obligation to that act."[89]

Were one able to feel pleasure in doing good and pain in evil, helping the intellect judge right from wrong, and yet still be unable for whatever reason actually to do the good, that one would not be under obligation. That is, a person must be able to feel, know, and choose the good to be a moral agent. Any person who has all three of these capacities is expected to accomplish all of the good that they know to do.

For Oberlinites, the notion of free will is the key for moral culpability. They believed that if the Reformed doctrine of the bondage of the will is true, there is no culpability on the part of human persons. If humans are incapable of doing the good that they intuitively sense and intellectually deduce, they are not held responsible. Thus, Fairchild, and

88. Ibid., 14.
89. Ibid., 15.

every other Oberlin professor, taught some form or another of the freedom of the will. An empowering notion, it not only caused the guilty to accept their own guilt and choose a life in and for Christ, but also helped the righteous to do all the good that they could.

For Fairchild, the doctrine of the unity or simplicity of moral action is simply the logical implication of his above definitions. All moral agents are held responsible to uphold all of the good (and shun all of the evil) that they know. In this framework:

> Two kinds of moral action, and only two, are possible. The agent may accept the right end of life, and thus his actions become right, virtuous; or he may reject the right end, and thus his actions become wrong, sinful. No neutral position is possible to a rational being, because when the right end is proposed to his intelligence, he must accept or not accept; and not to accept is to reject. Moral freedom lies in the ability to accept or to reject this end—an ability which is essential to moral agency.[90]

Thus it is that when he comes to his ninth chapter, "Unity or Simplicity of Moral Action," Fairchild answers in the negative the question of whether or not virtue and sin can co-exist in the same heart.

> Let it be remembered that all moral action is voluntary—that virtue and sin are found in the action of the will—in ultimate choice alone—that virtue is the voluntary choice or regard of good as good, or on its own account, and that nothing else is virtue–that sin is the voluntary refusal to choose or regard the good, and that nothing else is sin; and the conclusion seems inevitable that the two cannot co-exist, that where one is the other cannot be. The two forms of action are directly contradictory to each other, and, in the very nature of the case, each must exclude the other.[91]

---

90. Ibid., 19–20.

91. Ibid., 85. Later in this chapter Fairchild quotes Nathaniel Taylor, although noting that Taylor typically discards this doctrine. "[Every] moral being is doomed by a necessity of nature to place himself under the absolute dominion and control of the one or the other of these preferences. It is an ordinance of his very being, that he cannot serve both these masters, and must serve one." Ibid., 92.

Summary of the Revivalist Doctrines of Moral Government and Moral Simplicity

All Oberlinites, in some form or another, maintained similar doctrines of the moral government of God and the simplicity of moral action. Although both brought considerable criticism against them from many,[92] it was believed to be the only way to avoid the sloughs of religious antinomianism and social apathy. The systematization and imparting of these two fundamental revivalist doctrines empowered Oberlin graduates to preach with clear and even inspiring language. While they could be divisive in their application of these doctrines, Oberlinite revivalists often bore the distinctive stamp of their school with zeal. As we will see exemplified by A. M. Hills, such a stamp, drawing black and white lines, often earned the proponent her or his share of trouble.

REVIVALIST MEANS

Arguably just as important as revivalist theological method and content were revivalist *means*. A somewhat inaccessible term over one hundred years after being coined, the revivalists' "means" were a set of practical methods for bringing about revival. These means ranged from simple advice concerning sermon delivery to complex solutions for breaking through the most resistant crowds or individuals.

The major name connected with revivalist means is Charles Finney. His *Lectures on Revivalism*, and to a lesser extent his unpublished lectures on pastoral theology, clearly outline his programmatic and practical revivalistic means.

It was often said of Oberlin graduates that they bore the "stamp" or "imprint" of Finney. We have already seen instances of Hills' usage of the term, once in describing his childhood pastor and his wife, Rev. and Mrs. T. E. Monroe. In "Autobiography," he writes of this couple, "The pastor and his wife were both graduates of Oberlin College and had the Finney revival stamp on them . . . Our dear pastor . . . as much expected to have a revival every year as he expected to preach."[93] This way of describing

---

92. See Warfield, *Studies in Perfectionism*.

93. Hills, "Autobiography," 30 (19, 20). Also, cf. McWilliams, "Hills: A Life Sketch," 16 and Gresham, *Waves Against Gibraltar*, 27. Also, in "Autobiography," Hills writes of his own mother that she "got the Methodist stamp on her inmost soul." Hills,

the relationship between mentor and student highlights the perceived reality that many of the students of Finney embodied his style, approach, and delivery—in general, his means. It was these characteristics that drew students to Oberlin as much as, or perhaps even more than, mere doctrine. Profoundly shaped by the man Finney himself, students left Oberlin College bearing his stamp, his imprint.

Many who knew A. M. Hills personally said that he bore the Finney stamp or imprint. Indeed, the large majority of his interpreters, presenters, and eulogizers state as much while quite noticeably making no reference to doctrine.[94]

Obviously the phrase is based upon the subjective impression many had that Hills personally exemplified to them what they imagine Finney would have been like if they had known him. When put in this way, the phrase seems fraught with subjectivity. What is significant, however, is that *never* is doctrinal adherence what is intended by this phrase. The word "stamp" was used to connote a general likeness with regard to style and, as it relates to the immediate discussion, practical means.

Finney's Revivalist "Means" and Revivalism as a Means

As was mentioned previously, Finney felt that too many Christians subtly excused indifference to their own spiritual state, passively attending to the sacraments and church attendance without pro-actively attending to their own salvation and the salvation of others. This conviction was developed early and formed the foundation for the views he maintained the rest of his life.

From Finney's perspective, the use of the sacramental means in most settings contributed only to the passivity of the church, offering the partaker primarily a means to complacent procrastination.

It is significant that Finney chose the word "means" for his practical methods of bringing persons into the Christian life. Although he certainly would have resisted the idea, his practical means functioned as means of grace in a very real sense.

"Autobiography," 9 (6).

94. Hills' son, James, writes concerning Finney's influence on his father. McWilliams, "Hills: A Life Sketch," 80. Likewise, R. T. Williams writes of the stamp Hills left on his students. Ibid., 68. Gresham speaks of Oberlin's "imprint" on Hills. Gresham, *Waves Against Gibraltar*, 33.

Of course, Finney did not accuse the sacraments alone for the passivity of the church. Doctrine was also often a co-conspirator. Addressing quietism everywhere he perceived it, he charged Methodism, for instance, with passivity for their doctrine of prevenient grace. In Finney's mind, prevenient grace often functioned doctrinally for the Methodists the way the sacraments did liturgically in other churches; it gave an excuse to wait passively for God to turn the soul towards heaven without the necessary synergistic participation from the human side. To put it simply, Finney saw the various liturgical and doctrinal manifestations of preceding grace often serving to enable quietism and antinomianism. He maintained no conception of therapeutic grace that did not *first* include the will. He never conceptualized grace as a medicine for the soul that, regardless of the partaker's present disposition, would accomplish its end. For Finney, right disposition before God was antecedent to all growth in grace, and it was the human will that turned the disposition toward God.

Having said all this, however, it is perhaps one of the greatest ironies of Finney's theology that, while on the one hand he could be so contentious against the various expressions of preceding grace, he nevertheless maintained something of an alternative set of preceding means. Finney's revivalism worked practically that some means always preceded the conversion of a sinner. Shifting the locus of antecedent work from liturgical and doctrinal conceptualizations, Finney made the church and the minister the active participants that ushered in the grace of God. He writes, "The Church is required to use the means for the conversion of sinners. Sinners cannot properly be said to use the means for their own conversion. The Church uses the means."[95] For this reason, it is of the utmost importance that the church be instructed in the laws of spiritual revival and of its duties.

As we saw above, Common Sense philosophers sought to apprehend and articulate all of the physical, spiritual, and moral laws of the universe. One of the most prominent examples of the appropriation of scientific concepts and language is found in Finney's revivalistic means. His system of thought is permeated with appeals to scientific parallels, generally categorized under the heading of "law."

In articulating the dynamics that make up the laws of revivalism, one particular scientific first principle appears time and time again,

---

95. Finney, *Revival Lectures*, 12.

"cause and effect." This phrase, and the concepts underlying it, permeate both his systematic and revival lectures. In the former, Finney states that cause and effect is a universally understood first principle. Several times he cites it as an example of an undeniable, axiomatic truth. In one place, for instance, Finney states clearly: "A *first* truth, be it remembered, has this invariable characteristic, namely, all moral agents know it, by a necessity of nature, and assume its truth, in all their practical judgments, whatever their philosophical theories may be. Take, for example, the affirmation, or assumption, that every event must have had an adequate cause. This is a *first truth*; all men know it, and, in all their practical judgments, assume it, whatever their theorizings may be."[96]

While on the surface, Finney's appeal to cause and effect seems like merely a quick or obvious example to help illustrate what a first truth is, in reality it is much more than that in his system. This scientific notion is *central* to both his system and logic.

This is best exemplified in his *Revival Lectures*. A revival, in Finney's estimation, is the result of the right causes being put to work to produce the desired effect. Often comparing agricultural and spiritual laws, Finney writes:

> Revival is the result of the right use of the appropriate means. The means which God has enjoined for the production of a revival, doubtless have a natural tendency to produce a revival. Otherwise God would not have enjoined them . . . What are the laws of nature according to which it is supposed that grain yields a crop? They are nothing but the constituted manner of the operations of God. In the Bible, the Word of God is compared to grain, and preaching is compared to sowing the seed, and the results to the springing up and growth of the crop. A revival is as naturally a result of the use of the appropriate means as a crop is of the use of its appropriate means.[97]

In these statements, we begin to see how cause and effect applies to religion. Simply, for Finney, revival comes when the church puts into practice the means that will cause a revival. He contrasts this idea with the more traditional belief that revivals are miraculous, mysterious, or sovereign acts of God.

---

96. Finney, *Lectures on Systematic Theology*.
97. Finney, *Revival Lectures*, 5.

Finney's much more man-centered view of revival reversed the traditional conception completely, assigning the burden of bringing revival onto the church. In his estimation, a church should no more think of revival as a miracle or a sovereign act of God than does a farmer when reaping what he has sown and cultivated. The farmer, knowing and obeying the natural laws of planting and tending, can expect a good harvest when he has done his part. When he reaps a good harvest for his work, he will thank God for the blessing, but the farmer does not call it a miracle, (i.e., a suspension of the natural law). Again, he assumes the blessing of God in a good harvest, but nevertheless does not call it a sovereign mystery or a miracle that crops are in his field. A good farmer knows both the laws of agriculture and the tasks that are his to fulfill in accordance with the laws. No miracle, divine interference, or suspension of the natural laws is required when a farmer reaps what he has sown.

Finney vigorously argued that a revival is no more miraculous or mysterious than what the farmer experiences. Built into God's spiritual economy are the laws according to which revival comes. When the church tills, plants, and waters, so to speak, according to the spiritual laws of God and the psychological laws of human nature, it can expect to reap the harvest of a revival. In the scientific language of Finney's day, a revival is the natural effect of correctly applied causes. More often than not, Finney called these causes "means."

In his first lecture on revival, Finney presents the central means instituted by God to bring about revival. Under the heading "*The Agencies Employed*," he writes, "Ordinarily, there are employed in the work of conversion three agents and one instrument. The agents are God; some person who brings the truth to bear on the mind; and the sinner himself. The instrument is the truth. There are always two agents, God and the sinner, employed and active in every case of genuine conversion."[98]

Finney next clarifies the role that God plays in the process. God's agency in salvation is twofold. "By His providential government He arranges events as to bring the sinner's mind and the truth in contact."[99] Even more specifically, Finney continues, "God's special agency [is] by His Holy Spirit. Having direct access to the mind, and knowing infinitely well the whole history and state of each individual sinner, He employs

98. Ibid., 8.
99. Ibid.

that truth which is best adapted to his particular case, and then drives it home with Divine power."[100]

Concerning the specific role that humans persons play in the salvation process, Finney writes, "The agency of men is commonly employed. Men are not mere *instruments* in the hands of God. Truth is the instrument. The preacher is a moral agent in the work: he acts; he is not a mere passive instrument; he is voluntary in promoting the conversion of sinners."[101]

Likewise, for Finney, even the sinner himself has a role in the saving process. "The conversion of the sinner consists in his obeying the truth. It is therefore impossible it should take place without his agency, for it consists in *his* acting right."[102]

We see Finney's clearest instructions on means in his fourth lecture, "Prevailing Prayer." Here he actually defines "means" in a concrete way for the first time. He writes, "There are two kinds of means requisite to promote a revival: the one to influence men, the other to influence God. The truth is employed to influence men, and prayer to move God."[103] The two means that Finney makes reference to the most, the proclamation of the truth and prayer were the most important tasks the church could habitually do to usher in revival and eventually the millennium. These means were placed at the feet of a pro-active church and heralded as the very vehicle through which individual and mass conversions took place.

As powerful and effective as these two means are, however, the final and largest of Finney's means was revivalism itself. To put it simply, Finney's vision of the soon-coming millennium of peace could only be procured in the frenzied excitements of mass evangelization and revivalism.

Finney's rationale for why revivalism is a means in and of itself to bring about revival and worldwide Christianization is simple. "Men are so sluggish, there are so many things to lead their minds off from religion and to oppose the influence of the Gospel, that it is necessary to raise an excitement among them, till the tide rises so high as to sweep away the

---

100. Ibid., 9.
101. Ibid., 10.
102. Ibid.
103. Ibid., 49.

opposing obstacles. They must be so aroused that they will break over these counteracting influences, before they will obey God."[104]

This is not to say that Finney did not recognize the psychological downside to this approach. Indeed, he seems even to lament the need for revivalistic excitements, writing: "It is very desirable that the Church should go on steadily in a course of obedience without these excitements. Our nervous system is so strung that any powerful excitement, if long continued, injures our health, and unfits us for duty. If religion is ever to have a pervading influence in the world, this spasmodic religion must be done away with. Indeed, it will then be uncalled for."[105]

Even while offering a sharp self-critique concerning his own means, however, Finney's next statement becomes his final word.

> It is altogether improbable that religion will ever make progress among *heathen* nations except through the influence of revivals. The attempt is now in making to do it by education, and other cautious and gradual improvement. But so long as the laws of mind remain what they are, it cannot be done in this way. There must be excitement sufficient to wake up the dormant moral powers, and roll back the tide of degradation and sin. And precisely so far as our land approximates to heathenism, it is impossible for God or man to promote religion in such a state of things but by powerful excitements . . . Men being so reluctant to obey God, will not act until they are excited . . . Many are wedded to idols; others are procrastinating repentance until they are settled in life, or until they have secured some favourite worldly interest. Such persons never will give up their false shame, or relinquish their ambitious schemes, till they are so excited by a sense of quiet and danger they cannot hold back any longer.[106]

The above statement suggests that while Finney was somewhat reluctant to use revivalism's frenzy, he was nevertheless pragmatic in the spread of religion. The breadth and scope of his postmillennial vision required the most immediately effective means possible, and revivalism was this.

---

104. Ibid., 2.
105. Ibid., 3.
106. Ibid., 3–4.

Mahan's Concept of a Universal Reformer

Even with all of Finney's extraordinary means and personal abilities, the vastness of the Oberlin vision of universal reform *via* revivalism was too big a task for any single person. Indeed, it was going to take no less than an army simply to get started. Such a vast vision implied, therefore, a large team effort, so to speak. At Oberlin, it was understood that no one person was going to usher in the millennium. Indeed, it was not possible for any single person to possess enough time or energy to play even a small part in *every* reform that Oberlin envisioned. Among the Sabbath Schools, the physiological, peace, and educational reform movements, anti-slavery, the war against the heathen classics, and many others, the most that was expected of any person was to do her or his part in two or three areas while maintaining a supportive attitude toward all other reforms. Articulating Mahan's philosophy, Fletcher writes:

> The true reformer . . . was a *universal* reformer, seeking the correction of all evils. No man, said he [Mahan], could consistently be a temperance advocate and not an opponent of slavery nor an enemy of war and not a sponsor of moral reform. He recognized that the "great reformatory movement of the age" was legitimately divided into special departments, but insisted that it was equally true that all real reforms were "based upon one and the same principle, to wit, that *whatever is ascertained to be contrary to the rights, and destructive to the true interests of humanity, ought to be corrected*" . . . "Reform is manifold and yet it is one. E Pluribus unum."[107]

Again, one should not think that Mahan expected each and every graduate of Oberlin to be an active part of every kind of reform. Such would be impossible. So here is where Oberlinites were liable to apply something of a "body of Christ" metaphor. While each faculty member and student was expected to maintain the attitude of a universal reformer, each was also expected to be a part of only two or three reform movements.

This is best illustrated in Theodore Weld's letter to Lewis Tappan. "God has called some prophets, . . . *some apostles*, some leaders. Let Delavan drive Temperance, McDowell—Moral Reform, Finney—Revivals, Tappan—Anti-Slavery etc. Each of them is bound to make his

---

107. Fletcher, *Oberlin College*, vol. 1, 235.

own *peculiar* department his main business, and to promote *collaterally* as much as he can the other objects."[108]

Thus, it was that Oberlinites conceived of themselves as a part of a larger body, so to speak, each member doing its part to accomplish universal reform, but no one member trying to do everything. Even in the 1860s, Oberlinites genuinely believed that, if unified by an attitude of universal reform with each member doing its part, the reform of the entire world would happen.

SUMMARY

Chapter 3 has outlined a number of aspects of Hills' revivalist mentors at Oberlin and Yale. Having considered the revivalist theological method and content and Finney's means, we will next turn to the actual development of A. M. Hills' revivalist identity. In chapter 4, we will consider his development as a revivalist pastor and evangelist before 1895, when a turn of events procured his baptism with the Holy Spirit and subsequent slight theological change. Chapter 5 will consider Hills' development after 1895.

---

108. Ibid., 235. While any Oberlinite could be used to exemplify Fletcher's statement, one of the more interesting mixtures is found in Platt Rogers Spencer, who was a penmanship teacher and the inventor of Spencerian penmanship. Fletcher writes, "His early life was divided between the practice of writing and his battle with intemperance. Eventually he became a teetotaler and an abolitionist, an early member of the Ashtabula Anti-Slavery Society." Ibid., 361.

4

The Early Development of A. M. Hills' Revivalist Identity

HAVING CONSIDERED THE LIFE and mentors of A. M. Hills in chapters 2 and 3, we turn now to his actual sermons and publications. Chapters 4 and 5 will systematize the revivalist vision, doctrine, and means of A. M. Hills.

Roughly speaking, the dividing line between chapters 4 and 5 is his experience of sanctification in 1895. Because many aspects of his identity remained the same throughout the entirety of his life, this chapter will consider not only the development of his pre-1895 revivalist vision, doctrine, and means, but also those aspects of his revivalist identity that remained mostly unaltered by his experience of sanctification. Chapter 5, therefore, will consider only those ideas that were developed or radically altered after 1895.

THE LIFELONG REVIVALISTIC VISION, DOCTRINE, AND METHODS OF A. M. HILLS

In consideration of his early revivalist identity, it would be too narrow to consider Hills' theology alone. Indeed, as we have seen revivalism was and is much more than simply the sum total of its doctrines. A. M. Hills exemplifies this well. His identity includes not only a tight matrix of the doctrines that revivalists held most seriously, but also their overarching scholastic and millennial visions as well as their means. Because Hills' eschatological vision was as central to his identity as it was for his mentors, it will be the first to be considered.

The Eschatological Vision of A. M. Hills

In his article entitled "Millennial Views and Social Reform in Nineteenth-Century America," Donald W. Dayton opens with the statement, "We find it difficult today to grasp the extent to which millennial visions dominated nineteenth-century America. Our lives, at least for most of us, are no longer controlled by the religious currents that once cultivated bewildering variations on the millennial theme. But nineteenth-century America was different."[1]

The vision and works of A. M. Hills exemplifies Dayton's assertion well. While one might assume that a revivalist's soteriology provides the truest center of her or his system of thought, it is in fact eschatology that dictated most of Hills' logic and shapes his theological content. He embraced the postmillennial vision all of his life, and this made a defining impact on his overall system. Likewise, his appropriation of the broader eschatological themes of future judgment and eternal reward and punishment had a significant impact on his thought as well.

Thus, while Dayton addresses only the changes from nineteenth-century postmillennial to premillennial views, in order to appreciate fully A. M. Hills' thought, we will expand Dayton's statements to include *all* of the themes of eschatology. That is, Hills' system of thought is governed significantly not only by his millennial vision, but also by the broader eschatological themes of death, judgment, and future reward and punishment.

---

1. Dayton, "Millennial Views and Social Reform, 131. It is perhaps equally difficult for theologians and philosophers in the early twenty-first century to grasp how *functional* nineteenth-century millennial visions could be. Of course, part of this difficulty is a result of reading back into the nineteenth century the often speculative, dissipating, and impractical eschatologies of the twentieth century. Over the last one hundred years, perception has often been that only fringe movements have strong eschatologies. And as many twentieth century evangelical eschatologies are often perceived as more fit for tabloid covers than systematic theologies, it is very easy to dismiss the more functional eschatologies of the early and mid nineteenth century.

Hills and Postmillennialism

Hills contended for a postmillennial eschatology all of his life. As we saw in chapter 3, his Oberlin mentors maintained a vision of the coming thousand years of peace through the gradual work of the church under the power of the gospel and the Spirit. That Hills advocated this doctrine for the entirety of his life is exemplified in the publication of his systematic treatise, *Fundamental Christian Theology*, in 1931.[2] At the end of a very long life, he published the complete systematic definition of the position he had always maintained. Defining the "post Millennial Advent theory," he writes, "The nations of the earth are to be evangelized and all are to be converted, who ever will be converted, in this Holy Spirit's dispensation, by the present means of grace. The millennium means the triumph of Christianity in this world, the gospel being the controlling influence in human society, and in civic and national life."[3]

After defining his position, Hills immediately defends it. Always an apologist, Hills especially felt obliged to defend his position because, by 1931, it had already long been unwelcome in the Holiness Movement. One of several arguments, Hills writes:

> Post-millennialists accept what Jesus said about the expediency of His personal absence from the world (John 16:7). He plainly taught that His visible presence anywhere, would not be so helpful to His Church as the invisible but universal presence of the Holy Spirit in all Christian hearts. He never spoke one syllable about the insufficiency of the Holy Spirit and the gospel, and the present means of grace to win the world and establish His kingdom. He never intimated that His preachers and teachers and missionaries should go in the power of the Holy Spirit, with the gospel and the means of grace, and labor in vain, because all these Christian instrumentalities were never intended to succeed! God inaugurated these means and they will succeed![4]

Only a portion of his defense on the subject, nine more pages are offered, challenging holiness readers to consider the postmillennial position. Unfortunately, 1931 was far too late in the Holiness Movement's history for the doctrine to receive a serious hearing. By the fourth decade of the twentieth century, the Church of the Nazarene and the larger

---

2. Hills was eighty-three when it was published.
3. Hills, *Fundamental Christian Theology*, vol. 2, 351.
4. Ibid., 354–55.

Holiness Movement were predominantly either staunchly premillennialist or steadfastly ambivalent on the subject. The eschatological vision of the brand of revivalism in which Hills was trained was already mostly a thing of the past.

Hills' earliest millennial views are, of course, encapsulated in sermon form and are therefore anything but systematic. Indeed, his early postmillennialism is better understood as a vision than as a systematic doctrine. As we saw in the previous chapter, the eschatological vision of Oberlin was far from being a simple final chapter in a doctrinal treatise. Oberlinites wrapped their entire program for revivalism and social reform around the vision and hope of the millennium. In Finney's thought, the hope of a rapidly approaching millennium spurred zeal for the causes of both revivalism and reform often to the point of frenzy. It was not uncommon to hear him proclaim that the millennium could, or would, begin within a few decades or even years. This vision and hope captured the young A. M. Hills' theological imagination at a profound enough level to sustain itself for the rest of his life.

While Hills rarely makes explicit reference to the millennium or his postmillennial stance in his early sermons, the presence of it can be felt indirectly in the majority of his sermons, especially those highlighting Christian duty or social reform.

The most explicit reference Hills makes to the millennium is in "Temperance Address," dated August 3, 1880. Perhaps the most rhetorically exquisite of his sermons, "Temperance Address" represents Hills at his best. While only a single date appears on the title page, the actual manuscript bears the marks of a sermon that has been reworked at least once, although more than likely several times.[5] Painstakingly crafted, it is very likely that it is the address he used the year he spoke forty-two times across Ohio for the Woman's Christian Temperance Union on the subject of legalized prohibition.

The largest percentage of "Temperance Address" is multiple arguments in favor of prohibition legislation. Calling intemperance "*the sin of our land*," Hills paints it in the ugliest colors and goriest pictures available.

---

5. The actual manuscript is half hand-written and half pasted newspaper clippings. The use of the printed clippings suggests Hills was appropriating one of his own published sermons or articles.

> No sin has fewer apologies; the suffrage of the world is against it; drunkenness is universally reprobated. Yet it digs a bottomless pit of ruin in the sight of all mankind, paves the broad highway that leads to it with sighs, and groans, and broken vows, and lost health, and depraved manhood, and bleeding hearts; and then along the highway of blood, travel a *laughing, jeering, mocking* throng, deaf to all entreaties, and proof against all warnings; and it pours with shrieks and blasphemies, a very Niagara tide, in the chasm of remediless ruin.[6]

Calling upon his audience to be more than just patriotic and philanthropic, but Christian, Hills cites several ways in which to rid the country thoroughly of this "infernal traffic" that has "no moral right to exist" and upon whose forehead "Almighty God, Himself, has put the brand of his curse."[7]

Hills confesses that only three years prior he believed widespread education on the evils and dangers of intemperance, combined with a "strong public sentiment in favor of total abstinence," would be sufficient to rid the world of the use of intoxicants. In the last three years, however, Hills admits he has changed his mind. While he advocates continued prayer, the picketing of saloons, and the evangelization of traffickers and users, his main point of the sermon is to encourage the use of the ballot to stop intemperance.

Of course, in 1880 women did not possess the right to vote, so Hills' directs his comments toward two other sets of ears. First, Hills addresses the men in the W.C.T.U. audiences, to cast their votes in favor of their wives and prohibition.[8] Second, Hills also addresses any lawmaker who might be listening or reading to grant women the right to vote. "If man proves himself unworthy and morally unable to administer government and execute just laws while standing alone, then we must put woman beside him . . . If this evil must live, if the generation must continue to go down to darkness as they have done in the past, if tears must flow and hearts must break over the evils of intemperance, until we give woman the full ballot, then I say, let us give it, and may heaven speed the day! We cannot give it too soon."[9]

---

6. Hills, "Temperance Address," 2–3.
7. Ibid., 12.
8. Ibid., 23.
9. Ibid., 30–32.

In Hills' concluding remarks, one can almost hear what must have undoubtedly been an increase in the tempo and resolve of his tenor voice. He proclaims:

> To these glorious temperance women and all the friends of the blessed cause . . . The fanaticisms of yesterday are the reforms of today and the glorious triumphs of tomorrow . . . Do not doubt the promises or question the result. The victory is <u>ours</u>, as sure as the Lord reigneth and the kingdom shall be given to Christ. Human hopes shall not always be blighted; human hearts shall not always break. Truth shall triumph; this hoary evil shall sink beneath the execrations of men and the curse of a holy God; this old Earth which has so long groaned and travailed in <u>pain</u>, and echoed to the cries of <u>anguish</u>, and been wet with tears and blood shall yet be filled with righteousness and find its millennial peace.[10]

As is typical in Hills' early sermons, explicit reference to the millennium is virtually non-existent. In fact, the only use of it appears in last line of the sermon. It is not given any doctrinal or systematic treatment. The vision and hope of the approaching millennium, however, permeate the entire sermon. It is assumed between every line and recapitulated at the end as a closing reminder of the foundation upon which all reform efforts are built. Hills closes what must have been a moving address with a triumphant reminder of the world's eventual, and even inevitable prognosis, millennial peace. Again, this is not a systematic definition, but a living and inspiring vision of what most in Hills' audience believed the world would someday become as a result of their own tireless efforts.

In "Individualism in the Church," Hills offers another example of the use of the millennial vision in his early sermons. In this sermon, we hear one of Hills' clearest echoes of his millennial mentor, Charles Finney. At one point in this sermon, Hills almost sounds as if he is going to burst forth like Finney into a millennial prediction. He concludes his fifth of seven points with a rousing quote from John Angell James. "Were all members of Churches walking in holy conversation and godliness, sending forth the light of a beautiful example, full of zeal, laboring for the salvation of their fellows . . . what <u>revival</u> would come on! What prayer would ascend, and what showers of blessings would come down in their season! When our churches shall exhibit such scenes as these,

---

10. Ibid., 39–41.

then will God's work go on in the earth' [sic] And its progress will be with a speed hitherto unparalleled in human history."[11]

Again, the above citation in its entirety is a quote from John Angell James, and Hills certainly does not follow it up with a Finney-style, rousing crescendo that the millennium could arrive in but a few short years. Indeed, he does not even use the word millennium. A subtle inference to be sure, nevertheless, as in "Temperance Address," the overarching postmillennial vision of God's work and history's progress is clearly implied as the natural result of prayer and the work of Christians. Thoughtful listeners would have caught the inference, even without a specific reference to the soon-coming millennium.

The above quotes are an excellent example of the irony Hills demonstrates in his early sermons. The irony is that even while he was constantly guided by the vision and hope of postmillennialism, Hills seldom made explicit reference to it in his early sermons. This is, of course, easily explained. Hills' postmillennialism, as Oberlin's, was an extremely practical eschatology. Far from being simply a matter of doctrinal assent or scholastic speculation, it served less as a systematized idea than as a practical vision and a clear goal for the church. It functioned much more like the vision of a movement than the creedal affirmation of a denomination.[12]

The settings in which "Temperance Address" was offered best exemplify the fact that the doctrine of the millennium was more an overarching vision and a hope for a movement than a systematic doctrine. This sermon was a W.C.T.U. address and was more than likely never preached outside of a temperance union meeting. The W.C.T.U. was an interdenominational reform *movement*, not a division of the Congregational Church. Its single concern was the promotion of temperance, not the formation or proclamation of doctrine. While this does not mean they were anti-doctrinal, it certainly implies that their priorities lay in prayer,

---

11. Hills, "Individualism in the Church," 30–31.

12. A vision serves a very different function within the context of a movement than does an article of faith within a denomination. While a denominational article can be accepted by mental assent and fall to the periphery, a movement's vision takes on a life of its own and refuses to be ignored. In Hills' case, his postmillennialism serves his ecclesiological mission by providing a goal for which to pray and work. So integrally wedded is his postmillennialism to his ecclesiology that the former only appears in Hills' sermons on Christian duty and never in his sermons on doctrine. Cf. Hills, "Creeds–their Value," and "Creeds and Life."

picketing, political reform, and the evangelization of alcohol traffickers and users and not in the complexities of creedal formulation.

Not unrelated to the first, another reason for Hills' subtle and understated millennialism is how divisive such eschatologies can be. As a pastor, a local and state community leader, and an ecumenical spokesperson for temperance and other reforms, it is likely Hills felt discretion with regard to a divisive issue a better approach to unity and direction. Thus, he keeps his millennial views subtle and understated, generalized, but motivational.

While here we have seen the explication of A. M. Hills' postmillennial eschatology, it should be noted that echoes of the vision will be heard below in multiple places. Indeed, in many of his sermons where he addresses Christian duty, reform, or a social slippery slope that leads to the downfall of many, one can perceive the subtle challenge that Christians work toward societal, and even global, transformation. Thus, we will make mention of Hills' *implicit* postmillennial vision several times throughout the rest of this chapter whenever it surfaces.

Hills and the Coming Judgment

While A. M. Hills' postmillennial vision and hope can be found underlying many of his early sermons, the eschatological theme that receives the largest percentage of clear and explicit pulpit time is that of future judgment and the eternal destiny of dying persons. Hills' pastoral sermons and published books and articles are permeated with explicit exhortations, warnings, and even pleas for his listeners to consider the coming judgment, prepare for it, and live with it always in mind.

Chapter 3 explored briefly Finney's doctrine of the moral governance of God and the necessity of sanctions to secure its maintenance and justness. To recap succinctly, Finney believed that for God to be a just governor, both positive and negative sanctions had both to exist and to be enforced. This meant that the righteous would receive rewards and the unrighteous punishments. In Finney's system, these sanctions were both logically and biblically eternal, ultimately translating into a permanent residence for all persons in either heaven or hell.

Both in his early sermons and his later writings, Hills reveals strong adherence to the doctrine of the moral governance of God and to its subsequent implications with regard to sanctions. Unmoved by Congregationalism's shifting stance on the subject of hell from the mid to the late nineteenth century, Hills taught and preached the reality and necessity of eternal sanctions all of his life.

For Hills, unlike Finney, divine sanctions were a first truth of common sense. A sermon from Hills' first year of ministry, "God will Judge the World" is an abbreviated manuscript printed in one of Ravenna, Ohio's newspapers, *The Portage County Democrat*. The young preacher begins that on the previous Sunday, Easter, 1875, he discussed the topic of the resurrection, but ran out of time before his final point. Following up, Hills proclaims: "There is one other thought connected with the resurrection of Christ, which was not then considered, which it is well to bring before our minds. By that event, as the text [Acts 17:31] informs us, God has assured all men that he will judge the world. The day of that judgement is already appointed—when it shall be is one of the secrets hidden in the bosom of the Almighty. It is to come unexpectedly, like a thief in the night."[13]

Hills goes on to scold many other preachers of the day who, in his words, yield to the pressures of popular sentiment, withhold certain scriptural truths, and thereby contribute to the leanness of churches. Preaching only a partial gospel, they forget:

> This Bible doctrine of a future judgement is in perfect harmony with the universal consciousness of the race. All have some conception of a day when the deeds of men will be reviewed, and the good and bad separated, and to each allotted his apropriate [sic] reward. The inspired utterance of Paul on Mar's Hill [sic] was, therefore, only an authoritative announcement of what man, by his unaided powers had instinctively conceived to be true. Now if there is to be a judgement, it follows inevitably that the guilty will be condemned and punished. Otherwise the judgement has no meaning. We all knew also that we are guilty. There is, therefore, no hope for those who are out of Christ.[14]

Simultaneously appealing to both "universal consciousness" and "unaided powers" (i.e., common sense) and biblical revelation, Hills extends Finney's list of first truths. As we saw above, while he applied reflective logic to come to the *demonstrated* truth of divine judgment, Finney explicitly denied that it is a *first* truth. Hills' assertion that what the Bible teaches about judgment is affirmed by the universal conscious-

---

13. Hills, "God will Judge the World."
14. Ibid.

ness and unaided powers of the race is clearly an addition to his mentor's teachings, moving judgment and sanctions from their status as demonstrated truths to that of common, self-evident truths.

Finney's system of moral government combined the concept of just judgment with that of the necessity of sanctions. The divine sanctions are the only means of enforcement and the only assurance of justice in the moral universe. Hills contended for the moral governance of God as a central doctrine for the entirety of his life. He also, therefore, always maintained the logical corollaries of God's moral governance, that God would judge the world and eternally reward the righteous while eternally punishing the unrighteous. Heaven and hell were the only two options for the entire race of human persons. In Hills' logic, both were real and eternal.

Hills' evangelical dualism with regard to future destiny can be seen in his 1884 sermon outline, "The Solemn Alternative." Taking the text, "He that believeth on the Son <u>hath</u> eternal life; but he that believeth not the Son shall not see life but the wrath of God abideth on him," Hills opens his outline, "A joyous and an awful message here in same breath. A Pleasure to preach the one. The heart naturally shrinks from proclaiming the other. Both to be preached."[15]

Hills continues, stating the biblical condition for salvation, faith. "Notice—Belief in God's words, and trust in God is [sic] the great condition of salvation . . . We can not blame God for . . . making an eternal decree that 'without faith it is impossible to please God, and without belief and trust in him no soul shall ever be saved.'"[16]

After proclaiming a dozen or so scriptures showing that faith is the only condition for salvation, Hills moves to sections two and three in the sermon outline on the present salvation for those who believe. Section two opens, "Notice the result of believing, <u>hath</u>, <u>hath</u> eternal life. Present salvation. Durable salvation. Life! Life." This present and durable salvation will make the believer like a tree, "clothed in living green and loaded with fruit . . . a soul living as God designed it to live."[17]

Hills begins section four of the outline, "I turn now in sorrow to the other side. If you will not believe and trust so holy a God here is

---

15. A. M. Hills, "The Solemn Alternative," 1. Please note that the incomplete sentences are correct, taken directly from this sermon outline.

16. Ibid., 2.

17. Ibid., 4.

your doom. 'He that believeth not shall not see life but the wrath.'" Using again the word picture of a tree, Hills paints, "A tree girdled by lightening. Every twig shriveled. Every leaf withered. Existing but not living."[18]

Of course, such a withered existence is without parole. Hills continues that the lost will never again see life, not in a century, not even in an age. Graphically, he proclaims: "'Forever' written upon the gate of their prison house. 'Forever' stamped upon the clanking door. 'Forever' carved in deep lines of despair upon their hearts. 'Forever' written in the wreathing flames of their torment. 'Forever' greeting on every side their longing gaze. 'Forever' graven on the brows of their memory and eternally echoed in the pangs of their torture. The essence of hell is the thought of its duration."[19]

Hills' rationale for such language is in his conception of God's moral governance. Such a sanction is founded upon the justice of God. Hills concludes the sermon with an illustration of a New England dam that broke in 1874.[20]

> The rains had fallen upon the green fields of the hillside. The brooks and streams had watered the lowing herds. The accumulated and pent up waters had patiently turned the wheels and spindles in the factories. But in an evil hour these peaceful agencies burst forth through the broken dam and swept away factories and marts and homes and lives. So do the dews and showers of divine grace fall upon the lives of sinners. In a thousand ways does the mercy of God call them to repent. In 10,000 ways come reminders of forgiving love. But by and by the grieved and outraged love of God will lift up itself. The pent up indignations of the Almighty will break forth. O my God, what will the incorrigible sinner do when thou dost lift the arm of justice and whet the sword of vengeance, when thine anger burns to the deepest hell and thy fury is poured out like fire![21]

While certainly offering a vivid portrayal here, Hills should not be counted among those whose sermons were always littered with the threat of hell. He was, of course, a pastor for most of his early career and

---

18. Ibid., 6.

19. Ibid.

20. While Hills does not name the dam or the town, it is likely that he is referring to the May 16, 1874 Williamsburg, Massachusetts flood, where 139 people were killed when the reservoir dam broke.

21. Ibid., 7.

preached on many subjects other than eternal destiny. Rarely given to graphic descriptions, Hills was never gratuitous when speaking of hell. It was not a regular theme and, even when speaking on the subject, he never devotes more than a portion of a sermon to it. Of his manuscript sermons in existence, none reveal the use of the subject as a scare tactic, and there is no example of a sermon with the threat of hell simply sprinkled in at the end to elicit an altar response. Hills neither always preached on hell nor never proclaimed it. As a pastor, he addressed the theme when the scriptural text or topical theme insisted upon it.

Hills was certainly not alone in his proclamation of both heaven and hell, but in the Congregational Church, he was a part of a shrinking clan. Hell had often been a primary theme in Congregationalist and larger American revivalism. From Jonathan Edwards' "Sinners in the Hands of an Angry God" to George Whitefield and Charles Finney's vivid portrayals, hell was the obvious end to those who remained stubborn against the pleas of Christ in the good news. Thus, on this doctrine, Hills stood in theological and historical continuity with earlier revivalism.

Hills maintained his doctrine of sanctions for the entirety of his life. His experience of the Spirit baptism did little to change his convictions, save perhaps to strengthen them. Exhortations to consider the weight of eternity appear frequently in his books. In 1905, Hills published a series of ten sermons in book form, *Dying to Live*. In the third sermon, "Not Ashamed of the Gospel," he offers a list of the "truths that never can be eliminated and have any power left," the truths that are "as lasting as the love of God, as enduring as the needs of the soul." These include the fatherhood of God, the brotherhood of man, inherited depravity, the Savior's atonement for those who repent and believe, the Spirit's baptism for those who receive Him, and the "eternal retribution for those who will not be saved."[22] The post-1895 Hills holds his earlier convictions deeper than ever, radicalizing the balance of his former sermons, at least in this instance, by not even mentioning heaven.

Dozens of other such references could be made from his published books to illustrate Hills' lifelong convictions concerning judgment and eternal sanctions. One has only to read his *Fundamental Christian Theology*, however, especially the seventh chapter of part six, "Eternal Punishment of the Wicked," to see that he argued in favor of the necessity of sanctions even to the end of his life. After both logical and biblical

22. Hills, *Dying to Live*, 24.

defenses of his position, Hills concludes not only the chapter but also the two volume systematic work with this final paragraph. "That there is eternal sin, and therefore eternal punishment cannot be disputed. Be it an act of blasphemy, or a state of persistent impenitence, if unpardoned, it must be punished forever. The whole right-thinking moral universe may well ask the unanswered and unanswerable question, 'What else shall God do with it?'"[23]

While not the most positive or perhaps even appropriate way of concluding a systematic treatise, it at least illustrates well the reality that Hills saved a high place for the eschatological themes of future judgment and eternal sanctions for the entirety of his life.

In mining Hills' pastoral sermons for his early eschatology, one cannot help but notice that Hills makes many more explicit references to the themes of future judgment and eternal destiny than he makes to the millennium. To a very large extent, this is simply because postmillennialism was more of an overarching vision than a doctrinal tenet. Thus, while both sides of his eschatology are virtually omnipresent in his works, Hills *appears* to preach more often on the coming judgment than on the coming millennium.

Even taking this into consideration, one still notes that Hills speaks slightly more often of eternal eschatological issues than of earthly. The slight disparate ratio between these two themes is governed by a fairly simple logic, as exemplified in three sermons: "God's Question Answered," "Turning Back," and "What is Man?"

In the sermon "God's Question Answered," Hills takes his text from Ezek 33:11, "Say unto them, As I live, saith the Lord God, I have no pleasure in the death of the wicked; but that the wicked turn from his way and live; turn ye turn ye from your evil ways for Why will you die?"[24]

While this sermon is not Hills' usual manuscript, but only an outline, there is still enough of a skeleton to catch his logic. God's question is, of course, "Why will you die?" In the sermon, Hills attempts to answer this question for any listening soul, lingering about the church, refusing or procrastinating the making of spiritual decisions. Offering several possible answers for the listener, answer number four is, "Some of you will die because you childishly think more of the present than of

---

23. Hills, *Fundamental Christian Theology*, vol. 2, 431.

24. Hills, "God's Question Answered," 1. The Scriptural text is quoted directly from Hills' title page. Lack of punctuation, Hills'.

the future."²⁵ Hills continues in this outline sermon to scratch out the center of his argument. Such a person thinks more of "Present gratification of body vs. future blessedness of soul. Now/This life > vs. everlasting ages . . . Death bed is the true stand point from which to contrast time and eternity."²⁶

It is unfortunate that this sermon is only an outline with more fragmentary than full sentences. Nevertheless, the simple point comes through in Hills' use of the "greater than" sign. Simply, many will die in answer to God's question because they think more often and more highly of the present moment than of the eons of eternity. Often only a person on the deathbed, whose present days are completely spent, has a sufficient vantage point from which to weigh the seriousness of the swiftly-approaching eternity.

Hills addresses the relative weight of eternal and temporal things in an 1881 sermon on the subject of backsliding, entitled "Turning Back." "Men oftentimes become so absorbed in their <u>business</u> and their <u>professions</u>, even though they be the most <u>innocent</u> and <u>honorable</u> and <u>essential</u>, that they lose all true conception of the relative worth of the material and the spiritual, the temporal and the eternal."²⁷ Continuing a few pages later, he writes, "Satan entices souls. He leads them to forget God and the future and the eternal interests of the soul."²⁸

Interestingly, Hills does not blame forgetfulness of the coming eternity on intemperance, Sabbath breaking, or any other lesser or greater sin. On the contrary, contrasting several noble and necessary things of this present life against the weight of eternity, he concludes that nothing must keep a person from a clear perspective on the relative worth of this very brief life and the eternal one to come. All the things persons do during their lives, whether good or the bad, must never take away from the stark reality of the swiftly-approaching eternity. And while Hills never actually quotes it, one can certainly hear precursors to the soon-coming

---

25. Ibid., 3. Underlining, Hills'. Hills' notes on the title page indicate that he preached this sermon at least sixteen times. At some point, Hills manually edited this sermon, scratching out his original use of second person singular and replacing it with third person plural, taking some of the bite out of the sermon's rhetoric.

26. Ibid.

27. Hills, "Turning Back," 25.

28. Ibid., 28–29.

evangelical emphasis, "What good is it for man to gain the whole world, yet forfeit his soul?"[29]

The rationale for Hills' priority of concentration on future and eternal things over the present and temporal is fairly simple. Contrasting the relative length of even a long human life span against the infinite number of eons to come, one would easily, perhaps even self-evidently, arrive at Hills' conclusion that the life to come is of much greater importance. Hills offers an example of the vastness and potential horrors of eternal existence in a journal article, entitled "What is Man?": "All the vast waters of the Atlantic ocean [sic] could be passed through an aperture not larger than a straw of wheat. Nothing is needed but an infinity of time to accomplish the surprising result. President Finney used to say the lost soul during the sweep of eternity could suffer and doubtless would suffer, more than all the universe has suffered up to the present time. Nothing but constant suffering, and the eternal duration of a lost soul are needed to reach the appalling result."[30]

With such hearty and sincere convictions, it is of little wonder that Hills so identified with the calling of an evangelist for his entire life. Believing the only thing that will fit a person for eternal bliss is conversion, Hills often preached with this aim in mind. As a "revivalist pastor,"[31] he preached evangelistic messages. Between and even during other assignments, he often served as an evangelist. Indeed, whatever other title he held, Hills was always an evangelist.

From the above sermons and rationale one would think, therefore, that Hills' vision of social reform would have suffered as a result of what might be called the "eternity principle" and his personal emphasis on evangelism. This, however, was not the case.

There are two reasons Hills' resolve in favor of social reform remained steadfast against the logic of the eternity principle. The first reason is that Hills was a postmillennialist and, as such, simply believed that it was the Christian's duty to bring in the kingdom for its own sake. In "What it is to be a Christian," Hills speaks of Christian duty, echoing Mahan.

---

29. Innumerable evangelical sermons have been based upon this text, Mark 8:36.

30. Hills, "What is Man?" 1.

31. Gresham's third chapter is entitled, "A. M. Hills, Revivalistic Pastor." Gresham, *Waves Against Gibraltar*.

> There are vices to be <u>cured</u>, and great evils to be <u>corrected</u>, ignorance to be enlightened, and woes to be assuaged . . . Now the worldly are <u>deaf</u> to this call: but God expects his children to come out from among them and be <u>different</u>. He expects them to have a deep sense of their grave responsibility toward others, and to help on by holiness of life, and earnest activity, and importuning prayer, and generous benevolences, every institution and enterprise of the Redeemer's kingdom. The true Christian will gladly strive with all his heart to meet this just expectation. He will be a prayerful and upright man, a conscientious citizen, a true patriot, an earnest worker in the church, a friend of missions, and a zealous advocate of every true reform.[32]

In these sentences, one can hear that Hills embraced Oberlin's millennial spirit of a "universal reformer." He shared this vision, working for reform where he felt called, evangelism, temperance, and Sabbatarianism, while collaterally supporting other reforms for which he felt no personal call.

The second reason Hills never lost his zeal for societal reform was that he did not think of it as contradictory to his eternity principle. Indeed, the two sides of Hills' eschatology, the temporal and the eternal, worked in perfect harmony in his mind. It was for the very sake of the eternal destiny of a world of persons, whose lives were helped by or wrecked upon the righteousness or fallenness of the structures and institutions around them, that society and its vices had to be reformed. To put it simply, the spread of righteous reform meant that there would be fewer slippery slopes leading to hell.

The Slippery Slopes, Hell, and Social Reform: Pulling Together Hills' Eschatological Themes

As we have seen, concerns for the eternal destiny of human persons were foremost in A. M. Hills' mind. There being only one of two destinies possible for every person, one of eternal felicity and the other everlasting anguish, it was imperative that individuals not only apprehend this truth, but also be positively inclined toward the conditions for heaven. It was for this reason that many safeguards were conceived, both ideologically and practically, to help both those within the Christian flock to stay and those without to find fewer hindrances to coming in. In Hills' mind,

---

32. Hills, "What is a Christian," 31–33.

this is where concern for future judgment and work for present reform meet.

From Hills' perspective, while there is only one way into the kingdom of God, conversion, the world is replete with paths to destruction. While Hills never actually used the phrase, he envisioned a number of "slippery slopes" with inevitable destinations in damnation. This being his vision, Hills, as an evangelistic preacher, felt it his calling to warn travelers to get off the roads to destruction. His calling and identity, however, did not stop there. Taking it a step farther, he also saw himself as a reformer, whose job was to set up roadblocks, so to speak, at the entrances to all such slippery slopes.

Oberlinites were Arminians when it came to the possibilities of backsliding and even sinning to the point of rejecting saving grace. Sharing Oberlin's rejection of the various static forms of Calvinism for his entire life, Hills maintained the possibility of falling back from, and out of, even the highest heights of grace. Rejecting Calvinism's decrees as the determining factor in salvation and damnation, no complicated explanation was required for Hills to understand how persons are eternally lost. Without the complications of a high-Calvinist doctrine of decrees or of static salvation, his teachings required little sophistication. Simply, the devil lures away the unvigilant.

> Satan entices souls. He leads them to forget God and the future and the eternal interests of the soul. He keeps them, if possible, from Christ by breaking down every resolution they make to seek their Savior. If he fails there, he follows them over into the christian life, still assaulting their purpose to love and serve God. He plies them by indulgences, weans them by pleasures, distracts them by business, clouds them by doubts, stifles their aspirations, causes them to neglect their bibles, and give up prayer,—anything, everything to debauch the conscience and lure the heart, and induce surrender of hope and faith, forgetfulness of the future, and neglect of God. When this is achieved, the soul is quite ready to turn away from Christ, draw back from salvation, and with open arms, welcome death.[33]

With such a tireless and wily enemy, there were only two possible means for securing one's salvation. The first is the individual's duty and the second, the church's. First, the Christian person had to be just as

---

33. Hills, "Turning Back," 28–30.

tirelessly committed to God, the Bible, and the church. Hills draws a conclusion from what he has just said.

> The lesson to be drawn from this theme is not hard to find. It is a great thing to secure the salvation of one's soul. The very <u>entrance</u> to the christian life, and every step of its course, is beset with difficulties, oppositions, temptations, dangers. He only can hope to enter, and persevere, and finally win the crown of life who has that determination of mind, and preserves that inflexible purpose to follow Christ, and do right, and gain heaven, which will know no swerving and bend to no opposition, whose earnestness will never wane, and whose faith in final victory through the grace of God will never dim.[34]

Of course, all of the vigilant perseverance a single person can muster was not the only defense against falling. Fortunately, the Christian is not all alone, trusting in her or his own determination of mind and inflexibility of purpose alone. In Hills' vision, the church also has a duty to help in two ways.

In *Fundamental Christian Theology*, we see Hills' twofold understanding of how the church is to help. Under the heading "*Visible fellowship with the church would naturally seem, then, to be the duty of every true child of God,*" he writes, "The end of this fellowship is mutual helpfulness, and association in worship and mutual co-operation in the spreading of the Gospel and in extending the kingdom of Christ throughout the world."[35] Unfortunately, Hills does not elaborate these statements much beyond this. Because his systematic statements on the church predate the revival of ecclesiological studies in the mid and late twentieth century, he leaves the early twenty-first-century reader a little disappointed.[36]

There is, however, a wealth of ideas underlying Hills' brief sentences, and his decades of pastoral experience show a practical ecclesiology that adds commentary to what, today, is considered an underdeveloped systematic statement. His early sermons offer the missing explication

---

34. Ibid., 30–31.

35. Hills, *Fundamental Christian Theology*, vol. 2, 282.

36. This in turn often results in the unusual and unfortunate criticism that holiness theologians have no actual ecclesiology.

that one covets. Like so many of his generation, Hills lived and worked a better ecclesiology than he ever wrote down.[37]

Hills' systematic statement can be divided into the twofold duty of the church. In the first phrase, "The end of this fellowship is mutual helpfulness," we see the duty of the local church to help individual parishioners. In the second phrase, "The end of this fellowship is . . . mutual co-operation in the spreading of the Gospel and in extending the kingdom of Christ throughout the world," we see the social responsibility of church to reform the structures of a fallen world.

Of the first part, two particular sermons represent Hills' ecclesiology. In his 1878 sermon "Friendship with Christ," Hills opens with a brief description of the power and influence of *all* the relationships of life, including those found within the church.

> The relations of life are many and various. Men meet and mingle. Their lives are interwoven in ways innumerable, like the fine threads in a texture of surpassing richness and beauty. Never does human nature appear better than in the light of its social connections . . . The relation between parent and child . . . between husband and wife . . . between brothers and sisters, . . . between the state and the citizen, between the church and its members, between neighbor and neighbor,—all these are pleasant to contemplate and profitable to man.[38]

In the second sermon, "The Responsibilities and Relations of Life," Hills illustrates the reality of interpersonal influence. "Scientists assure us that Nature is one and matter is indestructable [*sic*]. This being so, nothing happens that does not have a bearing upon other things . . . Not a leaf flutters in the breeze, not a flower lifts its head from the earth, not a ray of light falls but awakens influences as lasting as time."[39] For this reason:

37. Here I mean something like what James W. McClendon's posits in his methodology of "biography as theology." Using examples like Martin Luther King, Jr. and Dag Hammarskjold, McClendon argues that a person's life can often speak a clearer (or even better) theology than do her or his writings. McClendon, *Biography as Theology*.

38. Hills, "Friendship with Christ," 1–2. Hills contrasts the depths of interpersonal relationships he is advocating with "cool, calculated acquaintanceship," where a "friendship" is sought because of the rank or eminence that can be gained from it. "Whoever looks upon it [friendship] as a kind of dragnet to bring in to himself whatever is desirable from society, help, or tribute, or flattery, or pleasure, or honor, does not know so much as the alphabet about the love of friendship." Hills, "Friendship with Christ," 5–6.

39. Hills, "Responsibilities and Relations of Life," 7.

> It is pleasant to think that just as bad men are increasing evil, so good men are enlarging the sway of goodness . . . Every tear you shed over the sin and suffering of the world is counted, every prayer is heard, every good act is felt and remembered. You are adding to the renovating forces of the world. No manly deed is performed in vain. You never give the grasp of kindly sympathy to one in need, but the touch of your palm thrills his being and inspires him with hope. Every word of tenderness to the sorrowing, every word of encouragement to the despairing, every noble endeavor is a living germ that cannot fail to grow. None of you can work so silently or in so humble a sphere, or live in such seclusion that your lives are wasted or vainly spent . . . The truth is, every man is like a soldier in the ranks; we touch men on all sides of us; we weaken or strengthen, we dishearten or encourage the great hosts of humanity among us according as we are false or loyal to duty, and recreant and true to the great interests of men.[40]

Of course, in these statements, one hears Hills speaking about more than just the interrelationships of fellow church members. Indeed, the same sympathy, encouragement, and loyalty are to characterize every relationship the Christian builds. Thus, the Christian, while certainly living out a godly life of deep, influential, and strengthening friendship with fellow persons in the church, is also expected to be a "friend" of the world. The Christian is called to exemplify the same empowering and transforming relationship with the world that she or he does with fellow church members.

That the fellowship and friendship found within the church provides personal support for those attempting to live a godly life is only the first (and perhaps even the least) of the two duties implied in Hills' systematic statement. In his ecclesiology, the church has a much broader mandate than simply to help along any individual that needs strengthening. The church is also to be a reform society, working for larger social changes to close down many of the entrances to sin. In "What it is to be a Christian," Hills writes: "All religion may be summed up in this—the faithful performance of known duty or implicit obedience to the manifest will of God. O how numerous these duties are! . . . We are all under a solemn obligation to make the most we can of our lives, for the glory of God and the blessing of humanity. There are vices to be cured, and

---

40. Ibid., 18–19.

great evils to be <u>corrected</u>, ignorance to be enlightened, and woes to be assuaged."[41]

"What it is to be a Christian" is dated six months prior to the above-cited "Temperance Address," where Hills echoes the W.C.T.U. agenda for full-scale temperance reform through personal and political means. In both of these sermons, Hills teaches his congregation to work against vices, evils, ignorance, and woes at the personal and systemic level. "[Christian duties] meet us every <u>hour</u>, in the family, on the <u>street</u>, in social gatherings, [and] in places of business . . . The true Christian will gladly strive with all his heart to meet this just expectation. He will be a prayerful and upright man, a conscientious citizen, a true patriot, an earnest worker in the church, a friend of missions, and a zealous advocate of every true reform."[42]

One cannot help but note Hills' underlying millennial hope in these sermons. He envisions a church, both evangelistic and reforming, working for a world of peace, where persons neither look for nor find vices that destroy both body and soul. To put it metaphorically, the second of duty of the church in Hills' sermonic ecclesiology is to close down the various roads to destruction, making it harder for the innocent, young non-Christians and Christians alike to find themselves on one of the slippery paths to eternal hell.

Hills' list of slippery slopes is numerous: there are the several roads of abject amusements; there is the use of alcohol and intoxicants; and there is the slippery slope of infidel education from an ungodly institution. In Hills' estimate, the first two of these would definitely sear the conscience and lead to eternal death, while the third was simply very likely to do so.

The Slippery Slope of Abject Amusements

Nowhere is Hills' pastoral concern for his laity more apparent than in his addresses to young persons. Originally a series of at least six sermons preached in the spring of 1881, only two have survived, sermons I and VI. In these sermons, we begin to see Hills' heart for young persons, a heart that would be deeply realized decades later as a college administrator and professor.

---

41. Hills, "What is a Christian," 29–31.
42. Ibid., 30, 32–33.

Although only the second of the remaining two is actually entitled "Amusements," both sermons address the topic of leisure activities. Not at all averse to amusements and recreation in general, Hills advocates a position in line with his Oberlin training. In "Lectures to Young People, No. VI. 'Amusements,'" Hills begins with a general affirmation of the necessity of amusements for recreational purposes. After citing a few vague, unnamed cases of strict asceticism and abstemious philosophical thought, Hills opens strongly:

> Let it be understood that any religious doctrine that frowns indiscriminately upon every form of amusement and pleasure is dangerous in the extreme. I am not standing here, you will soon know to defend unbridled license, or any ill-regulated enjoyments of whatever kind. I approve of nothing that is harmful either to body or soul. But . . . we might as well open our eyes to the indisputable fact that the Author of our being put into the very faculties of our minds and knit into the fibres of our physical natures the love of play . . . He has made us capable of responding pleasurably to an external world. He has given us senses and the means of gratifying them; he has given us minds and spirits susceptible of intense joy. Now why has he given us these powers and functions, if their exercise is necessarily wrong? We are driven to the conclusion either that God made a mistake in our creation, or that there are times and occasions when these faculties may be innocently called into play.[43]

The next four pages of this sermon are Hills' defense for human recreation. He defends it upon the grounds of medical and healthful necessity and even biblical texts.[44] Couched mostly in the rhetorical style

---

43. Hills, "To Young People, 'Amusements,'" 6–9.

44. "It aids to keep in healthful activity both body and soul." Ibid., 9. "Work and play are universal ordinances of God. The work is a necessity for any true life and the play is necessary for the most successful work . . . There are men who would live longer, and do more work and better work if they would take an occasional playday." Ibid., 10–11. "A wholesale condemnation of every kind of amusement is no honor to that Master who 'came eating and drinking' and does not praise the God who tints the sky of the morning, and paints with evanescent brilliance the clouds of evening, and carpet the earth with flowers." Ibid., 12. "God pauses betimes to inspect his work and enjoy it. And man, his child, has a right to leave the treadmill of toil and refresh himself occasionally with those things which God has given us richly to enjoy. No: a correct physiology and a sound theology are agreed in the condemnation of harsh asceticism, and join hands in an attempt to put amusements in their true light, and in the proper estimation of the people." Ibid., 13.

of common sense, though, he draws upon multiple secular and religious sources in the order in which he feels they will most effectively drive home his point.

Taking it for granted that the common sense of his listeners has affirmed the logic of what he has said to this point, Hills moves on to discuss exactly how play can become vice. He proclaims, "I now turn to caution you against venturing near the devouring Charybdis. Unquestionably, the tendency of our time, and especially of the younger generation, is toward excessive indulgence in amusements."[45] Hills continues for the next eight pages, listing the various kinds of entertainments that were, at that time, making themselves increasingly more accessible. From the step-up in toy production for children to the increasingly unrestrained gambling at the horse races, Americans were, in Hills' opinion, becoming too infatuated with leisure activities. It is for this reason that he offered this series of lectures and sermons to the youth. "The young ought to have some principles given to them by which they can safely guide themselves in their choice of pleasures, and in the amount of attention they can wisely and innocently bestow upon them."[46]

Hills offers seven principles over the next sixteen pages, all of which are germane to the present discussion of his eschatological themes. Hills' first principle is, "No amusement is innocent or permissible that does not prepare your mind and body for more and better work."[47] In Hills' economy, first and foremost, rest serves to further the work of God.

After a brief explication of the first principle of rest serving for better work, Hills continues with the second. "Amusements, however harmless in themselves, to be innocent must not engross too much of the time. Time is sacred,—the opportunity given of God to mortals for usefulness, for serving him and advancing his glory . . . If one hour of play will answer the end of recreation then it is a sin to take more. This is one of the strong temptations of young people—to waste time."[48]

---

45. Ibid., 14.

46. Ibid., 21–22.

47. Ibid., 22. Later, Hills concludes, "The work is the main thing. The recreation is a preparation for the work, and the amusement is only the means by which we seek the re-creation of the exhausted powers. Our amusements, then, to be innocent and lawful should send us back to our work fresher and stronger in mind and body." Ibid., 24.

48. Ibid., 25–26.

A few pages later, Hills offers his third principle: "Amusements to be innocent must, for the most part, be inexpensive."⁴⁹ Of course, Hills does not offer any advice on how much is too much, but simply continues that one should keep a proper perspective of the relative value of amusements in relation to more important necessities. One should think first of paying the bills, giving to philanthropic organizations, and saving as much as possible for future use as capital or for times of need. "However small a man's surplus may be, most of it ought to be devoted to these higher purposes, and to spend it all, or any very considerable portion of it in sport, is a most foolish and inexcusable extravagance."⁵⁰

When warning his congregations about the entrances to the various roads, a kind of slippery slope logic of "one-thing-leading-to-another" is almost always applied. Indeed, such is the very nature of a slippery slope. Once entered, the path becomes slicker, easier, and more seductive. Hills reveals this logic in the explication of his third point.

> When a young man spends lavishly on <u>amusements</u>, he soon becomes careless in <u>all</u> expenditures, and loses all sense of the <u>value of property</u>. And when a man sees no great value in <u>property</u>, he will see no necessity of labor to <u>earn</u> it, and then his feet are on the high road to <u>indolence</u>, <u>worthlessness</u>, and <u>dishonesty</u>. Probably more pilfering from employers on the part of clerks, more stealing from banks and railroads, more taking of bribes, more destruction of character, and more arrant knavery have grown out [of] extravagance in <u>amusements</u>, than have been occasioned by all other causes together.⁵¹

Hills places an extraordinary weight upon what many would consider a small thing, one's use of spare time and money for amusements. Of course, he places these statements immediately into the context of his eschatological vision. His next sentences reveal his mind on the relationship among the Christian, social reform, and amusements. "Nor is this <u>all</u>. The world is full of ignorance to be enlightened, of suffering and woe to be assuaged, of wickedness to be overcome. God has put us here to make the world cleaner, and happier, and better, and this is to be done largely by wise use of money. As his <u>servants</u> and <u>stewards</u>, he will call

---

49. Ibid., 29.
50. Ibid., 30.
51. Ibid., 31–32.

us to <u>strict account</u> for the use of our ability to make money, and for the way in which we have spent it."[52]

Hills continues with principle four: "Amusements, to be <u>innocent</u>, must be innocent or wholesome in their effect upon the soul,"[53] and, a few pages later, principle five: "Any amusement is unsafe which unfits you for ordinary pursuits." Offering examples of middle-of-the-night excitements that will weary a woman during her regular motherly duties or a man at his job the next day, Hills simply suggests that such amusements are wrong. "We should be <u>wedded</u> to our callings and thoroughly <u>devoted</u> to them; and we should no more permit any amusement to come between <u>us</u> and <u>them</u>, than we would suffer an artful jade to come between us and a devoted and faithful <u>wife</u>."[54]

Offering his sixth principle, Hills' proclaims, "All amusements should be avoided that will almost inevitably bring us into bad company."[55] Next considering the good of others, Hills offers his seventh principle. "We should not participate in amusements, which, though possibly safe <u>to us</u>, would be quite likely to ruin <u>others</u> who would follow our example . . . We are bound together in this great human family and the children of a common Father, and the interests of <u>each</u> ought to be unspeakably sacred to <u>all</u>."[56]

The Slippery Slope of the Theater

Completing thirty-seven pages of principles, Hills finally moves into the application of his thoughts to specific amusements. First, he applies his principles to the theater. Of course, the theater fails miserably to come even close to innocence. "The world has had the theatre for 2600 years, and it is always just going to be reformed, but never <u>is</u> reformed."[57]

---

52. Ibid., 32.
53. Ibid.
54. Ibid., 35.
55. Ibid.
56. Ibid., 36, 38.
57. Ibid., 39. "The fact is the theatre is incurably vile. It cannot be run without great expense, and to support itself it panders to the lowest tastes of the lowest classes. The morals of its plays are unchristian; religion is usually ridiculed. Crime and wickedness that would call down the wrath of God on their perpetrators are introduced to provoke laughter. The language is made spicy by oaths and profanity, and the conversations abound in profane allusions and vile double-entendres, and actresses and dancers are scantily dressed and all this to <u>draw</u>." Ibid., 43–44.

Incurably vile and still completely unreformed after two and a half millennia, Hills feels that the theater should not be frequented by any Christian who wishes to spend time and money wisely.

Of course, in Hills' estimate, the theater is so vile that it requires only a very few words of warning. For this reason, he quickly moves on to less obvious applications for his principles; Hills next turns to a more classical form of the theater, the opera. While he admits that he is a lover of great music, he regrets that, for the same reasons as the theater, the opera should be under the ban. Citing several examples, including *Don Giovanni* and *La Traviata*, Hills simply states that the stories and themes of many operas are often too vile and immodest, causing injury to the body, mind, and soul.[58]

The Slippery Slope of the Dance

Hills next considers dancing. Citing a Dr. Crosby, Hills distinguishes between two different classes of dance, the square dances and the round dances. Quoting Crosby, Hills preaches, "'In the former the sexes meet with perfect propriety—in the latter they publicly embrace. The former are modest, the latter are immodest and still worse.'"[59]

It is in his appropriation of Crosby's warnings concerning the dance that we see another excellent example of Hills' pastoral concern for the slippery slope. From the progressions Crosby paints, one would think the dance was the number one cause of all debauchery among women of the nineteenth century. Quoting Crosby and adding two other sources, Hills continues:

> "The foundation for the vast amount of domestic misery and domestic crime which startles us often in its public out crop-pings [sic], was laid when parents allowed the sacredness of their daughters persons, and the purity of their maiden instincts to be rudely shocked in the waltz." The chief of the New York police says: "Three fourths of the abandoned girls of New York were ruined by the dancing." The eminent Archbishop Spaulding declared that the confessional revealed the fact that nineteen twentieths of the fallen women began their descent in the ballroom.[60]

---

58. Interestingly, Don Giovanni is dragged to hell at the end of the opera for his life of wanton misdeeds. Cf. Mozart, *Don Giovanni*, Act II, Scene Five.

59. Hills, "To Young People, 'Amusements,'" 49–50.

60. Ibid., 50–51.

Perceived by Hills to be the most dangerous slippery slope of the age for girls, the round dance was to be completely shunned by Christians.

Over the decades, Hills became only more opposed to dancing, coming to his final position in his fifth book, *Pentecostal Light*. Slightly radicalizing his earlier position Hills makes *no* distinction between the square and the round dances as he did in earlier decades of his life. When listing the many things that grieve the Holy Spirit, Hills writes:

> What of dancing? I am compelled, of course, to speak of it as it is among all classes and under all circumstances. The least objectionable forms leads to the most objectionable; the social private dance leads to the masquerade or public ball . . . *The* SEX ELEMENT *is the charm of the dance, and the one thing that makes it even tolerable.* It is, therefore, *essentially* an evil thing. It leads, first, to impure thought; second, to improper conversation; third, to immodesty of action, and last, to immorality of living.[61]

True to his common sense method, Hills continues, "Of course, such statements coming from a preacher are likely to be challenged as untrue. Very well; let others, who are not preachers, speak."[62] Hills next continues not by quoting the Scriptures or any other cleric, but whatever sources would best commend themselves to his listeners' common sense. Quoting the editor of the *Utica Herald* of New York, Hills writes, "More young men and girls are ruined in this city at dances than by any other means. This is a severe indictment, but it is, nevertheless, true, *and the destruction of nine-tenths of the young women who are known to the police as 'street walkers' is due to the bad influence of the dance.*"[63]

Of course, after several secular citations, Hills quotes several Protestants and Catholics alike who tell the same kinds of stories and maintain his stance. After this, he concludes with perhaps the most powerful common sense source of all, firsthand knowledge. Hills writes that in his own rounds as an evangelist he has met many Christian leaders who have worked with girls who have fallen as a result of the dance. Some fell in a single night, some mothered children outside of marriage, and one pastor's daughter, after becoming pregnant the night of a dance, died in a hospital far away from home where she had gone in shame.[64]

---

61. Hills, *Pentecostal Light*, 80.
62. Ibid., 80.
63. Ibid., 81–82. Italics Hills'.
64. Ibid., 84.

In *Pentecostal Light*, Hills' pastoral advice on the slippery slope of the dance is simple. "For Jesus' sake, young Christians, for the sake of your own growth in grace, and for the sake of your Christian usefulness, give up, cheerfully, these perilous, inexpedient pleasures, or you will grieve the Spirit, and lose His companionship—the crowning blessing of life."[65]

The Slippery Slope of Billiards

In "Lectures to Young People," Hills next considers billiards. Of this game, he states:

> It is in itself the noblest game in the world. If billiard-tables did not cost but a dollar apiece and were in every home, the game would be perfectly harmless. But the tables are so costly that they are usually found only in saloons with the vilest and most dangerous surroundings. The use of the table must be paid for. The man that loses the game has to pay it. That introduces the element of gambling. It costs a thousand dollars to become even a modest player. The great expense, therefore, tempts the young to dishonesty. For all these reasons, then, it . . . should be thoroughly let alone.[66]

Exposing one more potential slippery slope leading at best to frivolity with God's entrustment and, at worst, dishonesty or gambling, Hills warns against the billiard table.

Of course, unlike his work against intemperance, Hills' concept of the reform of amusements did not extend beyond the application of education and moral suasion.[67] As a pastor, evangelist, and educator, he preached and taught against such things and held much sway in the churches and communities of which he was a part. His methods of amusements "reform," however, obviously never included the community ballot.

---

65. Ibid., 88.

66. Hills, "To Young People, 'Amusements,'" 59–60.

67. Hills' exact plan for the reform of amusements, so to speak, is found in "Temperance Address," where *before* he felt the ballot necessary to achieve the desired end, he fought against the use of alcohol with "wide spread intelligence, [that is, education] on the evils and dangers of intemperance and moral suasion among those who drink and a strong public sentiment in favor of total abstinence." Hills, "Temperance Address," 12. It is evident from Hills' sermons that his method for reforming various "amusements" invokes the same methods as he once used for intemperance.

The final "amusement" Hills considers in "Lectures to Young People" barely fits the description. Nevertheless, he feels compelled to speak about it, drinking alcohol.

The Slippery Slope of Intemperance

While, as was stated above, Hills was rarely given to graphic descriptions of hell, this is not true of his depictions of vice. One of the most graphic images Hills ever used is an illustration he borrows from Victor Hugo. While the whole citation is several pages long and too much to quote here in full, it will suffice to paraphrase most of Hugo's description of death by quicksand.

Walking along the beaches of England, a lone traveler happens into a sand that has an odd feel, but thinks nothing of it at first. It is only after several more steps that he sinks suddenly in a few inches.

> "He draws his feet out of the sand: he sinks in deeper. He pulls himself out and throws himself right and left; the sand is half-leg deep. Then he recognizes with unspeakable terror that he is caught in the quicksand in which man can no more walk than the fish can swim . . . If the beach is deserted, if there is no help in sight, it is all over. He is condemned to that appalling burial, long, infallible, implacable, impossible to slacken or to hasten, which endures for <u>hours</u>, which seizes you erect, free, and in full health, which draws you by the feet, which at every effort which you attempt at every shout you utter, drags you a little deeper, sinking slowing into the earth . . . The victim attempts to sit down, to lie down, to creep; every movement he makes inters him; he straightens up he sinks in; he feels that he is being swallowed. He to the surface of the beach moves, and shakes and disappears. It is the <u>earth</u> drowning <u>man</u>." Young men, intemperance is the social quicksand of modern life![68]

Hills continues by elaborating upon the debauchery and eventual death that intemperance brings. Paraphrasing Hills, at first, one walks freely and laughingly along the path of the drink. The eye delights at the sparkle, but even while the experimenter feels safe, he has already stepped into the quicksand, although he does not yet know it. It is only when the drinker treads in a little farther that he soon becomes aware of the reality of the drink.

---

68. Ibid., 62–66.

> Suddenly you are appalled to learn that the gossamer threads of indulgence have grown into the strong cords of an evil habit that has woven its meshes about your whole being. Your cords become chains; you tug at your fetters but they do not break. You still go <u>down</u>, <u>slowly</u>, <u>steadily</u>, <u>surely</u>, as if irresistibly drawn by some subtle infernal spell to a drunkard's doom. You <u>weep</u>, you <u>groan</u>, you call for <u>help</u>, but continue to go <u>down</u>. At last with diseased body, and bloodshot eye, and cursing lips and maddened brain, you utter your final shriek of despair and drop into a drunkard's grave and a drunkard's hell, perished forever from the sight and the memory of worthy men.[69]

Hills' description of alcohol usage is graphic, and his view on the Christian's relationship to it is unequivocal. In his earliest surviving sermon on intemperance, "Total Abstinence," Hills preaches:

> I wish to say at the outset that by temperance I do not mean "genteel tippling," but rather total abstinance [sic]. I do not find any other ground large enough for the sole of one of my feet to stand upon, either in the Scriptures or in human experience. One of the immovable and indestructible pillars of the temperance reform is the inspired word. Men try to find in the Bible license for a moderate use of strong drink. They read, "Let your moderation be known to all men." "Temperate in all things," etc. But the apostle no more told men to be moderate, or temperate in stealing and lying and licentiousness.[70]

Hills' convictions concerning even moderate tippling are equally clear. The first drink opens the door for many more, and somewhere along the path of moderate drinking are the chains of drunkenness and, eventually, the grave and hell. For Hills, the only common sense and biblical stance on the subject is steadfast abstinence.

For such a profoundly destructive personal and social problem, Hills feels obliged to advocate more than mere education and moral suasion. As we saw in "Temperance Address," this slippery slope of slippery slopes warrants no less than full blown attacks from every angle conceivable. Against intemperance, Hills advocates education *and* legislation.

---

69. Ibid., 67–69.
70. Hills, "Total Abstinence."

The Slippery Slope of Infidel Education

All of his life, A. M. Hills advocated the need for good and godly education. For Hills, this included both formal and informal education, schooling and personal readings. Of the latter, so emphatic was Hills on the importance of proper readings that he devoted an entire sermon to the subject in his series to young persons. The very first sermon of the series is entitled "Sermons to Young People: No. 1: Books and Readings."

Offering a proof-text of 1 Tim 4:13, "Give attendance to reading," Hills presents something close to the Oberlin rationale for their war on the heathen classics. Spending the first few minutes of his sermons extolling the power and virtues of good readings, Hills comes to his most serious point. "Now if the reading of good books can thus make epochs in lives what have we not to fear from bad books? A half hour's communion with an evil author has often kindled the fire of hell in a youth's soul which all his parents' prayers and tears were never able to extinguish."[71]

Hills goes on to cite several contemporary examples of young men whose imaginations were overly captured by pirate stories. All of the young men in Hills' stories went on to lives of crime, even as youths. Offering several stories to his audience, Hills chooses the bleakest one for last. He states that he got the story from one of the most noted professional men in the country about a friend the man once had. While the man's friend had once been a generous and noble person, studying for an honorable profession, he kept one infidel book in his trunk. Apparently, when advised to destroy the book, he kept it instead and read it again and again. Hills finishes the borrowed story:

> After a while he gave up religion as a myth. He gave up God as a nonentity. He gave up the bible as a fable. He gave up the church of Christ as a useless institution. He gave up good morals as being unnecessarily stringent. The next time I [the noted professional man] heard from him he was a confirmed inebriate. The last time he was coming out of an insane asylum—in body, mind, and soul, [an] awful wreck. That one infidel book killed him for two worlds.[72]

As tempting as it is to classify these stories as mere urban legends designed to scare young persons away from the potential hazards of the

---

71. Hills, "To Young People: Books and Readings," 10.
72. Ibid., 13–14.

wild west, they actually serve a much broader purpose for Hills. Indeed, his rationale for steering parishioners away from risqué novels is entirely eschatological, although his rationale here speaks nothing of eternal destiny. Later in the sermon, one hears an echo of his underlying postmillennial vision as well. Hills continues, encouraging the occasional reading of good quality novels,[73] although strongly warning against reading too many. Why? He reasons:

> Novels call out the sympathies and excite the emotions of the reader over the sufferings of imaginary characters, but the reader feels no sense of duty to relieve it. A <u>real</u> case of suffering not only excites pity in the soul, but also sets every faculty to work to devise relief. But an <u>imaginary</u> case calls out the pity, and yet allows the faculties of action to sleep on and take their rest. Now, it is hazardous to form a habit of <u>feeling</u> without <u>acting</u>. It blunts the sensibilities of the soul. By a law of the <u>mind</u>, the oftener one weeps over the <u>fictitious suffering</u> of the hero of a tale, the less inclined he is to feel for and alleviate <u>real distress</u>.[74]

As is most often the case in consideration of Hills' postmillennial vision, there is no mention here of the thousand years of peace. Nevertheless, the preacher is attempting to illicit a compassionate and proactive Christian response to the real sufferings of the world. In reading a novel, one may feel empathy, but in Hills' estimate, a Christian's priority is to weep for the real anguish of the real world and to work to "alleviate real distress." Thus, not only do risqué novels endanger one's eternal destiny, but even too many good novels can threaten the Christian' sense of social responsibility.

In conclusion, two particular sermons summarize Hills' concept of the slippery slope; "To Young People—Lessons from the Life of Lot" and "The Coefficients of Safety."

"To Young People—Lessons from the Life of Lot" is an allegorical application of the story of Lot. Drawing lessons from Lot's "downfall" and near destruction with the city of Sodom, Hills allegorizes that, like Lot, first one pitches a tent *toward* Sodom. Of course, at this point one does not yet even conceive of going into the city. Nevertheless, being

---

73. Ibid., 41. Hills names several novelists whose works one can safely read, as long as novel reading only makes up one in eight or ten books. Hills names Scott, Dickens, Thackary, Trollope, Read, George Elliot, Bulwer, Holmes, Hawthorne, Kingsley, MacDonald, and Mrs. Stowe.

74. Ibid., 39–40.

positioned *toward* the city easily leads to Lot's next step of being *in* the city. Next, Hills allegorizes, being *in* the city, it is easy and even natural to become *like* the city. On this downward progression, Hills comments:

> Such is the deceitfulness of sin, such the spell it gradually weaves over the soul, such its insidious growth in the heart. No one ever becomes desperately wicked all at once. Especially, does no good man, no convert, no reformed man, ever give up his good resolutions, ever backslide and fall in a <u>moment</u> or an <u>hour</u> . . . The great defalcation, the horrible crime, the fearful moral lapse does not overtake a man <u>suddenly</u>, as many suppose. The path to it is not a sudden plunge over a moral precipice; it is a long path down an inclined plane, each step only a slightly descending one, but all of them together bringing a man to the depths.[75]

This being the case, Hills warns against committing even the smallest of sins. Anticipating a negative response to his statements, Hills parries rhetorically that he is not bigoted or narrow in his exhortations. "No, nothing of the kind. [I offer these warnings] because all human experience discloses the stealthy, treacherous, but sure and awful growth of evil in the heart from small <u>beginnings</u> till it culminates in the wreck of the soul."[76]

Hills next illustrates how best to protect oneself from a Lot-like downfall. He points out that in warfare, if a fortress is of great importance, it is protected not by one, but by several concentric lines of defense. In the Christian's battle against sin, he imagines three lines of defense. Over the most inward line waves the banner, "I write unto you that ye sin not." In front of that, closer to the battle's front, is the second line of defense, above which is fluttering the flag, "Neither be partakers of other men's sins."[77]

The first line of defense, however, where the battlefront is and where the enemy's primary attack rages, is where the Christian must hold strongest in vigilant prayer. Above the first line waves the banner, "'Abstain from all appearance of evil.' So long as that first outwork is held . . . the soul is safe. But to yield that without a struggle to the enemy, is to make a virtual surrender to all . . . Don't sport with a <u>little</u> sin, unless you

---

75. Hills, "To Young People—Lot," 15–17.
76. Ibid., 17.
77. Ibid., 18.

are ready to abandon yourself to a career of wickedness, unless you are fully determined to court destruction and embrace death."[78]

In his sermon "The Coefficients of Safety," Hills applies a technological illustration to his warnings against sin. Offering a proof-text of 2 Sam 18:29, "Is the young man Absalom safe?" Hills proclaims how a Christian can guard against all possibility of sin.

Attached to the original handwritten manuscript of the sermon is a small newspaper clipping. While the clipping gives no indication of its original source, its topic is the title of the sermon, the coefficients of safety. Because it is pasted to the first page, the clipping was likely read as an opening illustration, explaining the concept. The clipping explains, that when designing ocean cables, engineers build them capable of withstanding more pressure than it is calculated they will have to endure. Originally, a safety factor of three or four was built into each cable, enabling them to sustain pressures three to four times greater than was anticipated. Because even this was discovered not to provide a sufficient enough buffer against break and loss, engineers later increased their safety values to six, seven, and even ten.

After explaining the concept, the clipping makes a spiritual application, asking, "What are the 'coefficients of safety,' what are the actual precautions and guards against deception, misleading, disaster and wreck? Permit us to leave the reader to figure out his own calculations in his own way."[79]

Never one to leave his parishioners to figure out their own calculations without help, Hills goes on to offer eight safeguards that will bring the soul, represented as "x," up to "9x." These eight he calls the "coefficients of *soul* safety."

The first is "Good habits—abstinence."[80] Every person who would bring their soul safety up to 2x should absolutely avoid both liquor and tobacco. The next three coefficients are good companions and influences, good literature, and good amusements. Why associate with persons of low character, read bad or dirty novels and vile papers, and amuse oneself with cards, billiards, the dance, and the theater when each of these alone are sufficient to wreck the soul?

---

78. Ibid.
79. Hills, "Coefficients of Soul Safety," 1.
80. Ibid., 2.

Hills continues that good principles, a good occupation, and a good ambition or purpose raise one's soul safety three more factors.

Finally, bringing the soul up to a safety factor of nine times its own original strength is "Good Anchorage—Christ." Hills comments, "We have been eliminating the elements of uncertainty . . . Man becomes safe as he has added grace to grace and virtue to virtue, and finally conscious still of weakness and uncertainty, puts on the Lord Jesus X, and clothes himself with the mantle of X."[81]

Together, these two sermons present clearly Hills' conceptualization of the Christian fight against sin. Not only does Hills exhort his listeners to choose a wisdom that avoids grave sins, but he also entreats them to shun even relative proximity to the entrances of sin.

Summary of the Eschatological Vision of A. M. Hills

Hills' eschatological vision was a complex mix of the hope of postmillennialism and a reverential fear of coming judgment. Far from being a straightforward systematic doctrine, Hills' two-sided eschatology was a governing center for his theology. A captivating vision, it defined the penumbra of revivalist ideas that Hills maintained all of his life. As we will see in chapter 6, this vision, and the integrally related matrix of doctrines and means that surround it, provided Hills with a revivalist canon against which he contrasted every other idea or practical measure.

The Revivalistic Means of A. M. Hills

The revivalists' vision of a transformed world was no small thing. Indeed, as we saw in chapter 3, Oberlin's vision of millennial peace and global reform would require nothing less than an army simply to get started. Of course, had their fundamental assumptions been correct, their vision would have been realizable. Basically, revivalism hoped for exponential growth out from its present centers until it encompassed the whole planet.[82] Firmly convinced of the possibility of millennial peace ushered in by the prayers and works of the church, revivalists felt that, even as big

---

81. Ibid., 4. "X" abbreviation for "Christ" Hills'.

82. For an interesting critique of this paradigm, see Walls, *Cross-Cultural Process in History*. Walls' appropriation of K. Scott Latourette's *A History of Christianity* could easily be extended to provide a critique of the assumptions underlying the nineteenth-century revivalist vision.

as the task was, they needed only to understand the laws of revival and to work the methods and means.

Following the precedent and the rationale set down by Finney, Hills maintained that the eschatological reform vision was best fulfilled by the overarching means of revivalism and that revivalism was best accomplished by Finney's "means."

As we saw in chapter 3, the use of the word "means" was not accidental. Specifically chosen to contrast with the typical Christian meaning of the word, Finney's alternative means brought the grace of God, so to speak, in a more revivalistic fashion.

The revivalist means, as they were appropriated by Hills, are best classified in three categories. The first means to revival and reform was the truth proclaimed. The primary locus of this means was the preaching moment, but it could also be extended to include any pastoral or lay, formal or informal presentation of the gospel.

The second means to revival and millennial reform was prayerful, steady effort. The locus of this means revolved almost completely around the armies of Christian laity, mobilized to do all they could, every minute of every day, to usher in millennial peace. For Hills, every Christian was expected to be a part, supporting revivalism and reform in any way possible according to one's gifts, abilities, and calling. Likewise, in Hills' mind, every Christian was expected to maintain the spirit of a universal reformer, supporting the revivalist and reform efforts of others through financial giving, prayer, and word of mouth.

The third revivalist means was closely related to the first, although it belongs to the sinner himself. The third means was the volitional acceptance, faith, and repentance of sinners, without which revivalism, and therefore, reform, never expands. Because the first and the third are so closely related as to be inseparable, we will consider them together, handling the second means separately.

The Means of the Truth and the Acceptance of the Truth, and the Obligations of the Preacher and the Sinner, Respectively

In revivalism, two particular moments were at the very heart of the institution, the preaching moment and the subsequent moment of the listener's response. Nineteenth-century revivalism, by its very nature, revolved almost entirely around these two moments. Finney's understanding of the relationship between evangelism and reform placed the preaching moment and the moment of response at the very center of his millennial vision. In his logic, only after a person has trembled in fear before God in the preaching moment and immediately thereafter repented and turned from wickedness to God is she or he more naturally ready to respond to a message of reform.

So central were these two means that one might argue that they constituted the two *sacraments* of revivalism. By its very nature, revivalism revolved around the guest preacher. The institution required protracted meetings or special scheduled services. At the heart of these meetings was, of course, not only the sermon, but the preacher. Proclaiming messages from the biblical revelation with common sense appeals from science, nature, literature, and human experience, the preacher attempted to embody the kind of Christianity being preached.

Of course, it was well understood that the proclaimed message of truth was only the first half of the salvation equation. Without the second moment of *response*, the proclaimed truth, as powerful as it could be, was not sufficient to save. Later revivalists like A. M. Hills almost entirely used the altar call as the locus of appropriate response. Functioning much like baptism, the "sacrament" of the altar response was the more typical revivalist initiation right into Christianity. Indeed, in the larger revivalist community, where the majority had walked the isle and knelt to plead for forgiveness, one joined the company of saints when one did the same. Baptism was not negated in this process, but the primary right of passage involved kneeling at the sinners' altar in penitent response to the proclaimed truth. Thus, revivalism's two "sacraments" or "means" were the preacher's truth and the sinner's response.

Oberlin students were sent out with these means fixed in their minds. Likewise, John 8:32, "And ye shall know the truth and the truth shall set you free," was equally fixed upon their lips. Like so many other Oberlin students, Hills felt his primary calling to be that of a preacher of the truth. Thus, he adopted a pragmatic rhetorical style that would stir a positive, immediate, and proactive response from his listeners.

That Hills embraced Finney's revivalist means is exemplified everywhere in his corpus. From his earliest existing sermons to the last words written on the subject in *Fundamental Christian Theology*, Hills maintained Finney's position and rationale with regard to revivalist means.

In his second year of pastoral ministry, Hills preached a sermon based on the above Johannine passage. Interestingly, and not unrelated at all, it was communion Sunday, reports the newspaper which printed the sermon. While only an abbreviation of the sermon was printed, there is still sufficient content to recognize Hills' contrasting of communion and the truth as means.

After reading the text, Hills proclaims, "The desire of freedom . . . has been universal. Perils have been encountered, sacrifices endured, and great deeds done in behalf of freedom. Christ came to offer freedom to the race by means of the truth."[83]

While not very much of the original body was printed by the newspaper, Hills' rousing conclusion is well outlined. Just prior to communion, Hills reminds his congregation that the elements typify all of the blessings Christ has given us. In a rhetorically powerful move, he states: "My friends, the world is full of sorrow. If Christ purposed to add one more drop to the bitter cup of human woe, or wring one more groan from hearts already breaking, I would never again enter a pulpit or speak his name in prayer. The world is yet full of bondage. If the religion of Jesus put the shackle on one of your faculties or made the least abridgment of the freedom of your soul I would never again proclaim it or in his name solicit love."[84]

Having fulfilled his obligation to proclaim the truth, Hills closes imploring his congregation to respond. "How long will you wear the yoke of a grievous bondage when Christ would set you free? How long will you be an alien who might be a child of God? How long will you make the atonement of no effect and look unmoved upon these emblems of dying love? How long will you refuse to receive Him whose very coming to the soul bringeth benedictions and perfect peace?"[85]

It is significant that Hills concludes this sermon, (and many others), with a plea for reception or acceptance of the truth. He does not close with any assurance of the therapeutic means of the sacraments. No such postponement is allowed. Implied in his question "How long" is another, "Why not right now?!"

Of course, the abbreviated version of this sermon for print in the newspaper leaves many holes. In fact, were it not for Hills' later writings, it might be difficult to hear the emphasis he puts here upon truth

---

83. Hills, *Portage County Democrat*, 8 September 1875.
84. Ibid.
85. Ibid.

as the means, as opposed to the sacraments themselves. Multiple later sermons, however, reiterate the same theme.

In his full manuscript sermon "No. 2- Resisting the Devil and Drawing Nigh to God," Hills contrasts the traditional and the revivalist sets of means more clearly. In this sermon, Hills' point revolves around the distance persons intentionally place between themselves and God and the only condition under which the soul is saved, its volitional movement toward God.

> So the <u>soul</u> may have its bible, its sabbaths [*sic*], its sanctuary privileges, its formal prayers, and all the means of grace ten times multiplied; but while it remains far from God,—too far to consciously feel the light of his countenance and the warmth of his love there will be little spiritual life, no blossoming out of christian graces, no ripening fruits of holiness whose end is everlasting life. But once let <u>God</u> be welcomed to the heart, and under the power of his sweet attractions, the most <u>ordinary</u> means of grace become instantly efficacious; the quickened spirit feels the drawings of its Savior, and follows on to know the Lord.[86]

In these lines, Hills is clear about the relationship between the typical means of grace and their revivalist replacements. The volitional move of the person is *always* prior to the efficacy of the traditional means. The only means that precedes the purposeful movement of a person toward God is the proclamation of the truth.

Thus, the proclamation of the truth by the preacher and the volitional acceptance by the listener are absolutely necessary in Hills' revivalistic worldview. The truth has to be proclaimed clearly *and* accepted actively. The appropriate response to the proclamation of the truth is the immediate acceptance of it on the part of the listener. In these two moments lie the beginning of the Christian life and personal transformation and also a microcosmic picture of the millennial vision.

The "truth" as Hills sees it is, of course, not just any idea that could be recognized as true. Truth has a specific shape and content. For Hills, truth means a specific matrix of doctrines—sometimes unwritten, but nevertheless systematic—a swarm of revivalist tenets in organic relationship to each other. In Hills' sermons, this revivalist matrix is taught and illustrated by scientific, common sense, and biblical language.

---

86. Hills, "No. 2- Resisting the Devil," 30–31.

One is hard pressed to find a pattern in A. M. Hills' pastoral sermons with regard to the relationship between natural and revealed theology. While systematically, natural understanding is often considered to be prior and foundational to revealed understanding, Hills uses both concepts liberally and occasionally as they best fit within the flow of his weekly text or his argument. It would seem that the listener's common sense could regard truth as truth, no matter if the source was natural or biblical.

While Hills' revivalist system underlies all of his sermons, its clearest encapsulation is in his two-sermon series on the "creeds." According to Hills' records, "Creeds—their Value" and "Creeds and Life" were preached five and four times each, respectively.[87] So important a sermon was "Creeds—their Value" that Hills preached it for the ordination sermon of R. A. Torrey.[88]

While the word "creeds" is used in the title and body of both sermons, neither sermon has much to do with what is typically understood by the word, the ecumenical creeds of the early church. Among the sixty-four hand-written pages of these two sermons, the doctrine of the Trinity is never mentioned, and the nature of Christ is given but a portion of one sentence, and that only on his divinity and oneness with the father.[89] In point of fact, the sermons have little or nothing to do with what is typically meant by the word. Defining his usage of the word, Hills writes, "A creed . . . is simply a definite statement of the truths believed."[90]

Although Hills defines creed differently than is typical or ecumenical, the word is neither haphazardly chosen nor lightly used. For Hills, the word represents the tight system of revivalist doctrines that by 1878 had achieved the status of an authoritative creed in many revivalists' minds, a status of even greater importance for the revivalists than the ancient creeds. Hills' creeds are simply the common sense, evangelical doctrines that were laid down a generation prior by the revivalists.

Both sermons are proof-texts of 2 Tim 3:16–17. In the first sermon, Hills considers only verse sixteen, "All Scripture is given by inspiration

---

87. Hills, "Creeds—their Value," title page; "Creeds and Life," title page.
88. Hills, "Creeds—their Value," title page.
89. Hills, "Creeds and Life," 6.
90. Ibid., 5.

of God and is profitable for <u>doctrine</u> . . ."[91] At the outset, Hills points out that a false dichotomy cannot be allowed between the theological teachings of the Bible and the ethical life.[92] Contentious toward those within Congregationalist ranks who, by 1878, were beginning to assert that Christianity is only a life and not a creed, Hills agrees that this is half-truth. "Christianity <u>is</u> a <u>life</u>; there is no disputing that. That is the <u>true</u> part. The <u>false</u>hood is the gross assumption that the <u>life</u> has no connection with the <u>creed</u>. Now I am free to assert that Christianity is <u>first doctrine</u>, and then <u>life</u>, and the doctrine always gives birth to the life."[93] Following the Pauline ethical principle of the relationship between the indicative and the imperative, Hills builds a revivalist system of ethics based upon the most central tenets and values of the revivalist mindset and lifestyle.

One can hear the doctrinal turmoil within Congregationalism broiling between every line of these two sermons. In accordance with his theological method, Hills builds his argument upon both common sense and biblical foundations. "Does it make no difference whether or not a man believes in a God, and a hereafter, and a future judgement, and future rewards and punishments, whether or not a man must be prepared by conversion to meet his God? Let your own best judgment answer me."[94]

Of course, while he commends his listeners' own judgment as sufficient to answer him, Hills immediately goes on in the sermon to state his own thoughts.

> Hear then my conclusions. This church is not a lecture association. I am not a lecturer. We do not gather here sabbath after sabbath [sic] to while away an hour in idle amusement. This is the church of the living God. We are bound together by a common and most sacred faith. The gravity of these occasions can not [sic] be overestimated. The truths proclaimed are of overwhelming, eternal moment to us all. The religion of Jesus as presented by its author attempts to deal with the gravest problems of human existence and human destiny. The bible attempts to answer the profoundest questions one ever put to his own soul. No mortal man can afford to forego or postpone the investigation of these

91. Hills, "Creeds—their Value," title page. Double underlining Hills'.
92. Ibid., 20.
93. Ibid. Unusual underlining Hills'.
94. Ibid., 28–29.

solemn themes. No man can afford to cease investigating till he has come to a conclusion which is satisfying to his soul."[95]

Giving a weight equal to that of eternally unending consequences, Hills places enormous practical value upon the doctrines taught by the revivalist tradition, common sense, the Scriptures, and his sermons, (i.e., the creed of revivalism).

In the second sermon of the series, Hills extends his text to include 2 Tim 3:17. "All Scripture is given by inspiration of God and is profitable for doctrine, for reproof, for correction, for instruction in <u>righteousness</u>; that the man of God may be <u>perfect</u>, thoroughly furnished unto all good works."[96]

Hills begins this second sermon with a reaffirmation of the importance of clear doctrine. By doctrine, he means far more than just what apprehensions every person can intuit naturally with a little help. Beyond the common sense certainties that every person possesses, one who would seek salvation must know revealed truths as well. If common sense tells a person that a day of reckoning is coming and that good will be rewarded and evil punished, then it follows logically that a person would want to know how to be safe at the judgment. Since, as Hills suggests, doctrine and life are organically related, correct living springing forth from correct thinking, it was reasonable to Hills that a person should want to seek correct understanding from the book that was given by divine inspiration for doctrine.

Thus, it is imperative that persons believe not only in the inspiration of the Scriptures, but also in the doctrines taught therein. Wrong thinking leads to wrong living, thus leaving the person in her or his fallen state. Hills writes:

> If a man does not believe in the inspiration of Scripture, does not believe that it is <u>the Word of God</u> then the book and all its marvelous utterances will have no more authority or interest for him than any other compilation of history, poetry, philosophy, and romance. If a man does not believe in the divinity of Christ he will come to the logical conclusion that . . . his death had no more to do with <u>us</u> than the death of any other man . . . If a man does not believe in the depravity or lost condition of man he will certainly come to the logical conclusion that man, not being lost,

---

95. Ibid., 29–30.
96. Hills, "Creeds and Life," title page.

does not need to be found and does not need a Savior . . . If a man does not believe in a hereafter he will have no potent motive for self-restraint, nothing to hold him back from giving loose reign to his leading impulse whether it be noble or base . . . If a person thinks there <u>is</u> a <u>hereafter</u>, but believes that there will be no <u>retribution</u> about which a man need to care very much, that belief will inevitably become a conscience balm making him at ease about the moral rectitude of his conduct and the final result of his short comings [sic].[97]

Quite obviously, these sermons extend considerably farther than the parameters of textual exegesis.[98] So in Hills' sermon on this Pauline text, we see the key ideas of *Hills* and *revivalism's* system of thought. These ideas are, of course, arguably scriptural; but they are unarguably put together by a revivalist mind of the mid and late nineteenth century.

The doctrinal themes in these two sermons reveal the core of Hills' revivalist theology, the "truth" to be proclaimed. Basing his arguments upon what were perceived to be universally accepted notions and their logical implications, Hills puts together a tight doctrinal core. From the above statements, we see that this core includes the fallenness of humanity and the implied, consequential need for atonement. From this arises the need for an atonement provided by Jesus Christ, whose divinity is absolutely necessary for his death to be of any redemptive value. Lastly, his doctrinal core requires the idea of future and eternal sanctions for there to be sufficient reason for persons to respond to Christ. Thus, common sense, applied logic, and revelation provide Hills with the truth to be proclaimed.

In these sermons, Hills' doctrine of inspiration is pulled in as the foundation upon which this creedal matrix is founded. Again, however, Hills' use of II Timothy extends beyond simple textual exegesis, which begs the question of whether his doctrines better represent nineteenth-century revivalism than the themes of the Pastoral Epistles.

This question aside, A. M. Hills certainly considered this basic core of revivalist themes to be both scriptural and, to a large extent, common knowledge. For Hills, these ideas are the heart of the truth that, when

---

97. Ibid., 2–5.

98. That is, while the text states that the Scriptures are useful for doctrine, Paul does not go on in the subsequent verses of 2 Timothy 3 to spell out the doctrines that Hills teaches in this sermon.

proclaimed and accepted, will set human persons and eventually all of humanity free.

The Means of Prayerful, Steady Effort and the Obligation of the Church

A considerable part of Hills' eschatological vision could be accomplished by the simple proclamation and acceptance of the truth. That is, at least *eternity* could be secured for any person who, after hearing the truth, would simply accept it by faith and live the rest of her or his life in accordance with it.

The sinner, however, is not the only one called to respond to the proclaimed truth; the Christian *also* is under an obligation. After seizing hold of the truth of forgiveness and divine acceptance, and thus moving from the kingdom of darkness into light, the newborn child of God immediately finds a new set of obligations to the truth. The Christian is obliged to hear the rest of the truth of religion and take action. This is how the millennium would come.

According to Finney's reasoning, reform becomes much easier after the conversion of a person or the majority of a community. The gospel changes the values and priorities of both. The newborn Christian is obliged, by virtue of her or his own common sense intuitions and newfound eternal and biblical values, to begin working to bring the millennium into reality. All Christians, the brand new and the more experienced, are expected to work to bring societal reform through the means of prayer and steady effort.

The earliest sermon Hills preached on this subject of the church bringing about reform through steady effort is dated within the first year of his first pastorate, March 24, 1875. Taking Luke 16:10 as his text, "He that is faithful in that which is least, is faithful also in much," Hills begins that too often Christians look for large tasks, great occasions, and great opportunities to do good. Since, however, great moments are so often few and far between, Christians neglect many small efforts.

Challenging this neglect, Hills proclaims: "We are utterly inadequate to measure the moral results of our acts. Life is not made up of a few great occasions, but rather of a vast number of unimportant days each hour of which has its trivial tasks . . . But are they unimportant? Each of those little duties and commonplace acts and thoughts are factors in the great problem of your life, and, taken together, they determine the grand result—your eternal destiny."[99]

Of course, not only does the Bible recognize this as true, but also common sense. "Again, fidelity in little things commends itself to our judgment as the best possible preparation for a great occasion or responsibility when it comes."[100] Likewise, God in creation demonstrates fidelity in small things.

> He has tipped the feather of a bird as accurately as if it had been the only object of His thought from the beginning. We tract life and organization in the microscopic animalcule as far as we can until it eludes us from its minuteness; but as it vanishes from our sight it is still perfect and touch with divine glory. The Dewdrop [sic] is as perfect and the Ocean [sic]. From all this we may infer that our christian character depends upon a proper estimate of the importance of little things, and our actions in the common circumstances of life. It is not so much how you act on some noted occasion . . . but how you act under the constant stress of daily duties.[101]

Of course, Hills' vision of duty in small things is more than simply the logical conclusion of his common sense methodology. It is eschatologically significant. In accordance with the postmillennial side of his eschatological vision, Hills continues that it is exactly in the incremental efforts of average Christians that the great evils of this world will be corrected. The Christian who works, (or even simply prays), for a transformed world will make a difference in this and the next life.

> The woman who refuses to pray for the cause of temperance in this town merely because her help would be but a little does not act on Christ's principle. Intemperance is the monster evil that stalketh abroad in our streets and wasteth like a pestilence at noonday . . . I assure you it is not by any spasmodic effort that you will ever put down this evil. It is only by patient and long continued labor, by the cheerful contribution of individual effort, by organized and unorganized endeavor, by by [sic] father's example and mother's prayers, and the training of the children and by the use of the strong hand of the law,—only by the help of all

99. Hills, *Portage County Democrat*, 24 March 1875.
100. Ibid.
101. Ibid.

these influences can the evil be stayed. May the Lord help us to so order our lives that we shall be "faithful in that which is least."[102]

In this sermon and many others, Hills reveals not only his concern for the eternal well-being of his parishioners, but also his larger postmillennial dream. His contrast between "spasmodic effort" and "patient and long continued labor" may well be a dig at Christians who, even as early as 1875, were beginning to adopt premillennialism or other eschatological views.

Of course, the exact identity of those to whom Hills is referring in this sermon does not really matter for his interpretation. From at least as early as this sermon, dated within his first year of pastoral ministry, 1875, until he died in 1935, Hills believed, taught, and attempted to motivate and mobilize Christians. He preached in hopes of empowering them to work patiently, prayerfully, and ceaselessly to shut down the entrances to sin in the world, with the eventual goal of bringing the Christian millennium into reality and saving a world of persons from eternal ruin.

Hills was gifted at motivating and empowering Christian workers for reform. As we saw in chapter 2, Mary A. Woodbridge thought very highly of her pastor's rhetorical skills, inviting him to speak across Ohio on behalf of temperance and prohibition. Even one hundred years after they were written, many of his sermons still exude the same simple eloquence, pith, logic, and savor that made them engaging originally. The work of Hills' first pastorate, especially with the Ohio W.C.T.U., solidified his identity as a reform mobilizer.

It is in the area of motivation and empowerment for mobilization that Hills especially shone. This is most likely because the *ad populam* eloquence with which he spoke was particularly empowering for the average person.

We saw in chapter 2 that, when Hills first came to Ravenna, he determined not to act as the previous pastor had, paying special attention to the "somebodies" of the church. In "Autobiography," he writes, "[I] determined that I would be the pastor of all but especially of the poor, the humble, the lowly, the nobodies; and if any body just had to be neglected it must be the well-off somebodies. In process of time it revolutionized the whole church and its standing in the community."[103]

---

102. Ibid.
103. A. M. Hills, "Autobiography," 57–58 (38).

This same identity as the "empowerer of the nobodies" revolutionized not only Hills' first pastorate, but also his entire ministry. He ministered to and empowered the poor and the "nobodies" in every pastorate, at Star Hall mission in England, and in his final denominational home, the Pentecostal Church of the Nazarene.

It is here where we see Hills' Christology, an understanding of Jesus, his identity, and his ministry, that made a profound impact upon many persons under Hills' ministry through the decades. It is, of course, difficult to assess whether Hills' ecclesiology is more rooted primarily in his Christology or in his eschatology. In any case, it is in Hills' reform vision and his appropriation of the laity, that his Christology is the most pronounced and the most profound.

Always sensitive to the perceived smallness that many of his parishioners would have felt in the shadow of so many societal problems of the nineteenth century, Hills found ways of re-envisioning the place of the Christian in the economy of God. Often painting in more vivid colors than his pictures of sin and damnation, Hills helped his people to see God's love for them, his grace over their sins, and his calling upon their lives for service in the reformation of the world. In "Christ Gracious," Hills paints the picture of his Christ.

> The Savior chose . . . humble men to be his disciples . . . He did not come to the ruling race, to the scholarly, philosophical Greeks, or the haughty, world-conquering Romans. He joined himself to a people whose nationality was most odious and unpopular. The Jews were even then the hated of all the earth . . . And yet Christ,—as if to shock the prejudices of all the world, was born a Jew and did not disown his nationality . . . And of these odious, hateful and hating Jews Jesus did not choose as he might have done. He did not gather his disciples from the ranks of the learned rabbis, from the ruling sanhedrin, or from the cultured Scribes and influential Pharisees. His first followers were mainly chosen from the poorest.[104]

Hills continues by listing the low credentials of Jesus' first disciples, men who were despised, scorned, ridiculed, maltreated, and held in public contempt. They were outcasts and apostates, "the offscouring [sic] of the offscouring of the earth. Yet these were the people to whom Christ

104. Hills, "Christ Gracious," 5–7.

united himself."¹⁰⁵ Of these, whose inferiority was not only intellectual and social, but also moral, Hills proclaims that Christ calls them friends, even "brethren."

Retelling the story of a Moravian missionary who, in order to reach a group of West Indies slaves, sold himself into slavery, Hills points out that "this missionary was but following the example of the Lord Jesus Christ, who took upon him the nature of <u>men</u>, <u>lived</u> with them, <u>suffered</u> with them, and is not ashamed to claim them as brethren."¹⁰⁶

Hills is clear to point out that such thinking is not in accordance with ordinary human conduct. Ordinarily, humans seek out persons of high rank and high mind, of strength and not of weakness. Contrary to this, though, is the principle, "It is the nature of the greatest <u>love</u> to care most for those who <u>need</u> most."¹⁰⁷

Not unaware or insensitive in the slightest to the reality of the highly feminine constituency of his congregations, (especially the Ravenna church¹⁰⁸), Hills often thoughtfully varied his Christology metaphorically to communicate better. Obviously attempting to find ways that would communicate the most clearly, he continues in "Christ Gracious": "Christ . . . sustains toward the whole human race the same feeling which the true parent has for the family. The mother lavishes her life upon her new-born babe not because of what it <u>has</u>, but because of what it <u>needs</u>, not because of what it <u>is</u> but because of what it <u>may become</u>. The fountain of tenderness is opened within her which pours itself out spontaneously upon the helpless nestler in her bosom."¹⁰⁹

Next moving beyond the love of Christ for individual persons, Hills illustrates how God can use anyone to help transform the world. "The feeble, the ignorant, the low—God loves them and has infinite compassion for them, and declares he is <u>not ashamed of</u> them. They are, in some way, a part of his plan. They enter into his purpose. His chief concern now is, having peopled the earth, how to bring all its teeming multitudes

---

105. Ibid., 7.
106. Ibid., 11–12.
107. Ibid., 14.
108. The report from *The Portage County Democrat* on Hills' installation and ordination service at Ravenna points out that for the service, "the church was filled to its entire capacity, it being noticeable, however, that the congregation was largely composed of ladies." *Portage County Democrat*, 3 June 1874.
109. Hills, "Christ Gracious," 15–16.

into conformity with himself till they are fit to be saints in glory. Out of the ruin and rubbish of this world Christ is building a kingdom wherein shall dwell righteousness."[110]

Hills illustrates this beautifully with an anecdote from Lord Macaulay of a particular cathedral in England. The story goes: "There is an exquisite stained window which was made by an apprentice out of the pieces of glass which had been rejected by his master, and was so far superior to every other in the church that according to tradition the envious artist killed himself with vexation. In this spirit does Jesus work. While others would select the beautiful, the strong and the good, his eye is also on the contemned material, and he will use in his kingdom even the refuse of society."[111]

In addressing whether or not this is an unworthy view of God, Hills simply asks:

> Pray tell me, then, in what, do you think, does the glory of God consist? Does it consist in calling worlds of dirt into existence and hurling them out into immensity on an endless journey, for his own amusement? In wearing a gleaming crown and emitting light from his countenance that shall outshine the sun? . . . Or does he rejoice in his unfathomable pity, and glory that the height and depth of his love can not be measured? Ah yes! It is his glory that he can bow himself down to the unworthy and the ungrateful, that he can wait upon imperfection and weakness, that he can pardon and heal, and pardon again and heal again, and continue to pardon and heal, till his little children lose their littleness, and the unworthy ones become worthy, because they have become like him. This is the true glory of the Lord Jesus Christ, and of this work he is not ashamed.[112]

In closing, Hills exhorts those who are weak or fallen in their faith and those who have only the first germ of faith planted in their souls to remember the graciousness of Christ, who is not ashamed to call them "brethren." Of the weak, and even the cowardly Christian, he is not ashamed. To even those who have only the first single spark of divine fire, he reminds, "Even they have a purpose to serve Christ."[113] Even to the ones whose hearts know the awful hardness of sin beaten into them,

110. Ibid., 16–17.
111. Ibid., 17–18.
112. Ibid., 20–22.
113. Ibid., 27.

Hills commends, "The <u>sun</u> never hung so patiently over the frozen earth in the springtime waiting for the starting of the <u>bulb</u>, as <u>he</u> hovers over men, <u>brooding</u> and <u>soliciting</u>, watching for the first germ of life."[114] Later in the sermon, Hills continues, "You are not living in a frigid zone of grace where the obstacles are many and the helps few, and the result is uncertain. You are in a very tropic of gracious influences where the <u>Sun of Righteousness shines</u> over you <u>the whole year round with healing in his beams</u>."[115]

In "Christ Gracious," Hills calls Christians deeper into the forgiveness and healing of God. Arguably one of his most moving sermons, it stands as the earliest statement of Hills' connection between Christology, ecclesiology, and implied eschatology. Christians young and old are encouraged to recognize their "purpose to serve Christ."[116]

A later and even clearer sermon on the Christian's duty to work to convert and reform the world, "Individualism in the Church—A Want in Modern Christian Life," reminds listeners that the locus of transformation is in the individual person. Addressing what he perceived to be a growing set of related problems that tear at the individual and her or his personal sense of duty, Hills opens, "There is a manifest want of <u>individualism</u> in church life and Christian activity, from which the kingdom of God is suffering untold and inconceivable detriment."[117]

Easily misunderstood over one hundred years later, Hills' seeming desire for more *individualism* in the church is simply an encouragement for Christians to develop the *personal* gifts within for larger service in the church and the world. The closest Hills comes to a doctrine of spiritual gifts, this sermon reminds the listener: "God intentionally makes men to differ. He bestows upon each a personality and an individuality all his <u>own</u>. Human beings, destined for immortality, are not made as bullets are run in a mold—all alike, to fill the same place, to do the same service, and to be used indiscriminately. We differ alike in natural endowments and in spiritual gifts."[118]

Hills continues that persons differ in form, features, tastes, inclinations, strength of will, balance of faculties, circumstances, parentage,

114. Ibid., 29.
115. Ibid., 31.
116. Ibid., 27.
117. Hills, "Individualism in the Church," 1.
118. Ibid., 2.

time of birth, domestic and social conditions, opportunities, and circle of influence.[119] This being the case, each has a unique mission to fulfill. "As might be expected from the foregoing, God rightly expects special service of each."[120] Quoting Horace Bushnell, Hills continues: "'Every human soul has a complete and perfect plan, cherished for it in the heart of God—a divine biography marked out which it enters into life to live.' We may conclude, then, that God has laid upon each special duties, commensurate with his individual gifts and opportunities. There is a post of duty for every man in the army of the Lord, which he alone can fill, and which he has no right to abandon, nay, cannot abandon to another."[121]

These personal duties require personal responsibility. "We are each called by discriminating, electing grace to do an especial work, which nobody else can do and which, if neglected by any one of us, will be forever undone; and the terrible responsibility of the failure will forever darken the guilty soul."[122]

In accordance with his twofold eschatological vision, Hills is attempting to motivate and mobilize the laity of his church to share the gospel with others around them and to work for societal change. Pointing out that it is impossible for Christian ministers to accomplish all that needs to be done, Hills states, "[There is an] all too prevalent disposition to relegate to ministers the sole work of converting men. This is a vile relic of popery and one of Satan's most satanic arts—this custom of regarding ministers as a class distinct from all others to whom are entrusted all the concerns of religion."[123]

As we have already seen, in Hills' understanding of religion, the preacher's obligation is to proclaim the truth and the listener's obligation is to accept and act upon the truth; the sinner is to repent and believe, and the Christian is to pray and act.

Unfortunately, and this was exactly why Hills wrote this sermon, few individual Christians take upon themselves the calling of an evangelistic reformer. Hills laments: "How utterly unlike the primitive church is this! . . . Today, societies are somehow looked upon as substitutes for persons; self is lost in the congregation; the church is expected to be

119. Ibid., 2–3.
120. Ibid., 6.
121. Ibid., 8.
122. Ibid., 11.
123. Ibid., 19.

active while the individuals too frequently suffer themselves to remain <u>in</u>active . . . and are losing their sense of personal responsibility, and even their consciousness of personal identity, and all due conception of the calling of God and the grand end of life."[124]

Hills continues that the world's enthusiasm for wickedness is too great for even a single Christian to hold back from service. After writing several paragraphs on the ends Satan and his followers go to fill the world with licentiousness, skepticism, and infidelity, Hills strongly asserts: "The truth is that by no other possible means can the religious needs of the age be met. We have so much evil to contend with, so gigantic in its strength, so diffused in its influence on all sides of us, and so infectious and malignant in its efforts that nothing short of the engagement, the energies, and the earnestness of the whole church can cope with it."[125]

The simple reality is, Hills points out, that there is too great a need for the professional ministers to be able to handle it all.

> O we sorely need today Christian physicians like Luke to write for Jesus, and Mary Magdalenes to run with glad feet and tell the sorrowing the joyful news that their Lord is risen, and seamstresses like Dorcas and Prisca—able to teach others "the more perfect way," and mechanics like Harlan Page, each bringing a hundred souls to Christ. We still need teachers like Mary Lion and servants like Onesimus, . . . We sorely need a countless multitude of <u>individuals</u>, who are always conscious of their individual responsibility to God, and who will not suffer their <u>personality</u> to be annihilated by church-membership.[126]

Again, as above, Hills is well aware of the vastness of the task and of his parishioners' feelings of ineffectualness. He closes, addressing these difficulties.

> You will doubtless feel your unworthiness, and be ready to cry out, "O Lord, who is sufficient for these things." This will drive you to the mercy-seat for the oil of grace that your light may shine, for the holiness of heart which will give you a sanctifying influence, for the anointed lips and the "tongue of fire" that you may speak with an unction from the Holy One, and for a mind illuminated and taught by the Spirit that you may fitly "hold forth

---

124. Ibid., 20–21.
125. Ibid., 24–25.
126. Ibid., 28–29. Again, note that over half of Hills' examples are feminine.

the Word of Life." When you are thus moved and prayerful and in sympathy with the mission of Jesus the means and the opportunities will open before you.[127]

Hills concludes his sermon reminding his church of the principles upon which his vision of Christian action is based. It is based upon nothing other than the principles his people claim to hold already, the canon of revivalist doctrines that Hills has always maintained.

> Consider the principles of your faith. You believe in the immortality of the soul, in the eternal evil and woe produced by sin, in the wrath of God, in the doom of the wicked. And you also believe in the love of God, in the redemption offered through Jesus, in the possibility of salvation for each soul, in the converting power of the Spirit, and in the ineffable and eternal bliss of heaven. You believe that it is God's will that all should be saved—and that, too, by human instrumentality. You profess to believe all this and dying men and women around you know it. And will you remain at ease in Zion and do nothing personally to point these dying souls to their Savior? Then your conduct is giving the lie to your creed, and you are helping to make all observers skeptics and unbelievers. They will not believe in the solemn doctrines of your Bible, and will not believe that you can believe them and still remain so supremely indifferent to their eternal welfare. Fellow Christians, we must either stop professing our belief in the stupendous realities of the eternal world, or we must act more as if they were true.[128]

While the two above sermons speak generally about means of the church, nowhere does Hills articulate more clearly the exact parameters of Christian activity than in "Temperance Address." In speaking to a Christian, and not just a patriot or philanthropic audience, Hills calls upon the members and non-members of the W.C.T.U. to pray and act to bring reform.

For Hills, prayer is so obvious a response to the evils of this world that it hardly receives explicit treatment in "Temperance Address." He simply assumes the prayerfulness of his listeners in two places in the address. "I trust that we are Christians who love the kingdom of Christ and pray for the peace and prosperity of Zion."[129] Again at the end, he

127. Ibid., 32–33.
128. Ibid., 35–36.
129. Hills, "Temperance Address," 10.

encourages, "Friends of prohibition, beloved sisters of the W.C.T.U., continue to labor and speak, and write and pray. Do not doubt the promises or question the results."[130]

However, while in "Temperance Address" Hills certainly assumes and encourages the *prayerful* effort of Christian workers, the majority of the sermon is on the W.C.T.U.'s community and political efforts. In all, Hills considers five ways in which Christians should continue to work: in laboring, speaking, writing, praying, and voting.

It should not be thought, however, that this list is all-inclusive in Hills' imagination. Simply, regarding temperance reform, and every other reform area, Hills is encouraging any activity that can be imagined by Christians for the transformation of the world. Included in the above "laboring" are all of the activities of reform movements like the W.C.T.U.: petitioning, picketing, praying, educating, evangelizing traffickers and users, and voting. Combined with the preacher's proclamation and the sinner's acceptance of the truth, the church's prayerful, incremental efforts for reform and evangelization would eventually bring the millennium of Christ's reign to earth and save numberless persons from eternal hell.

SUMMARY

A. M. Hills' vision and means form the heart of his revivalist identity. Far more than the sum total of a set of doctrines, Hills' revivalism was a tight matrix of ideas wedded to a practical ecclesiology of evangelization and social reform. Hills envisioned a transformed world where the divinely promised millennial peace would be accomplished by the proclamation of the truth in revivalistic preaching, the concomitant acceptance of the truth by sinners and Christians alike, and the steady, unceasing work of hundreds of thousands, and eventually millions and billions, of Christians.

Throughout the entirety of his life and ministry, Hills never wavered in these views. While he obviously never saw his vision come to reality, and even joined the Holiness Movement that largely rejected postmillennialism, Hills remained as unmoved by the waves of change and challenge as the rock of Gibraltar.

130. Ibid., 41.

Hills' revivalism involved the vision and means of a *movement*. His was a practical ecclesiology, not written succinctly in any denominational article of faith; but burned deeply into the imagination of revivalism. When his ecclesiology was wedded to his eschatological reform vision, it had an extraordinarily empowering effect. Here perhaps was Hills' finest moment—the preaching moment, when, in a vernacular eloquence accessible to many in the late nineteenth and early twentieth centuries, the prophet in him wove together a tapestry of God's ultimate ends with the average, even base, threads of humanity. It is unfortunate that the eschatologies and ecclesiologies of revivalists like Hills are perhaps the most misunderstood and most caricatured aspects of their religious identity. For this reason, these are also their least tapped resource. Accused of having bizarre eschatologies and non-existent ecclesiologies, Hills and the revivalists of his same ilk are overlooked in the histories and the historical theologies. Perhaps it is time for reevaluation.

5

The Tightening of A. M. Hills' Revivalist Canon

CHAPTER 4 CONSIDERED THE revivalist theology and means that were developed, preached, and lived out by A. M. Hills prior to his sanctification experience in 1895 and that also remained largely unchanged after this date. In chapter 4, we saw the continuity of ideas between his early sermons and his later books. It should be kept in mind that the ideas presented in chapter 4 provide the basic shape of Hills' lifelong revivalist doctrine and means. In this chapter, we will consider the only changes and additions that Hills ever allowed into that system, a Holiness Movement doctrine of sanctification.

Two lingering and difficult questions haunt the interpretation of A. M. Hills. The first question is how a man with so many Methodists in his family and schooling at Oberlin could have remained untouched by the doctrines of holiness and perfection seemingly all around him until he was nearly fifty. As we saw in chapter 2, both Hills' mother and his second wife were Methodists. Hills states that, while at Oberlin, he read Mahan's *Baptism with the Holy Spirit* in his senior year. Even though Oberlin perfectionism was already mostly a thing of the past, Hills sought Finney's council about the experience. Yet with all of this, Hills neither experienced a second work of grace nor even believed in or taught one until after his forty-eighth year of life.

The second difficult question is why such a staunch holiness "stay-inner" as Hills eventually "came out" from the Congregational Churches of America and joined the Pentecostal Church of the Nazarene. For almost seventeen years after his sanctification, Hills was of one opinion regarding holiness identity. He felt the Holiness Movement best served its calling when holiness people stayed in their respective churches and denominations working to leaven an understanding and experience of holiness right where they are. For nearly two decades, Hills steadfastly resisted the temptation to trade his interdenominational vision for a denominational one. Over a period of eleven years, he founded four holiness universities, each without any specific denominational affiliation. At these schools, he not only taught his interdenominational vision, but also exemplified it by staying with the Congregational Church. Then suddenly it seems from his autobiographical description, Hills curtly reports that one Sunday in 1912, "I rose up and joined [Bethany Church of the Nazarene]. I have never regretted it one moment from that day to this."[1]

The first of the two questions will be considered in this chapter, while the second will be answered in chapter 6.

SLIGHT REVIVALIST PARADIGM SHIFT: HILLS' HOLINESS APPROPRIATION

Hills spent the entirety of the year 1895 on three tasks. The first was, of course, simply to fulfill the duties of his job as an evangelist. Preaching sometimes as often as twelve to fourteen times per week, Hills showed an extraordinary capacity for work to accomplish this alone. Besides these labors, however, Hills also spent the spring of 1895 finishing his first book. A work of 401 pages, *Life and Labors of Mrs. Mary A. Woodbridge*, was finished in the spare minutes and hours between sermon preparation and presentation.

The third task Hills completed in 1895 was to read a very large proportion of the literature of the Holiness Movement. This reading, which spanned much of 1895, culminated in a religious experience on December 7, 1895, Hills' sanctification by the baptism with the Holy Spirit.[2]

---

1. Hills, "Autobiography," 196 (124).

2. Hills often spoke ambidextrously of his 1895 experience as sanctification or the baptism with the Holy Spirit. Because Hills uses both phrases synonymously, I will also use them interchangeably.

Hills admits in "Autobiography" that he was slow in coming into the experience of sanctification relative to the average holiness adherent. There are several reasons for this. Simply, Hills had many steps to go through before he was sanctified. A tough-minded Oberlinite, he had an intellectual conversion to make before an experiential one could take place. So first, he had to be sufficiently impressed with the literature for it to engage his attention. It had to speak his language, so to speak, addressing the several practical concerns that were troubling him in the mid-1890s. Second, after simply connecting with the literature, Hills had to make several doctrinal and epistemological shifts. With strong and sure convictions, Hills did not make these changes quickly.

Catching Hills' Attention: Characteristics of Holiness Literature

Hills was not a man easily swayed in his thinking; Oberlin graduates rarely were. Thus, in order for Hills to be moved into a new way of thinking, the new paradigm had to measure up to the revivalist canon he had already been developing for over twenty years. Holiness literature met every one of Hills' criteria.

First, in order for Hills to be swayed by a new idea it had to speak his language, the language of revivalism. If nothing else, the literature of the Holiness Movement was unquestionably revivalistic. Hills' list of sources for his first holiness book, *Holiness and Power*, reveals that most of the authors he read in 1895 were Methodist or holiness preachers for the National Camp Meeting Association for the Promotion of Holiness. A few of the authors he quotes in *Holiness and Power* are John Inskip, William McDonald, Phoebe Palmer, Hannah Whitall Smith, Amanda Smith, Daniel Steele, Isaiah Reid, John Wesley, and Bishops Simpson and Foster. That the Holiness Movement was revivalistic in nature fulfilled Hills' most important criterion for acceptance.

Second, in order for anything to catch Hills' attention it had to be practical. It had to address the concerns and problems that he himself was facing. The holiness literature met this criterion on three counts. It addressed Hills at the personal, professional, and theological levels.

On the personal and professional levels, Hills confesses in his brief 1898 autobiographical sketch in *Pentecostal Messengers* that, by 1894, he was struggling with hurts in the past, especially those from his premature resignations at the Olivet and Springfield churches. These last two pastorates had been hard on Hills, whose first two of ten and six year tenures had been great successes. In *Pentecostal Messengers*, Hills claims to have led one thousand souls to Christ in Ravenna and Pittsburgh, but no such successes are counted in the Olivet or Springfield churches. Likely feeling underappreciated and deeply frustrated with both of these pastorates, he writes, "After two long pastorates of sixteen years, the later rapid changes were disheartening and bewildering. My heart was humbled and subdued, and I began to cry out for God, more of God!"[3] In need of healing and help through what might be categorized as a "midlife crisis," Hills was ripe for the promises of the Holiness Movement.

Hills' hunger for "more of God" had a positive as well as negative side. In "Autobiography," he says nothing of the pain of the resignations, but simply writes that he was hungry for a greater enlargement of his ministry. "God's Spirit had graciously come and awakened this intense craving [for righteousness] in my poor heart, not when I was idle and barren, but rather when I was intensely busy, preaching twelve to fifteen times a week, and constantly winning souls."[4] After reading Mahan, A. T. Pierson, and Moody's experiences and their subsequent ministerial increases, Hills continues, "I reasoned, if this blessing was so good for Moody why would it not be a great benefit to me? I wanted to <u>be more</u> and <u>do more</u> for God."[5]

Addressing both personal and professional needs, the literature on holiness through Spirit baptism captured Hills. His readings promised help at a point when he was both personally and ministerial at his lowest.

Perhaps equally significant, the doctrine of the baptism with the Holy Spirit caught Hills' attention because of its ecclesiological and eschatological implications. To put it simply, it provided the power for the church to accomplish its mission of world evangelization and global reform.

One of the inherent problems of the vision of world reform by revivalism is the impermanency of revivalism's byproducts. Finney recognized the inherent problem of revivalism itself as a means. It seems that the high watermark revivalism set while in the frenzy was rarely sustainable for long periods of time across an entire community after the protracted meetings ended. Longing for not only spiritual stability but even for a diminishing need for the revival frenzy, Finney writes, "It is

---

3. *Pentecostal Messengers*, 37.
4. Hills, "Autobiography," 123 (78–79).
5. Ibid., 125 (80).

desirable that the Church should go on steadily in a course of obedience without these excitements . . . If religion is ever to have a pervading influence in the world, this spasmodic religion must be done away with."[6]

Part of the problem with the very concept of a revival is, however, that it implies peaks and valleys. Such a conceptualization is less problematic, of course, and can even go completely unconsidered, while the swing is upward. Unfortunately, the reality of many revivals was that they almost necessarily included an emotional valley subsequent to the peak experience. The lull of spirituality prior to a revival of religion was often paralleled by a lull of emotional stamina afterwards; and while the churches were certainly fuller than they were prior to the protracted meetings and communities were certainly better, the revival itself was not enough to fuel universal community reform. Revivalism's energy was persuasive, energizing, and genuinely reforming, but still liable to entropy. Thus even in the most responsive cities and areas, their hope of *universal* reform was nowhere ever fully accomplished.

This post-revival letdown, so to speak, posed a substantial problem to postmillennial systems that leaned upon revivalism to bring about the vision. Assumed in the vision of a soon-coming millennium procured by revivalism was the necessity that the revivals' effects remain in place where they were used. Even though many were converted and entire communities improved significantly, when a lull followed a revival, it at least partially frustrated the dream of securing the millennium by revival. It called revivalism's means into question when it could not maintain its high pitch of spirituality and community transformation in an area.

Maintaining Finney's paradigm of universal reform *via* revivalism all of his life, Hills ran into the same frustrations his Oberlin mentors had a generation prior. The effects of Hills' revivals were not nearly as lasting as he coveted. After three year-long terms as an evangelist for the Congregational Church, Hills, like many Oberlinites, longed for a religious experience that would not only assuage some of his own personal issues, but that would also cement revivalism's fire and sense of duty into Christianity's less enthusiastic or doctrinally corrupt adherents. Likewise, just like many Oberlinites, Hills found his answer in a doctrine of perfectionism.

Another problem that the literature on holiness addressed for Hills was that its pneumatology offered a revivalist answer to the dissonance

---

6. Finney, *Revival Lectures*, 3.

he had been feeling with his own denomination's doctrinal fluctuations for nearly three decades. As we will see in much greater detail in the next chapter, by the last decade of the nineteenth century, many ideas that had previously been relegated to common sense were becoming less and less common. This became even more problematic for evangelicals like Hills, whose list of universally apprehended truths was broadening just when American philosophy's list was shortening to what would eventually become a zero. What made it worse for Hills was his perception of how much of Christianity was leaving his position to embrace the newer methods and ideas. Indeed, it was not just the "tobacco-befogged and beer-soaked German rationalists"[7] on the other side of the world, but Hills' own fellow Congregationalists, who were resisting common sense and embracing the new philosophies. The Holiness Movement's pneumatological epistemology gave Hills a revivalist answer to this problem.

These concerns, and the hope Hills thought he found in the holiness literature, were sufficient to catch his attention. The search for spiritual permanency, both personal and social, prepared Hills to hear the Holiness Movement's message of sanctification. This, however, did not ensure his transition. While he was intrigued enough by the literature to continue in it for a year, searching for the answer to his and the church's problems, Hills still had two major doctrinal paradigm shifts to make before he could be fully open to sanctification.

Hills' Two Doctrinal Paradigm Shifts

The first doctrinal transition Hills made during his readings in 1895 was away from Oberlin's doctrine of moral simplicity. In his pastoral sermons, we see the dualistic marks of this doctrine in many places. The clearest example is in the sermon "Recompense of the Reward."

> When man's thoughts range out into the other life, and he contemplates the reward of holy living that awaits the righteous he desires them. But looking at this world, as he does most of the time, desire says, "Give me present ease, pleasure, indulgence, worldly honors, sensual gratification." It is however, impossible to be both carnally and spiritually minded. The world and heaven will not dwell together in our bosoms. We cannot have the devil and Christ for joint masters. There must be a choice between

---

7. Hills, *Pentecostal Light*, 8–9. For Hills' views on alcohol and intoxicants' effects on the thought processes of the mind, see Hills, *The Tobacco Vice*.

them. Men must choose, and the character of their choice determines the character of their lives.[8]

A similar dualism is in "What it is to be a Christian."

> [God] has taught, as plainly as anything <u>can</u> be taught, that there is to be a <u>radical difference</u> between the numbers of his church and unbelievers . . . Throughout the whole Word of God the broad distinction is clearly made between the people of the world and the people of God. The two classes are distinct; they are not actuated by the same purpose; they are not marching under the same banner; they are not following the same leaders; they are not moving on to the same destiny. The one class are represented as "brought <u>nigh</u> to God"; the <u>other</u> are far from God; the <u>one</u> are his <u>friends</u>, the <u>other</u> are his enemies; the <u>one</u> are his <u>children</u>, the joint-heirs with Jesus Christ of his <u>glory</u>; the <u>others</u> are <u>the children of wrath</u>.[9]

Later in the same sermon, Hills continues, "God looks upon the race as divided into two great companies which are separate from each other and unlike in their <u>conduct</u>, their <u>purpose</u> and their <u>design</u>."[10]

In these and many other sermons, Hills' anthropology is simple. There are only two sets of persons, those who are in the kingdom and those who are not. Hills is likewise equally clear about what separates the two, the conversion experience. "<u>Conversion</u> might be called the act of leaving the company of worldlings and joining the children of God."[11] Of the converted, he states, "God will not accept the partial consecration of any man. He demands, he <u>ought</u> to demand, he <u>must</u> demand entire obedience, unreserved submission, the whole-hearted consecration of the soul to himself. The offer on the part of the poor sinner of anything <u>less</u> is any <u>insult</u> to the Infinite Majesty of the Eternal."[12]

As we saw in chapter 4, with most of his early doctrines, Hills does not offer a *systematic* presentation of Oberlin's or his doctrine of moral simplicity. These examples do, however, represent Hills' sermonic distillation of the idea. Prior to 1895, Hills taught a fairly straightforward

---

8. *Portage County Democrat*, 21 April 1875.
9. Hills, "What is a Christian," 6–8.
10. Ibid., 10.
11. Ibid., 12.
12. Ibid., 17.

dualism of kingdoms, ideas, and ethics, with a two-way door between them of conversion and backsliding.

To a very large extent, this dualism did not change after Hills' sanctification experience. Indeed, there always remained a large gulf between the saved and the unsaved for Hills, those who followed Christ and those who did not, those who would enjoy the thrills of eternal heaven and those who would have to endure the torments of everlasting damnation. At some point in 1895, however, Hills made a transition into the Holiness Movement's threefold anthropological distinctions.

A necessary accident of the Holiness Movement's two-works soteriology, holiness adherents taught what they believed to be Paul's distinctions of 1 Corinthians 3. Holiness divines taught that there was the unconverted and the wholly devoted disciple, the worldly and the spiritual man, respectively. Beyond this, they also taught a third kind, the in-between person, converted, but only partially devoted or consecrated. Typified in holiness literature often by the anemic believers of the Corinthian church or by the dense disciples of Jesus before Pentecost, they called this type a carnal Christian.

Hills reveals not only familiarity, but agreement, with this new set of distinctions in *Holiness and Power*, finished only weeks after his sanctification. While references to his new understanding abound throughout the 386-page treatise, the clearest is in a quotation from Andrew Murray. Quoting Murray's *Spiritual Life*, Hills confirms his newfound identification with the holiness doctrine. "*The believer must be convicted, and brought to the confession of his being in the carnal state.* You know that before a sinner can be converted, he must be convicted of sin; he must know and confess his transgressions and his lost state. Just so, believers must see that they are in a wrong state; before they get into the spiritual life they must be brought under conviction of the shame and evil of this carnal state (I. Cor. iii. 1–3)."[13]

That Hills believes the above concept, (and for him, doctrinal shift), is necessary for sanctification is exemplified in the list of eight conditions he offers those seeking the blessing. The very first condition he borrows from Amanda Smith—the conviction of want. Hills gives nine pages to this condition. Only conditions nine and eight, faith and consecration, respectively, receive more comment. Hills completes his commentary on the importance of this condition with the above quote from Andrew

---

13. A. M. Hills, *Holiness and Power*, 223–24.

Murray and a few personal admonitions that carnal Christians vanquish satisfaction with their present condition. Thus, however long it took during the year of 1895, Hills made a transition from the twofold anthropology of the simplicity of moral action to the Holiness Movement's doctrine of a lower and a higher Christian state.

While the transition to a threefold anthropology was significant preparation for Hills' sanctification, there was a second and more significant paradigm shift that had to take place to actualize the experience. Hills' most significant doctrinal transition was from a moralistic to a soteriological doctrine of sanctification.

Hills *did*, of course, have a view of sanctification prior to 1895. Unsystematic, and mostly peripheral to the whole, his early understanding of holiness surfaced only when Hills preached on the subject of Christian duty. Again turning to his "What it is to be a Christian," we see Hills' clearest statements on holiness prior to 1895. Taking the text, "Wherefore come out from among them and be ye separate, saith the Lord, and touch not the unclean thing, and I will receive you, and will be a Father unto you, and ye shall be my sons and daughters, saith the Lord Almighty," Hills reveals his doctrine of sanctification, or more accurately, his doctrine of the Christian duty of purity by separation. As we saw above, the sermon is fraught with Hills' dualistic worldview. He is adamant that the world is full of only the friends of God and his enemies, the wholly devoted and the wholly unconcerned.

Early in the sermon, Hills speaks of what God wants for his church. "It was the great design of Christ . . . 'to purify unto himself a peculiar people, zealous of good works' to save those should believe on him 'from this present evil world.' In his great intercessory prayer, Jesus said to the Father—'They are not of the world even as I am not of the world. Sanctify them through thy truth.'"[14]

Using the Scripture as merely a proof text, the rest of the sermon teaches nothing on the subject of how Christ's work purifies his people or how the Father will sanctify the Son's disciples through the truth. Instead, Hills proclaims exactly how the *believer* is to purify and separate her or his own *self*. Since God makes such a broad distinction between the two classes of persons on the planet, Christians, (and non-Christians, as well), should take special care to move far away from the camp of God's enemies and far up into that of God's fully-devoted friends.

14. Hills, "What is a Christian," 6–7.

Hills offers several principles that listeners can apply to help them purify themselves by separation. "The very <u>first principle</u>, which might almost be said to include all others is a coming out from the world by a voluntary act of separation. This is plainly stated in the text, 'Come out from among unbelievers and be ye separate.' God expects his children to be a chosen generation, a royal priesthood, an holy nation, a peculiar people. That is,—a distinct and definite line is to be drawn between <u>their</u> character and the character of the children of the world."[15]

Later Hills states, "Another fundamental principle of the <u>christian religion</u> [is] <u>the giving up of everything that is inconsistent with or a hindrance to a genuine christian life</u>." He continues that this is both a revealed and a reasoned truth. "No principle of religion is more <u>rational</u> or more clearly revealed. God will not accept the partial consecration of any man. He demands, he <u>ought</u> to demand, he <u>must</u> demand entire obedience, unreserved submission, the whole-hearted consecration of the soul to himself."[16] No business that is evil can be carried on, but must be abandoned immediately. Any honorable calling must likewise be abandoned if God calls a person to something different. "Whoever is not willing to give up anything at the request of Christ is not his true disciple."[17]

This principle especially applies to relationships. Hills continues: "This same principle . . . will lead a true Christian to seek their <u>companions</u> and <u>associates</u> among the followers of the Lord Jesus. No Christian can safely select his intimate friends and bosom companionships [sic] from the ranks of scoffers and triflers and lovers of pleasure more than lovers of God without grieving <u>Christ</u>, and doing violence to their own religion. 'Be ye not unequally yoked together with unbelievers . . .'"[18]

"A <u>third</u> principle of the Christian religion is this—<u>the faithful performance of every known duty</u>."[19] Two pages later, Hills continues, "All <u>religion</u> may be summed up in <u>this</u>—the faithful performance of known duty or implicit obedience to the manifest will of God."[20]

Next, considering aspects of stewardship, Hills proclaims:

15. Ibid., 9–10.
16. Ibid., 16–17.
17. Ibid., 20.
18. Ibid., 23–24.
19. Ibid., 27.
20. Ibid., 29–30.

> Another principle of the Christian religion is,—fidelity to our privileges and possibilities. We are all under a solemn obligation to make the most we can of our <u>lives</u>, for the glory of God and the blessing of humanity. There are vices to be <u>cured</u>, and great evils to be <u>corrected</u>, ignorance to be enlightened, and woes to be assuaged . . . God calls upon <u>all</u> to cultivate the gifts that are <u>in</u> them, to do what they <u>can</u> during the short period of this earthly life in the service of God and humanity.[21]

Making reference a second time in this sermon to the "true" Christian, Hills states, "The true Christian will gladly strive with all his heart to meet this just expectation. He will be a prayerful and upright man, a conscientious citizen, a true patriot, an earnest worker in the church, a friend of missions, and a zealous advocate of every true reform."[22]

In his final remarks, Hills laments that the churches are not full of such true Christians. Crying out, he concludes, "O may God <u>help</u> us, may God <u>help</u> us to 'Come out from among them and be separate, and touch not any unclean thing of sin.'"[23]

Again, while Hills clearly recognizes the reality that many in the church do not live up to such a high standard, we nevertheless hear echoes of a doctrine of moral simplicity. *True* Christians are those who are fully separated in the ways outlined. Ironically, Hills seems to recognize the presence of a kind of Christian that falls short of being "true." He does not, however, have any name or category for this kind.

It should be noted that this sermon is book-ended by the language of sanctification, separation, and purity.[24] Thus, the body of it can easily be considered an unsystematic explication of these themes. What is most significant is the moralistic nature of the whole of the explication. Nowhere in the entire sermon does Hills refer to sanctification, separation, or purity as the work of God. Each of the four principles fall clearly under the category of Christian duty. Christians are to: 1) separate themselves voluntarily; 2) give up inconsistencies and hindrances; 3) perform faithfully every known duty; and 4) make the most of their

---

21. Ibid., 30–32.
22. Ibid., 32–33.
23. Ibid., 34.
24. Ibid., 6, 7 and 34.

lives for the glory of God and the blessing of humanity. Hills completely moralizes both the texts and the concept of sanctification.

The moralistic nature of Hills' early views on sanctification offers a clue into the question of how he could have a mother, a second wife, and many personal acquaintances who were Methodists and not have any understanding of sanctification. In fact, he *did* have a doctrine of holiness, so to speak, a moralistic one. A view of sanctification to be sure, it was simply not the one he discovered in the literature of the Holiness Movement of the late nineteenth century. Falling under the category of Christian duty, the themes of sanctification and holiness were not a part of Hills' soteriology until after 1895. Prior to this year of holiness readings, Hills' understanding of sanctification was anthropocentric and works-oriented; afterwards he held a soteriological and grace-centered version.

Unfortunately, in "Autobiography," Hills does not go into the particulars of this transition. He simply states that having already spent the spring of 1895 reading holiness literature, he decided to kneel in prayer and give himself away to God for the baptism with the Holy Spirit. He recollects, "[I] wrote in my book, 'O my God, Savior and Sanctifying Spirit, I receive Thee. Come in and fill my soul.' A. M. Hills May 29, 1895. The influence of that act was a refreshing to my soul all the Summer through, and had I then *believed* with all my heart, I might have received the blessing at once; but I retained a lingering *doubt*."[25]

Hills continues, however, that it was six more months before he understood fully the importance of faith in the process. While perusing a pastor's library in Massachusetts, he ran across an address, "The Sin of Unbelief," by Henry Varley. He writes: "It went to my heart. I determined not to be shut out of the blessing any more by a wicked unbelief so cruel and dishonoring to Jesus. I went to the Thursday evening meeting filled with my own converts, and publicly confessed my sin to that congregation meeting, and declared that I would take God for full salvation. They may have thought I was getting batty and becoming a Methodist fanatic. But at any rate I was becoming desperately determined."[26]

At this point in the autobiographical sketch, Hills recollects that he had previously read S. A. Keen's *Faith Papers*. Quoting from Keen's

---

25. Hills, "Autobiography," 125 (80). Italics mine.
26. Ibid., 126 (81).

treatise, Hills recalls the final hours before his sanctification. Two nights before his eyes fell upon Keen's phrases:

> Are you a child of God seeking <u>Full Salvation</u>, seize upon some declaration of God's word such as "The blood of Jesus Christ His Son cleanseth from <u>all</u> sin." Apply it to your own heart; confess to your own heart, to Satan and to God that it is to <u>you</u>, even <u>you</u>, because the Lord hath spoken it. Refuse to [listen to] the lying voice of Satan that it is not so. Let no inward feeling or outward sign dissuade you from your voluntary choice to count God's word true to yourself. And according to such faith it shall be done unto you. Have you given all to Christ? Are you longing to be fully saved, are you persuaded that "Tis the promise of God full salvation to give,/ Unto him who on Jesus, His will believe?" You may at once begin to sing: "<u>I can</u>, <u>I will</u>, <u>I do believe</u>/ That Jesus saves me now."[27]

Hills writes that these last lines were upon his heart and lips the entire next day, December 6, 1895. He retired for the night still repeating Varley's recommended phrase again and again. The next morning before he even got out of bed, a suggestion came to him that he should simply thank God for the blessing as if it were a thing already received, as F. B. Meyer had advised in a book. Hills writes, "I began to do it, when speedily the Holy Spirit came to bring the witness that <u>God is true</u>. <u>A tide of joy swept into my soul</u> and I cried out, 'O bless the Lord! <u>Praise the Lord! He does come and fill my soul!</u>'"[28]

Hills' struggle to grasp sanctification as an extension of God's gift of salvation by faith can be heard all the way up to the last hours before his experience. This simple re-conceptualization was the last transition he made prior to the experience. Having finally grasped both of the interrelated ideas that a converted soul can still be far from God *and* that this same soul can be cleansed by simple faith, Hills' baptism with the Holy Spirit was actualized.

The fruit of one year's worth of reading, seeking, and praying, one of course wishes that "Autobiography" included more details. But Hills does not seem to have understood the exact reasons these changes took so long for him. He simply interprets it as God's will for him so that he would be a better teacher and preacher on the subject. He recollects:

---

27. Ibid., 126–27 (81). Underlining Hills', and not Keen's.
28. Ibid., 127 (81).

> I have always been thankful that God did not let me get the blessing by any easy method . . . God made me <u>study and study for long weeks and months</u>; and when at last I did reach the goal of my longings, I knew the literature of the subject, what the blessing <u>is</u>, and <u>why it is necessary</u>, and <u>what are</u> the difficulties of <u>obtaining it</u>, and <u>how they are overcome</u> by <u>dying to self</u> and <u>surrender to Christ</u>, by <u>consecration and faith</u>, to be <u>God-owned, God-filled</u> and <u>God-used</u>. In other words the difficulty I had of obtaining <u>the blessing fitted me to be a teacher of others</u>![29]

Seemingly oblivious to the obvious reality of how stubborn he was in doctrinal matters, Hills simply attributes the slowness of his coming into the blessing to God's providence.

Hills' transition from a moralistic to a soteriological understanding of sanctification is an interesting commentary on the "Methodisms" of his youth and adult life. Unfortunately, Hills offers too little about his mother's theology, and nothing is known concerning his second wife's. What can be implied, however, is that his early understanding of holiness is likely a relatively clear window into the doctrines of holiness that surrounded him.

John L. Peters comments on the state of Methodism with regard to the doctrine of sanctification by the end of the Civil War. By 1866, he writes, "It was felt by many that the church itself was in a slough of spiritual despond. Discipline, it was asserted, was sorely neglected, the class meetings were going or gone, there was too much conformity to secular practices and goals, and revivals were in disfavor."[30]

Of course, these symptoms did not suddenly burst onto the scene, but in fact had been growing for decades. Of the generation prior, Peters cites two main schisms within Methodism that reveal just how moralistic the doctrine of sanctification had become.

> The history of these two churches [the Wesleyan Methodist Church and the Free Methodist Church] illustrates the growing tendency of the holiness emphasis of this period to identify sanctification with an individualistic puritanism. As time passed, the proof of orthodoxy tended to become strict adherence to a set of stringent and sacrosanct regulations. Thus the Wesleyan Methodist Church . . . reflects in its history, a system relatively liberal at the outset but which grew increasingly insistent upon

---

29. Ibid., 129 (82–83).
30. Peters, *Christian Perfection and American Methodism*, 133–34.

the observance of rules as it became a more distinctively holiness church. The Free Methodist Church, on the other hand, ... began with a fully enunciated set of stringent regulations.[31]

A. M. Hills' mother, a Free Methodist until her marriage to Henry Hills in 1840, likely simply reflected and taught her son the holiness doctrine from that stage in American Methodism's story. While even less is known about Hills' second wife, it is arguable that, likewise, she reflected the doctrine of holiness of her Methodist church.[32] What is certain of these two is that neither brought to their relationship with Hills what could be characterized as the late nineteenth-century Holiness Movement's version of sanctification by the baptism with the Holy Spirit.

Of course, all of this begs the question of whether or not the late nineteenth-century American Holiness Movement's version of sanctification, one of perhaps dozens of variations, and certainly among the most radicalized, is truly what Methodism had "always proclaimed." Hills is adamant that part of the reason it took him so long, even while regularly mingling with Methodist ministers, was that they had not been "faithful to their treasure committed to them . . . They did not <u>live the truth</u> themselves, nor proclaim it to others. I [Hills] was taught it by a Congregational layman."[33]

One thing is certain, many in the Methodist family of movements and denominations *then* would not have agreed with Hills or the Holiness Movement on the particulars of sanctification. Ironically, many who presently stand in the tradition and even denomination of A. M. Hills, receiving ministerial degrees from the universities he founded, would not agree with him on which holiness message is the true treasure committed to the Methodists.

In any case, Hills' Spirit baptism was an extraordinary religious experience for him and transformed him personally, ministerially, and doctrinally. It was an experience that he always wished he had found prior to his twenty-third year of ministry.

---

31. Ibid., 130.

32. Hills simply states, "She was one of thirteen children herself, and knew children, and knew God, being a member of a Methodist Church, and had the Old fashioned type of piety, which meant something!" Hills, "Autobiography," 76 (49). In no other place does Hills refer to his second wife's former denomination.

33. Ibid., 122 (78).

The fruits of Hills' Spirit baptism were immediate and very profound personally. He writes, "There was a great enlargement to my field of labor. My ministry to Christians was enriched and deepened and extended beyond measure. A whole realm of new texts were [sic] opened to me with a new meaning which I had never thought of preaching on before. I may truly say I had to learn to preach over again because of the realms of new truth that opened up to my mind."[34]

Not only did sanctification offer Hills a fresh perspective on the Bible, however, it also gave him a significant career boost. Within only five years of the experience, Hills had several published books and had already taught at Asbury College and founded Texas Holiness University.

Another fruit of his sanctification experience, healing for past wounds, also seems to have come in 1895. That is, even while he never says as much in *Pentecostal Messengers*, the fact that Hills even recollects his negative feelings and wounds in the context of the story of his Spirit baptism implies that he must have received help in this area.

A thoroughly rejuvenating second wind, Hills' sanctification was the only catalyst that initiated the major doctrinal shifts of his life. We have already seen the intellectual shifts that were necessary prior to his sanctification; there were also a series of shifts that took place subsequent to this experience. Hills' newfound experience not only changed his anthropology, soteriology, and epistemology, but it even encouraged his postmillennial hope. These shifts can be seen in his books, especially those that were written within the first ten years after his sanctification.

Because it took him an entire year of reading to understand the literature on sanctification, Hills felt that the message could have been simpler and clearer. Desiring this blessing not only for himself, but for the entire world, Hills decided to write clearer books on the subject than had ever been written. Two of these books reveal his post-sanctification doctrinal changes.

THE IMMEDIATE EFFECTS UPON HILLS' REVIVALIST IDENTITY

Hills' revivalist theology was slightly altered immediately after his sanctification in two ways. The first way is exemplified in his first book on the

---

34. Ibid., 128 (82).

subject, *Holiness and Power*. In it, Hills' postmillennialism gets a second and bigger wind.

Hills also altered his epistemology slightly as a result of Spirit baptism. This is best illustrated in his book *Pentecostal Light*.

Holiness and Power: Hills' Eschatology Finds its Second Wind

It might be said that writing his second book, the 386-page *Holiness and Power*, was an easier task than getting it published. While it took Hills only four months to write this treatise, finding a publisher was a longer task. Hills' first attempt with a Congregationalist publisher in Boston failed. As we will investigate more in depth in chapter 6, Congregationalism was moving away from revivalism, (and especially *holiness* revivalism), at the exact same time as Hills was moving deeper into it. The Congregational press was, thus, not interested at all in publishing a treatise on Spirit baptism.

In "Autobiography," Hills writes that he offered the book next to one or two holiness publishers, but again, with no success. Finally, a Methodist holiness evangelist, E. S. Dunham, advised him to take it to Martin Wells Knapp of Cincinnati. Hills did this, and the book was accepted. In fact, he was so pleased with Hills' works that Knapp published not only *Holiness and Power* but also several other books even though Hills never embraced the more radical vision of *God's Revivalist*.

Holiness and Power met with remarkable success, especially for the first book on the subject by a brand-new holiness adherent. Heralded by many as an instant holiness classic, it sold thousands of copies and, by the end of Hills' life, had been translated into nine languages.[35] It is in *Holiness and Power* that we see Hills' first doctrine of holiness and its eschatological implications.

As we saw in chapter 4, Hills' postmillennialist stance remained unaltered throughout the entirety of his life. Nothing changed his belief that the church, *via* the means given it by God, under the power of the Holy Spirit, could evangelize the world and usher in millennial peace. This is not to say, however, that Hills' eschatology remained absolutely untouched by his experience of Spirit baptism. In fact, the experience of sanctification actually encouraged his eschatology slightly.

---

35. Since Hills' death, it has been translated into at least one other language, Portugese.

As we also saw in the previous chapter, Hills was fairly reticent to speak explicitly of the millennium. While his eschatology undergirds the whole of his system, Hills rarely, for pastoral and ecumenical reasons, made explicit reference to his millennial views.

This did not change after his experience of Spirit baptism. The reason is quite obvious. By 1895, the Holiness Movement was no more interested in postmillennialism than was Congregationalism. Most had already made a complete transition to premillennialism or were embracing what would euphemistically come later to be known as "pan-millennialism."[36]

For Hills, the doctrine of sanctification by the baptism with the Holy Spirit had eschatological implications written all over it; the multiple implications of scriptural holiness and Spirit-imbued power for evangelization and world transformation were too obvious for him to ignore. Life on the "higher plain" seemed to secure the missing stability in revivalism, promising a grounding for the ups and downs of the revivalist means. The offer of fiery Spirit baptisms like the day of Pentecost likewise anticipated a power that, if allowed to become the norm for an exponentially growing number of Christians, could eventually encompass the whole world. Thus, the implications of sanctification for Hills' revivalist system were simple; millennial peace through mass evangelization was looking more and more possible. What the church of the coming twentieth century needed was simply the same Spirit of the first century.

We see Hills' recently re-invigorated eschatological hope in the very first words of *Holiness and Power*. Hills opens the book, expressing the same values and paradigm that he always has, eschatologically-inspired revivalism. The church, with the present means available through the Spirit, is to evangelize the whole world, thus ushering in the millennium. The only difference is now Hills will be introducing Spirit baptism as the functional key to mission zeal and empowerment. A holiness primitivism is added to the mix as the new revivalist means to accomplish his older revivalist goals. He writes:

> When Jesus rose from the dead the whole Church of Christ could assemble in one upper chamber. At the time of his ascension it

---

36. An obvious pun, pan-millennialists believed that it will all "pan out" in the end. In point of fact, pan-millennialists were simply those who thought eschatology was a waste of time and energy and used humor to sidestep the issue.

numbered one hundred and twenty. Of all the ages of history it was the age of universal corruption. Outside of Judea, idolatry reigned supreme . . . The masses were sunk in helpless degradation, without means, without learning, without protection . . . The early disciples had no wealth, no social position, no prestige, no Government aid, no help from established institutions. They were themselves despised and feeble folk, without influence, without skill, without education, without a New Testament, or even the Old Testament in the hands of the people . . . But those early Christians had the . . . indwelling, *sanctifying Saviour and the anointing of the Holy Ghost*, and with that equipment they faced a hostile world and all the malignant powers of darkness, and conquered. Within seventy years, according to the smallest estimate, there were half a million followers of Jesus . . . In other words, with Holy Spirit power upon them, they increased more than four thousand fold in threescore years.[37]

Such statistics were the exact kind of numbers Hills needed for his millennial vision. Hills' juxtaposition of the first-century context with first-century evangelistic growth is the hope of his new message of Spirit baptism. Simply, if the early church, with only a few disciples and the entire world against it, could grow by exponential leaps of hundreds and thousands within a few weeks and years, how much more could hundreds of thousands of Christians in the present context. In fact, for the first time in his career, Hills dares to predict, "Is it too much to say or believe that if the Protestant churches and ministry had a similar anointing of Holy Ghost power to-day, we could take the world for Christ in ten years."[38]

Interestingly, as we saw in the previous chapter, even though Hills was a child of Finney, he never offered a prediction in his early sermons. Hills' newfound Pentecost-centered, expansivistic primitivism empowered his vision, re-energizing his eschatological goal of world evangelization and pushing it to a new level. He finally found the secret to the success of the early church. All that was needed was a careful proclamation of the early church's experience of renewed Spirit baptisms.

Of course, the same logic worked conversely as well, helping Hills understand why the church of the late nineteenth century was so disap-

---

37. Hills, *Holiness and Power*, 17–18.
38. Ibid., 18.

pointing according to his measures. Simply, most were substituting any number of things for the baptism of the Holy Spirit.

As he would continue to do in later books, Hills spends a few pages in *Holiness and Power* simply reviewing the evangelism records from several denominations' annual church reports. From his own church's yearly records, he cites, "The last four Year Books show that on the average for the last four years there have been over thirteen hundred Congregational churches annually that did not receive an addition by profession of faith. The Year Book of 1895 shows fourteen hundred and eighty-three such churches."[39]

Hills continues that perhaps the most poignant of Congregational statistics is the state of Massachusetts, where no equal exists for "cultured ministry, or better equipment for Christian work, or a more intelligent constituency or more promising opportunities for winning souls." Beyond this, Hills writes, Massachusetts had a superabundance of one hundred and ninety-seven ministers. Yet with all these benefits, Hills points out that there have been for several years an annual average of 140 churches that did not report a single convert. "If that early Church in Jerusalem had had a like success, they would have had four converts the first year! . . . Such work in churches would not be very liable to hasten the millennium."[40]

Hills' conclusion is simple. "Truly, something is needed besides church organization and machinery and culture and pulpit oratory. These unspeakably sad facts above cited ought to call the Church to its knees in humble supplication for the mercy of God and the outpouring baptism with the Holy Ghost. The only escape from our spiritual impotency . . . is a journey back to Pentecost."[41]

Pentecostal Light: A New Pneumatocentric Epistemology

Only two years after the publication of *Holiness and Power*, Hills wrote *Pentecostal Light*, highlighting another implication of sanctification. As one might gather from the title of the book, Hills addresses the epistemological implications of the baptism with the Holy Spirit.

---

39. Ibid., 26.
40. Ibid., 26–27.
41. Ibid., 29.

As we saw in chapters 3 and 4, much of nineteenth-century revivalist thought embraced Common Sense philosophy. Affirming the inherent nature of a person to apprehend internally or at least recognize certain truths, revivalists built a system of doctrines upon certain foundational ideas. As we saw in chapter 4, Hills embraced not only the earlier revivalist list of universal apprehensions, but even extended the list.

As quoted above, Hills writes that a whole new set of scriptural texts opened up to him as a result of his sanctification. He continues that this had the effect that in some ways he had to learn how to preach again. Comparison of the themes and biblical texts of his early sermons with his later writings reveals the appropriation of many pneumatocentric passages. Two of the key biblical texts for Hills' new holiness mindset were John 16:13 and the second and third chapters of 1 Corinthians, especially verse 2:14. All of these highlight the agency of the Holy Spirit in human understanding.

As we saw in chapter 4, especially in the two sermons on the subject of creeds, correct doctrine and concomitant, appropriate ethics could not be divorced in Hills' estimation without eternal consequences. Of course, in his early years, the appropriation of the truth lay in his own careful proclamation of the truth, the church's steadfast prayers, and to a large extent the listener's own common sense.

Such a system was becoming more difficult to embrace in the changing America of the late nineteenth century. The flood of immigrations brought a plethora of differing ideas, questioning the underlying assumptions of Common Sense. While American philosophy made changes to account for this, Hills, who had spent over fifty years of his life with the assumptions of Common Sense, made only slight theological changes.

Pentecostal Light opens with the assertion that the present age is the dispensation of the Holy Spirit. Just before his ascension, Jesus spoke of this coming epoch of time, a time that would be inaugurated only after his departure. Jesus' teachings about this time and the Spirit, Hills writes, are recorded in John 14 and 16.

> "It is expedient for you that I go away: for if I go not away, the Comforter will not come unto you; but if I depart, I will send him unto you. And when he is come, he will reprove the world of sin, of righteousness and of judgment . . . When he, the Spirit of truth, is come, he will guide you into all truth . . . He shall glorify

me: for he shall receive of mine, and shall show it unto you. The Comforter, ... whom the Father will send in my name, he shall teach you all things, and bring all things to you remembrance whatsoever I have said unto you ... He shall testify of me" (John xiv. 26; xv. 26; xvi. 7–15).[42]

In the first chapter of *Pentecostal Light*, Hills offers seven reasons the reader should pray for the Holy Spirit. In reasons two and five, Hills elaborates on the enlightenment that the Spirit will bring. Of little surprise, the Spirit reveals the same revivalist tenets that Hills has always maintained are common sense universals. While common sense and self-education in the themes of the Scriptures will teach the person the basic tenets of the Gospel, the Spirit will bring these things to life in the soul. Hills writes:

> We need to pray for the Holy Spirit that we may have a better appreciation and a clearer perception of the truths of the Bible. "The Spirit shall teach you," said Jesus ... By perusing the Scriptures daily, and pondering the revelations God has made of *Himself*, of *Christ*, of redemption, and of things *unseen* and *eternal*, in the same way in which we study algebra and history, much indeed of a certain kind of biblical knowledge can be gained. Such study should not be neglected. But yet there is a heart-acquaintance with truth and experience of it, a spiritual insight in the Gospel, an apprehension and comprehension of Divine things which it can never give ... Rev. A. B. Simpson says: "It is wonderful how the untutored mind will often, in a short time, by the simple touch of the Holy Spirit, be filled with the most profound and Scriptural teachings of God, and the plan of salvation through Christ."[43]

Again illustrating the point that Spirit illumination will teach the soul the revivalists' doctrines and values, Hills quotes Godbey, whose fiery sanctification experience changed his whole system of priorities from those of a typical Christian leader to those of a revivalist.

> The fire swept through me day and night, from the crown of my head to the soles of my feet. I preached four to six time a day, moving in a revival cyclone the encircling year. I was compelled to bid farewell to my [one thousand dollar] library, give up sermon-making, and devote all my time to saving souls. Consequently,

---

42. Hills, *Pentecostal Light*, 3.
43. Ibid., 7–9. Italics Hills'.

> I consecrated all my fond aspirations to understand the Bible, and went forth, content to cry, "Behold the Lamb of God, that taketh away the sins of the world!" having forever abandoned all my cherished aspirations to understand the Bible. Anon, to my unutterable surprise, I find myself surrounded by preachers and people with open Bibles, listening to my expositions of the inspired Word. That God would use me as a teacher of the Bible seemed to me a paradoxical dream. But what is the solution of the mysterious problem? The Holy Ghost has revealed to me His Word. The spiritual gift of knowledge is the golden key which unlocks the Bible.[44]

Hills continues by echoing Godbey's commendation of the illiterate female preachers of the Salvation Army and their American counterparts, the illiterate circuit riders of the poor backwoods, all of which "enjoy a purer Gospel and a more vital Christianity than [those in] the wealthy stations."[45] Why? The answer is simple. "The poor, illiterate circuit-riders are taught by the Holy Ghost, while the learned pastors are taught by men."[46]

The Godbey quote continues, naming several "giants" of spiritual learning, few of which are actually remembered by history or Christianity as the most influential thinkers or theologians of their day. Godbey, and thus Hills, mentions only revivalists. Bob Burks, D. L. Moody, Amanda Smith, and the above mentioned illiterate Salvation Army women and circuit riders, are the only "deep divines" that make the list. Hills' underlying assumptions are not surprising; the Holy Spirit will guide the prayerful mind not only into Christian truth, but more specifically into the revivalist mindset.

Of course, the Spirit's help regarding understanding and truth is not wholly inanimate. Hills' fifth reason people need to pray for the Holy Spirit is so that they might properly appreciate Christ himself. He reminds the reader, "Jesus said: 'When he is come, he shall glorify *me*.' He magnifies the person and offices of Christ to the soul."[47] Well aware of the various objections against pneumatocentrism, Hills counters: "None need fear that by exalting the person and work of the Holy Spirit Jesus will thereby be obscured. The fact is, only by honoring the Holy Spirit

---

44. Ibid., 10–11.
45. Ibid., 11.
46. Ibid.
47. Ibid., 17.

and receiving him into the heart can we have any adequate appreciation for our blessed Saviour [sic]. Had the Holy Spirit been duly appreciated and honored and prayed for, Unitarianism, that so degrades the person and atoning work of Jesus, would never have been heard of."[48]

The above verses, and new interpretative uses of them, provided Hills with a new grounding for his revivalist tenets just as their commonness was disappearing in the waning decades of the nineteenth century. Even while Common Sense and philosophical foundationalism were eroding, Hills did not have to change his doctrines with the changing philosophical scene. In his new epistemology, all of Hills' older revivalist tenets could be conserved. In his new epistemology, the Holy Spirit, which would reprove the world of sin, righteousness, and judgment, would teach the person saving truths, even if universal consciousness failed to do so. The Spirit of truth would guide the person into all truth, glorifying the Son's person and work, clearly teaching all who would listen that Jesus is God and that his atoning work is sufficient for all the world, saving any person from eternal punishment. To put it simply, in his new pneumatological epistemology, Hills could preserve *all* of his revivalist tenets and practices without having to change them in the slightest. Thus, even as the philosophical changes of the early twentieth century made their weight more apparent, Hills' revivalist doctrines and identity remained well intact.

There is a natural, negative corollary to Hills' position on Spirit baptism and knowledge. As it is true that those who are taught by the indwelling Spirit are privy to certain levels of spiritual knowledge, the inverse is also logically true; those who do not have or reject the Spirit consequently do not have help in their understanding. A slight shift away from the notion of inherent, common sense knowledge, Hills' new pneumatological epistemology gave him an impenetrable circle of logic and an explanation for why growing numbers did not recognize saving truth as he proclaimed it. For Hills, the answer was right there in Paul's comments to the Corinthians. "'But the natural man receiveth not the things of the Spirit of God: for they are foolishness unto him; neither can he know them, because they are spiritually discerned' (I. Cor. ii. 14)."[49]

Hills used this simple rationale to explain not only Unitarianism, but also any complex or unsophisticated idea that ran contrary to common

48. Ibid., 17–18.
49. Ibid., 7.

sense or biblical revelation as he understood them. Failure to recognize the Spirit's place as illuminator will inevitably lead to lost apprehensions concerning Christ, his salvation, and the whole matrix of related ideas. One did not, however, have to be so blatant as the Unitarians to lose the illuminating effects of the Spirit. In the final chapter of *Pentecostal Light*, "Grieve not the Spirit," Hills weaves together his older system of ethics and slippery slopes with his new pneumatological epistemology.

Here, Hills conflates three biblical texts to relate the seriousness of human resistance against the Spirit. He writes:

> [God] entreats us: "Quench not the Spirit," "grieve not the Spirit," for "my Spirit shall not always strive with man." We have the fearfully solemn power to do it, to brace ourselves in successful resistance to every redeeming influence of the Spirit of God . . . O solemn, awful thought! Dear reader, in all the range of your eternal years nothing will ever come to you so supremely important as the ministrations of the Holy Spirit. He comes to enlighten, to guide, to regenerate and to sanctify. Don't resist Him. He who deliberately and persistently and finally does it is forever lost.[50]

Hills immediately continues that the reader is now faced with a serious question: "How is the Holy Spirit resisted and grieved?"[51] Hills offers eleven ways in which the Spirit is grieved and his benefits lost. Misplaced ministerial priorities, procrastination or refusal to follow the truth as proclaimed, the defense or even courting of errors, and the deliberate violation of conscience make the top of the list, although there does not seem to be any order of seriousness. As mentioned above, Hills' usual slippery slopes make the list, the theater, card playing, dancing, and alcohol and tobacco usage. Also, as one might expect, from the top of Hills' list of means, the Spirit is grieved when prayer is neglected. Improper use of the Bible also drives the Spirit away. One should never use the Scriptures in a conceited, irreverent, or flippant fashion. The Spirit is grieved when sought as only a means to an end. Those seeking only the gifts or power of the Spirit will certainly miss both. Hills continues that the Spirit will not abide in a church where mismanagement takes place. Along a similar line, on an individual level, no person

---

50. Ibid., 66. 1 Thess 5:19; Eph 4:30; and Gen 6:3.
51. Ibid.

should expect the presence of the Spirit who mismanages her or his own finances, wasting what God has given by refusing to tithe.[52]

Last, but certainly not least, Hills assures the reader that the Spirit is grieved when his best work among men is depreciated. Hills writes: "The Spirit is called 'Holy' because it is His chief work to impart holiness to fallen men, and keep them in it. 'The masterpiece of the Holy Spirit is the completed holiness of a soul born with a propensity to sin.' When one fights the doctrine of sanctification as a possible experience, and says malignant things about it and about all who advocate it, they are approaching perilously near the sin of blasphemy against the Holy Ghost which hath never forgiveness."[53]

While his list of slippery slopes has certainly grown, Hills' logic remains the same. Quite simply, the slippery paths that can damn the soul in the next life are the same ones that grieve the Spirit far away from a person in this life. The effect is simple; not only does grieving the Spirit leave the soul bereft of the much needed sanctification, it also keeps the Christian stunted in growth and the soul and mind in unpurified and unenlightened states, respectively. Even a Christian can be incapable of recognizing and appropriating the great truths of Christ's nature and atonement.

The eleventh and final grief of the Spirit reveals just how important sanctification has become for Hills. Believing it to be the Spirit's greatest work and the only key to global evangelization and the millennium, Hills expressly warns against any system or idea that would denigrate this hope or lead Christians away from the holiness message.

In both *Holiness and Power* and *Pentecostal Light*, we see just how central the Holiness Movement's doctrine of Spirit baptism is for Hills. Not only did it become the heart of his preaching, writing, and identity, but the message of holiness also altered Hills' soteriology, anthropology, and epistemology and bolstered his eschatology.

While on the surface, it appears to have expanded his doctrine and his audience, Hills' sanctification, and the subsequent addition of Spirit baptism to his revivalist worldview, in fact narrowed his revivalist identity slightly. That is, even while the success of *Holiness and Power* expanded his preaching influence into holiness and Methodist churches,

---

52. Ibid., 73–98.

53. Ibid., 98–99. Hills does not cite the quotation within the quote, although the sentence is marked as another's.

Hills' overall message quickly narrowed to the general theme of holiness. Holiness became the subject of most of the rest of his books. Even the biographies that he later wrote address holiness, two of them on holiness leaders and the third on Finney. To his canon of revivalist doctrines and means Hills added a new, powerful, and even commanding agent. Holiness dominated his thinking for the rest of his life, and rightfully so. Sanctification by the baptism of the Holy Spirit was the only remaining hope for his millennial vision. Global Christian success in mission would be Hills' only vindication against those who asserted that either his postmillennial vision was inherently flawed or that his revivalist methods were unable to deliver what they promised.

It is for this reason that Hills became very sharp toward any system, doctrine, theologian, or philosopher that would challenge his message. At stake was the Spirit's power, the Bible's truthfulness, and the revivalists' worldview. Thus, Hills was very straightforward and often even contentious toward contrasting positions. And by the last decade of the nineteenth century, there were many contrasting opinions.

The year of 1895 was not the easiest year to discover holiness. Hills was sanctified the very same year that Phineas Bresee left the Methodist Episcopal Church to found the Pentecostal Church of the Nazarene. The National Camp Meeting Association was already being called any number of pejorative terms for its distinctive emphases upon sanctification and revivalism. Class and methodological differences were exerting great stresses within the several denominations of the Methodist family of churches.

Besides all the turmoil from without, the Holiness Movement, (and revivalism in general), saw much splintering that same decade. The Keswick and Holiness Movements were beginning to bristle. Within only a few years after the turn of the century, Pentecostalism branched off from the Holiness Movement, claiming not only a large percentage of the holiness constituency, but also "hijacking" their beloved doctrine of the Pentecostal baptism with the Spirit.

Of course, these challenges only served to engage the apologetic side of Hills' mind. Coming onto the holiness scene so late in his life, Hills wasted no time in developing a doctrine of holiness and arguments in favor of its importance. Believing that if his Oberlin mentors had preached it as clearly as he himself could, he would have "entered Canaan" earlier, Hills set forth to write and preach with the kind of clarity he would like to have had for himself at an earlier stage. He put his message into the language he spoke, the language of the age of science. His works and sermons on holiness were, therefore, clear on the conditions for the blessing. *Holiness and Power* and *Pentecostal Light* were the first of a whole series of books, including three biographies, which proclaimed holiness in the clearest possible language.

HILLS' MATURE DOCTRINE OF SPIRIT BAPTISM

Hills' mature doctrine of Spirit baptism reveals a tight system of hamartiological and soteriological ideas. Because Hills often begins with the problem of sin and moves to the cure, we will start there as well.

The Twofold Hamartiology of Holiness Theology

In order to understand fully Hills' doctrine of the baptism with the Spirit, we must start where he does, with the sin problem. Hills is not unique among holiness thinkers of his era in his assertion that there are two distinctive accomplishments that grace affects for a person that specifically address the twofold problem of sin. Hills opens *Scriptural Holiness and Keswick Teaching Compared* with a chapter entitled "Definitions."

Citing Adam Clarke, Hills asserts, "Sin exists in the soul after two modes or forms: (1) In GUILT, which requires forgiveness or pardon; [and] (2) in POLLUTION, which requires cleansing."[54] In the next paragraphs, Hills teaches the essential difference between these two and presents several synonyms for both. One distinction he makes between sin as guilt and sin as pollution is that the former is often called "sins" in the New Testament, while the latter is often referred as "sin." Sins are the actual wrong deeds accomplished and evil thoughts harbored by humans, while sin is the propensity within persons that drives them to commit sinful actions and harbor evil thoughts.[55]

There is, of course, nothing unique or original in Hills' appropriation of the general twofold hamartiology of the Holiness Movement. Likewise, the same is true of his twofold soteriology, which addresses both aspects of the sin problem.

---

54. Hills, *Scriptural Holiness and Keswick*, 10.
55. Ibid., 10–11.

It is sin, and not sins, that takes up the majority of Hills' discussion on Keswick teaching, for in his estimation, it is the greater of the two problems. Throughout his books, Hills offers multiple synonyms for this inward problem of sin as pollution. In his exegesis of multiple Scriptures, he sees it called by many names. In Romans and Hebrews alone, he identifies or develops almost eleven synonyms for sin.

> In Rom. vi. 6 it is personified, and called "the old man." In Rom. vii. 17, it is again personified and called "sin that dwelleth in me" ... In Rom. vii. 23 it is called "the LAW of sin." If for the word "law" we substitute "a uniform tendency," which is its meaning, we shall get a flood of light upon the evil thing. It is the strange spirit of the devil put into every child by race inheritance, a UNIFORM TENDENCY to do wrong and run after sin and run away from God. In Rom. viii. 2 the figure is intensified, and it is called "the law of sin and death." ... In Rom. viii. 7 it is called "the carnal mind which is enmity against God." ... In Heb. xii. 15 this evil thing is called "a root of bitterness." ... In Heb. xii. 1 it is called "the sin that doth so easily beset us." ... In Heb. iii. 12 it is called "an evil heart of unbelief in departing from the living God."[56]

From this uniform tendency, this root, the old man, arises the actual outward manifestations of wrongdoing, or more simply, sins.

Thus, we see in Hills' theology the idea of sin as a twofold problem. This being the case, what is needed is a twofold solution.

The Twofold Salvation for the Twofold Problem of Sin

Hills' mature soteriology addresses the problems of sin on both levels, because, in his understanding, the grace of God is sufficient to deliver from both sins and sin. For the double problem is a double remedy. This double cure is accomplished at two different events in the Christian life. The first of these is regeneration, when the unbeliever first comes to faith in Christ. In Hills' estimate, the work of God in this instant is extraordinary and should never be diminished. Of this transforming moment, Hills writes:

> "*Regeneration is that moral change in man wrought by the Holy Spirit, by which he is saved from the love of sin, the practice of sin, and the dominion of sin, and is enabled with full choice of will*

---

56. Ibid., 15–16.

> and the energy of right affection, to love God and to keep His commandments" ... [When] we repented and sought regeneration, we gave up *expecting* to sin ... The whole moral attitude of a true child of God will be changed. He hates what he once loved, and loves what he once hated.[57]

In these statements, we see Hills' high regard for regeneration. The only problem is that while it certainly accomplishes an extraordinary transformation in the new convert, regeneration does not cleanse the soul from inward pollution. It does not dig out the root of bitterness, crucify the old man, or eradicate the carnal mind that is enmity against God. While "a justified and regenerated man is under obligation to live just as well outwardly as a sanctified or holy man," the grace of conversion does actually cleanse the soul of its inward pollution. "Obedience to God in outward conduct is refraining from actual sin, voluntary sin, the first form of sin. But that is not Bible holiness or sanctification. By itself it is only the experience of justification or regeneration."[58]

Here Hills is suggesting that regeneration can and will help change outward behavior. He is adamant, however, that a greater work is needed, one of inward cleansing. This is where his doctrine of sanctification enters. At some point in the *believer's* life, subsequent to regeneration, the Christian must receive a second experience of saving grace that will cleanse the soul of its propensity toward sinning. From Hills' new perspective, this cleansing of the inherited, inward law of sin is the greatest instantaneous work that God can accomplish in a person's life.[59] God's "much more" grace[60] is sufficient to save to the uttermost,[61] pardoning sins and cleansing sin. This is "the second blessing, properly so-called,

---

57. Ibid., 19–20. Italics Hills'.

58. Ibid., 22–23.

59. I say the "greatest *instantaneous* work that grace can accomplish" because, for Hills, the only grace that is greater than this is the *gradual* work of God after this second instant. This gradual work, subsequent to Spirit baptism, Hills calls "the fulness of the blessing" or the being "filled with all the fulness of God," and he implies that it takes most of the rest of the person's life for God to accomplish it. Hills calls it a "popular heresy" to consider sanctification as the final attainment of progress. Cf. Hills, *Pentecostal Light*, 41.

60. Hills, *Holiness in Romans*, 15–26.

61. Hills, *Pentecost Rejected*, 61.

deliverance from the root of bitterness, from inbred as well as actual sin."[62]

Just as he finds multiple synonyms for the inward sin principle, Hills also cites multiple biblical and theological equivalents for the work of God that cleanses the soul of sin. His two most frequently used synonyms, "sanctification" and "baptism with the Holy Spirit," can be seen in this definition of the second blessing.

> ENTIRE SANCTIFICATION IS A SECOND DEFINITE WORK OF GRACE WROUGHT BY THE BAPTISM WITH THE HOLY SPIRIT IN THE HEART OF THE BELIEVER SUBSEQUENTLY TO REGENERATION, RECEIVED INSTANTANEOUSLY BY FAITH, BY WHICH THE HEART IS CLEANSED FROM ALL INWARD CORRUPTION AND FILLED WITH THE PERFECT LOVE OF GOD.[63]

In this definition, we see Hills' interchangeable usage of the two terms "entire sanctification" and "baptism with the Holy Spirit." He sees the two terms as synonymous, accomplishing the much-needed second work of inward cleansing. An interesting conflation of holiness concepts and pentecostal imagery, again, it is no way unique or original to Hills. In *A Century of Holiness Theology: The Doctrine of Entire Sanctification in the Church of the Nazarene 1905–2004*, Mark R. Quanstrom writes, "The biblical paradigm for the holiness movement's understanding of entire sanctification at the end of the nineteenth century was Pentecost." Drawing from Donald W. Dayton's work, Quanstrom points out that this paradigm had begun taking shape since before the American Civil War.[64] By the end of the century, it found its full fruition as a kind of "holiness orthodoxy," emphasizing "entire sanctification as an instantaneous second work of grace that eradicated the sinful nature . . . Entire sanctification was identified as the baptism with the Holy Spirit and that baptism with the Holy Spirit, according to these early descriptions, resulted in almost glorified human persons."[65] As it relates to the subject of this present study, Quanstrom locates the four leading thinkers and craftsmen of holiness orthodoxy to be Daniel Steele, J. A. Wood, Asbury Lowery, and A. M. Hills.

62. Hills, *Holiness and Keswick*, 27–28.
63. Ibid., 29. Capitalization Hills'.
64. Quanstrom, *Century of Holiness Theology*, 33.
65. Ibid., 24.

Convinced that Spirit baptism is always given in an instantaneous manner, Hills joined a chorus of holiness theologians in scouring the Scriptures for examples of this *via salutis*. Many passages in both testaments are cited as revealing this twofold soteriology. From allegorical usages of crossing the Jordan River to Paul's accusation that the Corinthian church is still a carnal, milk-drinking church when they ought to be spiritual, solid-food-eaters, holiness thinkers produced multiple scriptural examples of followers of God who fell short of the fullness of God's help and salvation.

As well, they also found many examples of those who did not fall short of God's full salvation. Some of Hills' favorite examples are the apostles of Jesus. While they all fell desperately short of their calling while Christ was with them, the same was not true after the cleansing, sanctifying Spirit came to them at Pentecost.

Philip is a clear example. "The prayer of Jesus for the sanctification of His disciples was answered at Pentecost. They were immediately *cleansed* from the pride and self-seeking and cowardice and impatience that had characterized their former lives . . . Philip went down to the city of Samaria and had a gracious revival."[66]

In *Holiness and Power*, Hills relates that while he was still with them, Jesus rebuked the disciples regularly.

> [He] found it necessary to reprove them for unbelief, instability, selfishness, a worldly, secular spirit, a retaliating spirit, a cowardly and vacillating spirit, and repeated feelings of jealousy. These manifestations of the "indwelling sin" — the "carnal" nature — troubled the Master, and He prayed for them that they might be "sanctified." When the Holy Ghost came upon them that "old man" of sin was crucified, and they were sanctified. He took the cowardice out of Peter, and the unbelief out of Thomas, and the overgrown ambitions out of James and John. The "Son of Thunder" became the "Apostle of Love."[67]

In Hills' estimate, the disciples of Jesus in the twentieth century are much like his disciples before Pentecost—greatly in need of the cleansing work of God. "Human hearts are just what they have always been, estranged from God and filled with carnality and sin, no better and no worse than the human hearts of other times . . . [But] the blessed 'Third

---

66. Hills, *Holiness and Keswick*, 35. Italics his.
67. Hills, *Holiness and Power*, 71.

Person of the Trinity," the ever-adorable Holy Spirit, is not dead. He can still cleanse the believer's heart in the Pentecostal Chamber."[68]

As seen above, holiness thinkers of the late nineteenth century regularly connected pentecostal language and imagery with some kind of subsequent work of grace. Hills pulls these two themes and others together with great ease in *Pentecostal Light*. While pointing out that believers need to pray for the Spirit so that they may be purged from sin, Hills writes:

> Malachi prophesied of Christ that "He is like a refiner's fire, . . . and he shall purify the sons of Levi, and purge them as gold and silver, that they may offer unto the Lord an offering in righteousness" (Mal. iii. 2, 3). John Baptist [sic] said of Jesus: "He shall baptize you with the Holy Ghost and with fire." We are told in Acts that at Pentecost "there appeared unto them cloven tongues like as of fire" (Acts ii. 3); and that this Holy Ghost fire "purified their hearts" (Acts xv. 9). "Being sanctified by the Holy Ghost." [sic] (Rom. xv. 16).[69]

With no apparent effort at all, Hills weaves these texts and ideas together. Concerning holiness adherents, Quanstrom observes, "Pentecost was not understood as a singular event in the context of salvation-history. Instead, Pentecost was a personal event that was to be a part of every believer's salvation experience. A 'personal Pentecost' became normative for all believers according to holiness teaching, and this personal baptism of the Holy Spirit was considered the occasion of entire sanctification."[70]

Hills used multiple biblical and theological synonyms to refer to the inward sin principle and God's cleansing work. In *Holiness and Power*, he offers several of these synonyms along with the names of those who coined the terms. Paul called it "the fullness of God." John Wesley, along with the Apostle John, called it "perfect love." Mrs. Jonathan Edwards referred to it as "the full assurance of faith." A. B. Earle called it "the rest of faith." Asa Mahan, "filled and thrilled by 'the refining and sin-killing Spirit,' chose Pentecostal language and called it 'The Baptism of the Holy Ghost' . . . Finney, with a floodtide of rapture flowing over his soul, used the language of Christ, and called it 'Entire Sanctification.' But the work,

---

68. Hills, *Pentecost Rejected*, 19.
69. Hills, *Pentecostal Light*, 21–22.
70. Quanstrom, *Century of Holiness Theology*, 33.

by whatever name it is called, is essentially the same. It is God's act of cleansing the soul."[71]

The conflation of various biblical and theological motifs under the single umbrella of soul cleansing, (and even putting the word "entire" into Christ's mouth), begins to give us a clear picture of Hills' priority in his doctrine of Spirit baptism. *Primarily*, it should be thought of as a cleansing work of grace, which serves the regenerate believer by removing the inward propensity toward sinning.[72]

HILLS' FINAL REVIVALIST NARROWING—HIS ERADICATIONIST WRITINGS AGAINST KESWICK

The final narrowing of Hills' revivalist identity was precipitated by the culmination of two factors. The first is simply the extent of Hills' own personal experience of sanctification. As we saw above, Hills' baptism with the Spirit profoundly influenced every aspect of his life and ministry. At the lowest point in his life it gave him not only a personal boost, but a considerable professional one as well, propelling him into new spiritual heights and also into new career opportunities.

The second factor is the timing of Hills' sanctification. The ten years immediately prior to and after the turn of the twentieth century saw the splintering of holiness revivalism into various camps. Of particular significance to Hills' final narrowing was the Keswick movement's complete disassociation with the National Camp Meeting Association for the Promotion of Holiness.

Hills' Eradicationist Development

While Hills is very careful to maintain the basic holiness understanding of the twofold problem of sin and its double cure, there is still another major dilemma in and with the modern church that is addressed in almost every one of Hills' books, the problem of powerless Christian

---

71. Hills, *Holiness and Power*, 71–72.

72. While it is clear from multiple places that Hills' doctrine of sanctification by the Spirit's baptism primarily purifies the soul of sin, it would be far from accurate to say that this is all that it accomplishes. The baptism with the Holy Spirit also accomplishes multiple other positive and negative works in the believer. Cf. Hills, *Pentecostal Light*, 6–29; *Holiness and Power*, 237–72.

witness. Not only must every Christian seek God for forgiveness and sanctification, but also for help to proclaim the truth.

In *Pentecostal Light*, he laments, "I am persuaded there is a serious difficulty lying at the very roots of our modern church life. Our resources are so vast and our opportunities are so many, while our triumphs are comparatively so few."[73]

In *The Secret of Spiritual Power*, Hills writes of those ministers who sneer at the second-blessing baptism with the Holy Spirit. "It is a sad accompanying fact that the ministers who do it are scarcely saved from the deserved contempt of the world for their barrenness. This is the need of the hour in all our churches. Our ministers are conspicuously weak when they might be giants for God. Our churches confront an impudent, scorning world in conscious helplessness."[74]

Hills thought he saw this problem of powerlessness exemplified at Moody Bible Institute. Frustrated after a trip there by students calling him names loud enough for him to overhear, Hills sat down to write a book, *Pentecost Rejected*. In it, he outlines the problem of powerlessness and how this directly relates to Christianity's unwillingness to accept "Pentecost," the cleansing work of God. Quoting an article in the September 1901 "The Pentecost Century," Hills writes, "We have one dire disease — *Spiritual famine* — lack of witness of the Spirit, lack of personal experience, lack of spiritual power . . ."[75] The next pages in *Pentecost Rejected* include statistics of denominational growth during the decade of the 1890s. In Hills' estimate, the statistics reveal meager effectiveness and overall powerlessness.[76]

Powerlessness in witness leading to barrenness in ministry is the third great problem of the Christian church and the individuals within it. So great a problem is it that, again, it is mentioned in almost every one of his books.

One might expect that if the three greatest concerns of Hills are sins, sin, and powerless witness he might have advocated some kind of "three-blessings" soteriology; but this is not the case. According to Hills' new soteriology, the third great problem of Christianity, powerlessness,

---

73. Hills, *Pentecostal Light*, 28.
74. Hills, *Secret of Spiritual Power*, 11.
75. Hills, *Pentecost Rejected*, 16.
76. Ibid., 16-19.

is actually solved in the second blessing. Concomitant with the cleansing of inward sin by the Spirit is the endowment with power.

Again, Hills and many other holiness divines scoured the texts of the Bible looking for precedent, and again Acts 2 became a central proof-text. In *Pentecostal Light*, Hills makes the connection.

> We ought to pray for the Holy Spirit that we may be endued with power from on high. This was Jesus' parting charge to the disciples — they were to pray till the Holy Spirit came to endue them with power to win souls. They did pray until the Holy Spirit was poured out, and Pentecost was the result. They continued to pray, and "there were added to the church daily those that were being saved." What do Christians need *now* more than this power to save men which the Spirit can impart? Individually and collectively, we stand so impotent in the presence of sin and sinners. We have little power to cast out demons and to bring many to righteousness. The sermon at Pentecost resulted in the conversion of three thousand souls. A wit has scornfully said it now takes three thousand sermons to convert one soul.[77]

Hills' connection of cleansing with Spirit baptism is nowhere more clearly demonstrated than in *Pentecost Rejected*. The book opens with these words.

> So long as the early Christian Church frequented the Pentecostal chamber, her career was one of unbroken triumphs. While her leaders were sanctified, and her preachers spoke their gospel messages with the power of the Holy Ghost sent down from heaven, the march of her progress was steady and irresistible; nothing could stay her triumphant course. While the early Christians were taught to look forward to a second sanctifying work of grace by the baptism with the Holy Spirit as the normal Christian experience, their zeal was unflagging; their life was pure; their courage was perfect. The cross and the sword could not make them halt . . . The Church, while it repeated and renewed its Pentecosts, was full of an irresistible energy, and moved to conquest against the power of darkness, 'fair as the moon, glorious as the sun, and terrible as an army with banners.' It was not until the Pentecostal chamber was forsaken, and its experiences discounted, and the leaders of the Church began to trust to the natural rather than the supernatural, and substituted oratory, and scholarship, and genius, and Pagan pomp, and governmental friendship for the

---

77. Hills, *Pentecostal Light*, 26–27.

baptism with the Holy Spirit and the Enduement of Power, that the Church fell. History repeats itself. As Pentecost was rejected then, so it is being rejected to-day."[78]

In chapter 2, Hills continues by explaining *exactly* what it is that is being rejected in "Pentecost rejected." It may be exemplified in his friend and Moody president R. A. Torrey's position in the book "How to Bring Men to Christ." In Hills' understanding, Pentecost rejected is Torrey's idea that "'the baptism of the Holy Spirit is always connected with testimony or service. The baptism of the Holy Spirit has no direct reference to cleansing from sin.' . . . Brother Torrey absolutely and emphatically denies that the Pentecostal experience cleanses the heart, and declares that it only empowers for larger service."[79] Torrey's position, to the horror of Hills, explicitly rejects the concept of inward cleansing and reduces the baptism of the Spirit to power alone. Advocating a *holiness*-centered understanding of the Spirit baptism, Hills felt that to reject cleansing was to reject the heart of God's most profound work and, ultimately, to reject the whole of the experience.

In chapter 3, Hills offers pages of scriptural examples of what he means by "Pentecost." In every case, he connects a synonym for inward sin with some form of cleansing language.[80] Further, throughout the rest of the book, Hills connects Spirit baptism with inward cleansing. Thus, "Pentecost rejected" is any definition of Spirit baptism that rejects the "perfect work" of God's grace and the primary duty of the Holy Spirit to cleanse the soul of inward sin.[81]

Hills' visit to Moody Bible Institute, and the students' response to his doctrine of the cleansing pentecostal baptism, marked the beginning of a strained relationship between Hills and Torrey. So central was the cleansing motif to Hills' doctrine of Spirit baptism that Moody's rejec-

---

78. Hills, *Pentecost Rejected*, 11–12.

79. Ibid., 30–31.

80. The "old man crucified" and "the body of sin destroyed." The "spirit of disobedience," "the law of sin," "the constant tendency to sin," "the body of death," "the law of sin and death," "the carnal mind," "a root of bitterness," "the sin that doth so easily beset us," "an evil heart of unbelief in departing from the living God," "depravity," and the "curse" are all mentioned as synonymous with the inward propensity to sin. The removal of these may be called "cleansing," "the circumcision of the heart," "the purging away of the dross," "the purging as gold and silver," and "sanctification without which no one shall see the Lord." Ibid., 69–73.

81. Ibid., 73.

tion of it left Hills with many critical words for his own friend.[82] It seems, Hills' biographer remarks, that among the groups represented by Hills and Torrey, "neither side was skilled at compromise."[83]

We see the same staunch, cleansing-priority logic exemplified in Hills' critique of his own mentor, Charles Finney. Again, Hills' contentiousness is governed by his uncompromising stance that cleansing, and not empowering, is the primary work of the Holy Spirit. Near the end of Hills' biography of Finney, the semi-hagiographic language stops and the critique begins. Hills asserts:

> Finney failed to connect the obtaining of sanctification with the baptism with the Holy Ghost. Sometimes he almost got the truth, as his directions to seekers occasionally show. But his discussions, *as a whole*, show that he never fully grasped the idea that the heart was cleansed of indwelling sin by the baptism with the Holy Ghost. So it came about that, with all his matchless gifts as a preacher and teacher, he was not eminently successful as a teacher of sanctification . . . Had Finney held correct Scriptural opinions of what sanctification is, and how it is obtained, he would have been the mightiest preacher of holiness the world has yet had since St. Paul, just as he was the most successful soul-winner of the centuries. As it was, a few souls here and there sought and received the baptism with the Holy Spirit, and obtained the Divine witness to a cleansing of heart under his preaching.[84]

Hills' argument with his mentor, Finney, is the same as with his friend, Torrey. Neither maintains a doctrine of Spirit baptism that understands the cleansing of the heart as the primary aspect. Both inevitably lead believers to seek power without necessarily seeking purification. The result is simple; believers never arrive at true Spirit baptism—they never arrive at holiness or power.

Hills, of course, is not at all rejecting the category of power. Quite to the contrary, as was stated above, Spirit baptism remedies both the problems of inward sin and powerless witness. A personal pentecost will both cleanse and empower. This is exemplified in the very title of Hills' first book on holiness, *Holiness* and Power. Of the two themes, however, holiness has the clear priority. It is no coincidence that the title of the

---

82. For the fuller story see Marsden, *Fundamentalism and American Culture*, 94–96 and Gresham, *Waves against Gibraltar*, 127–28.

83. Gresham, *Waves against Gibraltar*, 127.

84. Hills, *Life of Charles Finney*, 226–27.

book is not *Power and Holiness*. Hills rejects his friend's position because Torrey claims that the Spirit gives power for purity. Hills' logic is the exact opposite of what he believes Keswick is teaching. The fullness of power comes when the believer is fully purified. Thus, in Hills' theology, purity is to be sought, so that once it is granted, power may be given.

Understanding Hills' rationale here is one of the keys to the holiness mind. Hills genuinely believed that only a small measure of spiritual power accompanies a small measure of inward purity. The minister, evangelist, or layperson who allows sin to linger will not have much power for witness or global transformation. According to Hills' vision, the world is in desperate need of the gospel's *full* potency, carried along by a full measure of the power and persuasiveness of the Holy Spirit. "People are pouring like a Niagara-tide through the gates of sin and death into an awful hell. God has set His heart upon turning that stream of life heavenward. Any child of God who will faithfully fall in with God's wishes and plans and conditions of success will become a winner of souls. I solemnly declare again, to the honor of the old Gospel and the glory of the Holy Ghost . . . barrenness is utterly needless."[85]

Unfortunately, Hills laments, most ministers, evangelists, and laypersons have but a portion of the efficacious anointing in their preaching and witnessing. The reason for this lack is simple—they have not been made clean vessels.

Hills, here, challenges many of the options open to the interpretation of the relationship between holiness and power. He challenges the Keswick position that Spirit baptism provides power that in turn suppresses sin within. Hills also challenges Phoebe Palmer's notion that "holiness *is* power,"[86] or that "purity and power are identical."[87]

Hills is adamant that personal spiritual power does not bring about purity, but vice-versa. He disagrees with all of the above positions and argues for a specific order of salvation. "Baptism [in the Spirit] can not be received unless one is 'cleansed,' 'sanctified,' made 'a holy man.' This is the very Pentecostal blessing we are writing about. The Holy Spirit would not dare to fill and empower an unclean, unholy, carnal man; he

---

85. Hills, *Pentecost Rejected*, 20.
86. Palmer, *Promise of the Father*, 206; Palmer, *Four Years in Old World*, 395.
87. Palmer, *Gift of Power*, vi.

would be sure to abuse the power by using it in a carnal selfish, wicked way."[88]

A similar order can be seen in his book *The Secret of Spiritual Power*, perhaps Hills' clearest book on the subject. Hills spends eight chapters and two-thirds of the book explaining the New Testament view of holiness before getting to the topic of the title of the book, spiritual power. His rationale for doing so is simple—because purity precedes power.

Before the ninth chapter entitled "It Brings Power," Hills offers, for his eighth chapter, "What Holiness Is." He is clear that the work of God cleanses the heart of all unrighteousness. It purifies the heart from all sin. "And the blessing indicated by all these scriptures is connected unmistakable with Pentecost. It was the baptism with the Holy Ghost that cleansed the hearts of the disciples, making them 'sanctified,' 'pure,' 'holy,' 'perfect.'"[89]

Hills continues in this chapter: "It is not difficult to find reasons why God wants this Holy Spirit cleansing wrought within us. He hates sin and every trace of the work of Satan within our souls. He loves, like any parent, to have us reproduce His perfect likeness, and reflect to the moral universe His glory. He wants us to be at our best, and clothed with power for service, and this we never can be while sin dwelleth in us."[90]

After spending eight chapters on holiness, chapter 9 finally arrives at the topic of the book, spiritual power. Hills reflects: "Power is universally coveted. Men love to gratify ambition and be dominant. Achievement will bring notoriety and publicity; conquest will be succeeded by renown . . . Oh yes! people want power. It will bring honor, prominence, and gain. Everybody is after it . . . Jesus promised power to His disciples. But be it noticed that their hearts were first cleansed by the Holy Ghost. It is not safe to entrust carnal men with power. It would almost certainly be abused and perverted to selfish ends."[91]

Hills is not making here any naive assertions that "power corrupts." To the contrary, humans who are *already* corrupted by their inward sin will use whatever power they have to further their corrupt purposes. For Hills, this principle is certainly true of the unbeliever, the one who knows nothing of Christ. More significantly, however, it is even true of

---

88. Hills, *Pentecost Rejected*, 27.
89. Hills, *Secret of Spiritual Power*, 47.
90. Ibid., 50.
91. Ibid., 52.

the regenerate disciple, who knows Christ and whose outward sins have been forgiven, but whose inward sinful compulsion has not yet been removed. Concerning the condition of this one, the carnal Christian, Hills is clear. Divine power and anointing will be granted only to the purified person—the Christian whose heart has been cleansed and can, therefore, be trusted with power.

Hills offers an example of the disciples John and James, who before Pentecost argued over being first in the kingdom of God. Of these two, Hills speculates briefly:

> Had they secured such positions, without an increase of grace, they would most likely have been ruined. But the great gift of power to the disciples was wisely postponed until their hearts were cleansed by the Holy Spirit. Then they were free from selfishness, and would use their extraordinary power with an eye single to the glory of God. Peter could then preach his moving sermon, not at all for Peter's exaltation, but for the glory of Jesus. The whole apostolic band, suddenly clothed with an unwonted power that made men marvel, could remain sweet, humble, and modest without a touch of that sense of self-importance which so often disfigures the character of carnal men.[92]

Having quite emphatically insisted upon the order of holiness leading to power, Hills continues by explaining exactly the purpose of pentecostal power. "What then is the power which Jesus gives? It is a power to bear witness for Jesus. 'Ye shall be witnesses unto me both in Jerusalem, and in all Judaea [sic], and in Samaria, and unto the uttermost part of the earth.'"[93] Unfortunately, Hills laments, the quietness of most Christians betrays the reality that they have not yet been baptized with the Spirit. They are silent in the prayer meeting and silent in their private conversations about spiritual life. "There is no gushing spontaneity and overflow of soul, no burning fire within that will not suffer them to keep silence. But let these same believers come to a Pentecost, and they would at once be like the early disciples of whom it is written, 'And they were all filled with the Holy Ghost, and began to speak.'"[94]

Hills is adamant that this view of the baptism with the Holy Spirit is the only way to move people from regeneration to sanctification

---

92. Ibid., 52–53.
93. Ibid., 53.
94. Ibid., 54. Hills own scriptural citation ends here.

and from ineffectual silence to Pentecostal-Peter power. Sin must be removed by Spirit baptism so that power for witnessing may reach its highest mark. The Holy Spirit must be sought with *holiness* in mind.

Hills' full soteriology thus includes conversion (the forgiveness of sins) and sanctification (the removal of the sin nature with a concomitant endowment with power). While both conversion and sanctification are profound events in the Christian life, the latter of the two opens the believer to the greatest possibilities of purity and powerful service. Hills is adamant that this understanding is the clearest way to proclaim the message of uttermost salvation and that teaching or preaching anything else will lead only to less effective spiritual development. [95]

SUMMARY

The year 1895 was the most life-changing year in A. M. Hills' life. Not only did it see the publication of his first book, but more significantly, it was the year he experienced sanctification by the baptism with the Holy Spirit. This experience launched his career in new directions, eventually moving him into the holiness circuits and holiness education.

This year also marked the beginning of a more subtle transition from a broadly conceived, Finney-like revivalism to holiness forms. In this transition, a gradual move to a narrower revivalist identity took place. Believing he had found the experiential answer to the church and even the world's problems, many of his earlier revivalistic themes became eclipsed in, or at least subsumed under, his new doctrine of holiness. Moving from an insignificant appendage of Christian duty to the center of his system, the theme of sanctification dominated his subsequent books and articles.

---

95. In the preface to *Holiness and Power*, the editor says of Hills, "When the truth dawned upon him in all its preciousness, it seemed to him that he could point out the way to receive the desired blessing of the Holy Spirit more fully and plainly than other authors had done." Hills, *Holiness and Power*, 7.

6

The Hills Controversies, or Where Does Hills Fit?

A. M. HILLS WAS not a man unacquainted with controversy. It seemed to find him all his life. There are three reasons for this. The first is the obvious reality that Oberlin graduates like Hills could always be counted on for a good fight. It was often said of Hills that he bore the Oberlin and the Finney "stamp," a distinctive identity that he in turn imprinted upon many of his students. Oberlin graduates were distinctive; they were different and often held these differences proudly and even contentiously. Thus, simply as a graduate of Oberlin, Hills was never afraid to fight over issues he felt were essential.

The second reason that controversy seemed to find Hills is his own personality. Without delving into any specific profile, it will suffice to say that, personally, Hills was a fighter. In his remembrances of his teacher and later friend, R. T. Williams writes of this personality characteristic.

> Dr. Hills was a man of great strength, but I could not say he had no weakness. Perhaps no man has ever lived who was entirely free from weakness. One's strength is often his weakness, or it may become so, and this was true of Dr. Hills. He had very strong likes and dislikes toward things and people. This was his strength, but it was also his weakness. If he liked a doctrine he would almost die for it, and if he did not like it he would work equally as hard to defeat it. If he liked a person he was ready to put his arms around him with deep feeling and affection, and protect and promote him to the limit. If he was convinced that a person was wrong, or insincere, he would denounce him in terms that could always be

easily understood . . . His likes and dislikes always ran deep, and were a source of very great strength to him, as well as a potential possibility of danger.[1]

In his remembrances, J. B. Chapman writes similarly. "I always felt that when I did not fully know the reasons for the doctrines I taught and the ethics to which I adhered, that I must be right or Dr. Hills would let me know. His silence was my assurance. I did not know what he would say about certain things, but I knew he would speak out if he found us running up a blind alley."[2]

Hills' son, James A. Hills, speaks of this same characteristic of his father, calling his outspokenness "sincerity" and "rugged frontier idealism." "I am deeply impressed by the absolute sincerity of my Father. What might have seemed to others as a certain hardness and inflexibility was but the natural outgrowth of the utter lack of deception in his mental and moral makeup. With him a thing was either right or wrong, however disagreeable the facts were. I cannot remember of his ever being insincere or double-dealing in his relationships with others. This trait of open-hearted dealing goes back to his early frontier life of rugged idealism."[3]

Of course, James Hills also recognizes the Finney stamp on his father as well. He continues: "Perhaps another reason for his outspoken ways was due to the tremendous influence of Charles G. Finney over him. One could not honor and respect such a great man, as my Father did Mr. Finney, without absorbing his attitudes and ideals. President Finney was stalwart, inflexible, and fully committed to both the living and preaching of the uncompromising ideals of God's kingdom, without fear of the world, the flesh, or the devil. My Father followed in his footsteps."[4]

By nature and nurture, Hills was a straightforward theologian, preacher, and leader. The positive side of this was a confidence that those who knew him said he possessed and that he was able to instill in others. The negative side was, as we saw in chapter 2 and above, that the com-

---

1. McWilliams, "Hills: A Life Sketch," 70–71.
2. Ibid., 75.
3. Ibid., 80.
4. Ibid. James Hills continues that his father' straightforwardness and simple sincerity characterized not only his doctrine, but his personal religious life and his preaching as well.

plexities of his pastoral and university settings often left him frustrated, requiring perhaps more subtle relational gifts and graces and greater political refinement than he possessed. Straightforwardness served him well behind the pulpit as an evangelist. In a college presidency, however, such unambiguous simplicity was much less appreciated.[5] Taking the above obituaries at face value, it might be said that Hills would have considered greater political savvy on his part to have been insincere or even dishonest. Whether for good or for ill, however, Hills was by nature and by nurture straightforwardly outspoken.

The third reason that Hills found himself in so many controversies is simply the awkwardness with which he fit in the various settings he placed himself. His theology resists most categorization. Indeed, the only category that sticks without qualification is "revivalist," a broad enough passport, so to speak, to have allowed him free passage in and out of all the revivalist movements of the early twentieth century. Drawing from so many diverse revivalist sources, Hills is probably better defined as an interstitial figure than the quintessential representative of any specific paradigm. For example, several of his key theological works bear either the words "fundamental" or "pentecostal" in them. Yet, as we will see in this chapter, Hills does not easily fit into either the Fundamentalist or the Pentecostal camps.

Chapters 4 and 5 reviewed the central doctrines, values, and means that Hills held most dearly. Characterizing these as revivalistic in every particular, these two chapters distill the core of Hills' doctrine, means, and larger revivalist identity. Thus, any interpretation of Hills and his works must be weighed not only against the doctrine of holiness of his later years, but also against the larger revivalist canon that he developed and maintained throughout his entire life. Only in combining his holiness years with his earlier, unchanging development can the interpreter see the full Hills. Chapters 4 and 5 together represent an unequivocal canon of doctrines and means against which Hills' measured everything. While many other doctrines lingered around the periphery of his larger system, those set forward in these two chapters represent the nonnegotiable heart of his revivalist worldview. As we will see in this chapter,

---

5. James Hills writes, "This quality of absolute sincerity was a great handicap to him in dealing with others. He supposed they would be equally as honest, which very often was not the case, and he became an easy victim for designing schemers and 'politicians', whether in church or college circles." Ibid., 80–81.

none of the other revivalistic movements of the early twentieth century taught his exact system. For this reason, depending on their relative proximity to his revivalist canon, Hills was, to a lesser or greater extent, ill-disposed toward them.

In this chapter, we will consider the controversies of A. M. Hills' later life. Specifically, we will see the arguments he maintained against three movements: the Keswick-Holiness Movement, Pentecostalism, and his own Congregational church. In each case, Hills' frustration stemmed from their respective distance from his own version of revivalism.

HILLS AND TORREY: ERADICATIONISM VS. THE KESWICK MOVEMENT

There was probably no more sour a controversy for A. M. Hills than his first; the dispute he had with R. A. Torrey, a Yale classmate and personal friend. The two were so close that Hills was asked to preach Torrey's ordination sermon. Both held so many overlapping concerns, from the general fear of apostasy inherent in Common Sense to apologetic and revivalistic styles, that they became close friends as well as colleagues. Thus, it was difficult for Hills to state his case against Keswick without consequences in their personal relationship.

Explicit Dissimilarities between Hills and Torrey

As revivalists, Hills and Torrey ran such parallel tracks that, were it not for what an outsider might consider a minuscule difference, most would think they were in the same camp entirely. The only problem is that *they* considered their variations on the subject of Spirit baptism of central importance. As we saw in chapter 5, Hills' doctrine of Spirit baptism was the newfound key to the cleansing of the spirit, without which power for worldwide evangelization and transformation would not be granted. As we also saw, while his understanding of Spirit baptism brought *both* holiness and power, Hills was adamant that it is primarily a cleansing work. Needless to say, Hills, who held all of the pieces of his treasured core with a fierce jealousy, was disturbed by his friend's teachings, summed up for Hills in a single phrase, "The baptism with the Holy Spirit is always connected with testimony and service."[6]

6. Torrey, *Baptism with the Holy Spirit*, 14. Torrey explicitly urges this when speak-

Of course, the tensions were heightened to an acute degree when Hills spent several weeks visiting Moody Bible Institute over which Torrey presided. As we saw above, Hills was greatly disturbed by the whispering he overheard while there. His visit to Moody was crystallized forever in his mind by a pointed statement made by a young man one day who happened to be sitting two tables over from Hills. The statement was made loudly enough for Hills to recognize that it was intended to be overheard; "The doctrine of the eradication of the carnal nature by the Holy Spirit is one of the most damnable heresies that ever cursed the Christian Church!"[7]

In Hills' assessment of the moment, the young man appeared only to be parroting someone else. Hills assumed that it was one or more of the professors at Moody and further began to assume that the school adhered to the Keswickian interpretation of holiness. When not a single representative from Moody came to a ten-day holiness convention in the Chicago area in 1901, Hills' suspicions were confirmed.

Hills, of course, addressed this perceived false teaching at his usual speed. Immediately upon his return to Texas, he sat down and wrote an entire book. In it, he unashamedly asserts that those who do not teach that Spirit baptism is primarily for cleansing are simply rejecting the whole idea; they are rejecting Pentecost. As straightforward as ever, Hills entitled the book *Pentecost Rejected*.

As we saw in chapter 5, the book articulates the fairly common late nineteenth-century Holiness Movement's conflation of the Methodist doctrine of sanctification with the pentecostal language of Acts. An obvious projection of the Holiness Movement's experience and doctrinal system onto a primitive church historiography, Hills is clear that as long as first-century Christians sought Spirit baptism for inward cleansing, their exponential expansion remained unchecked. Conversely, Hills asserts, when they stopped seeking this blessing of holiness, their power was cut and their expansion slowed to a crawl. Hills' rationale is simple for why God withdrew his spiritual power from those early Christians. He sums it up in a single phrase in *The Secret of Spiritual Power*; "It is not safe to entrust carnal men with power."[8]

---

ing of those who maintain a more Methodist or holiness interpretation of Spirit baptism. Cf. Hills, *Pentecost Rejected*, 30–31.

7. Hills, *Pentecost Rejected*, 64.

8. Hills, *Secret of Spiritual Power*, 52.

With such a logic in place, Hills simply could not understand other pneumatologies that did not relate the Spirit's gifts of holiness and power as his did, especially in revivalist systems so close to his as Torrey's. Perceiving a very serious oversight on the part of Torrey, Hills felt that explicit correction was in order.

It should be noted, however, that Hills *did* handle Torrey with much more grace than other theologians with whom he disagreed. The reason for this is not only because they were friends, but also because Torrey was a revivalist, and Spirit baptism was the only revivalist doctrine or method over which the two had explicit disagreement. Seemingly contradictory, right alongside the gale force blast that Torrey and other Keswick leaders receive from Hills, we also hear his affirmation of the same in *Pentecost Rejected*.

> We feel sorry to be obliged to criticise [sic] the teaching of these brethren. Brother Torrey and I were fellow-students at Yale. I preached his ordination sermon. Our first pastorates were within twelve miles of each other. In more ways than one he has brought me into a debt of gratitude to him. His writings and Brother Meyer's were specially helpful to me when I was seeking the baptism with the Holy Spirit. I love them both for the good they are doing to others and for the guidance and help they brought to me in one of the critical seasons of my life. I profoundly believe they are better than their theory about the work of the Spirit. But I am sure that they are wrong when they deny His power to cleanse the heart, and that the result of their teaching in this respect is deplorable.[9]

On the surface, *Pentecost Rejected* is a contradictory juxtaposition of strongly contentious rhetoric and partial affirmations. Hills admits that at an earlier stage, when he was first seeking after Spirit baptism, he found the Keswick writings, along with the Methodist, useful. His rapidly maturing thought on the subject, however, brought him to a new line of reasoning that was, doctrinally speaking, mutually exclusive to the Keswick position on Spirit baptism. For Hills, cleansing from inward sin is the first and only criterion for God's blessing of power.

Keswick's more Calvinistic orientation and view of sin, however, would not allow them to embrace fully the Holiness Movement's radicalized version of cleansing, at least not without modification. The mod-

---

9. Hills, *Pentecost Rejected*, 63.

ification that was required was a view of sin where its presence could be assented in light of Calvinist orthodoxy, while its effects practically overcome. In the turn-of-the-century Keswick view, the Christian could either speak of the suppression of sin or the empowerment of the individual over sin, but would not take it as far as to affirm the complete removal or eradication of sin. While on their part it was an extraordinary concession for Calvinist thought and clear evidence of the extent to which Methodism's message permeated American and British theology, Hills felt that the Scriptures, Christian pneumatology, and his and many others' experience taught more than Keswick would allow. Convinced that his presentation of the gospel of full salvation could bring about the sanctification of the whole church, Hills warred with the advocates of Keswick the rest of his life.

Thus ends Hills' *explicit* statements in refutation of Torrey. On no other subject or doctrine does Hills openly disagree with his friend. This is not to say, however, that there are not other unspoken differences. This leads us directly into the discussions of Hills' relationship to Torrey and the movement with which the latter is most recognized, fundamentalism.

Unspoken Dissimilarities between Hills and Torrey

A brief look into the unspoken dissimilarities between Hills and Torrey is illuminating. Perhaps the most profound and far reaching of their differences is their respective eschatologies and eschatological attitudes.[10] Two perspectives could not be any farther apart than postmillennialism and premillennialist dispensationalism. Hills' postmillennialism, an optimism of grace on the cosmological scale, saw the millennium as the responsibility of the church. Against dispensationalism, he writes: "Postmillennialists hold that the Old Testament nowhere supports the idea of two gospel dispensations. It very minutely describes *one* dispensation worked by the power of truth and the presence of the Holy Spirit,—the Gospel preached by Jesus and His apostles. The prophets describe it in scores of glowing passages, as blessedly successful; but they are silent as

---

10. Again, as in chapters 3 and 4, a differentiation is made here between an eschatology and an eschatological attitude. The former simply means the explicit doctrinal convictions of a person, while the latter represents something less explicit or concrete, an overarching disposition that usually transcends mere doctrinal formulation in vitality and importance.

the grave about a second one, entirely different, with risen saints and preachers to convert the world."[11]

Hills continues with an optimistic, revivalist attitude, "[Jesus] never spoke one syllable about the insufficiency of the Holy Spirit and the gospel, and the present means of grace to win the world and establish His kingdom. He never intimated that . . . all these Christian instrumentalities were never intended to succeed! God inaugurated these means and they will succeed!"[12]

This optimistic view of history, the church, the gospel, and the kingdom could not be any farther from the dispensationalist's negative attitude toward the same. *The Fundamentals*, of which Torrey was the general editor, reveals his systematic theology. He endorses A. T. Pierson's chapter "The Testimony of the Organic Unity of the Bible to its Inspiration" when Pierson writes: "The Unity [of the Bible] is Dispensational. There are certain uniform dispensational features which distinguish every new period. Each dispensation is marked by seven features, in the following order: Increased light; Decline of spiritual life; Union between disciples and the world; A gigantic civilization worldly in type; Parallel development of good and evil; Apostasy on the part of God's people; [and] Concluding judgment. We are now in the seventh dispensation, and the same seven marks have been upon all alike, showing one controlling power—Deus in Historia."[13]

The essentially different positive and negative views toward history and the church are but the tip of the iceberg, however. Their respective eschatological attitudes shaped their view of everything else, from social reform to larger doctrinal commitments. Of course, it is very easy to overlook and, therefore, understate the importance of eschatology in defining religious thought at the turn of the twentieth century. Too often today, eschatology is accounted among the vestigial appendages, an accident of other theological or social hermeneutics. Far from being a secondary doctrine for revivalists of that day, the post and premillennial worldviews were, simply that, *worldviews*—differing holistic superstructures, issuing forth in large-scale divergent associate doctrinal and ethical commitments. Hills and Torrey illustrate just how important overarching eschatologies were at the beginning of

11. Hills, *Fundamental Christian Theology*, vol. 2, 354.
12. Ibid., 355.
13. Torrey, *The Fundamentals*.

the twentieth century. The doctrinal and ethical ideas rolling around inside the premillennialist tumbleweed greatly differed from those themes and agendas swarming a postmillennial eschatology. Having vastly different centers of gravity, the two pulled into their orbits vastly different doctrines and ethics.

Donald W. Dayton's contrastive analysis of the eschatologies of Charles Finney and Dwight Moody in "Millennial Views and Social Reform in Nineteenth-century America" illustrates well the underlying differences and how these organically relate to social activism, (or inactivism, as the case may be).

At the outset, Dayton points out, "On the surface, the difference between these options is merely one of timing, of the ordering of eschatological events."[14] He immediately continues, however, that beyond the mere chronological level there is a great difference between the two. "In nineteenth-century America the choice of one or another of the millennial options usually revealed a fundamental mindset—a view of the world and faith—as distinct as one of the paradigms of H. Richard Niebuhr."[15]

Of postmillennialism, Dayton writes, "Usually implicit in such an understanding was the expectation that this millennium would be ushered in through existing Christian agencies in continuity with human effort."[16] This combination of millennial outlook and social activism is vastly different from the premillennialist attitude that emerged in the decades after the Civil War. "The new chronology [of premillennialism] implied a discontinuity between present human effort and agencies of the gospel and the coming age—and involved to some extent a shift from prophetic to apocalyptic categories and Scriptural sources."[17]

14. Dayton, "Millennial Views and Social Reform," 132.
15. Ibid., 132.
16. Ibid.
17. Ibid., 133. Dayton quotes Paul Hanson that prophetic eschatology is "a religious perspective which focuses on the prophetic announcement to the nation of the divine plans for Israel and the world which the prophet has witnessed unfolding in the divine council and which he translates into terms of plain history, real politics and human instrumentality; that is, the prophet interprets for the king and the people how the plans of the divine council will be effected within the context of their nation's history and the history of the world. On the other hand, 'apocalyptic eschatology' focuses on the disclosure (usually esoteric in nature) to the elect of the cosmic vision of Yahweh's sovereignty—especially as it relates to his acting to deliver his faithful—which disclosure the visionaries have largely ceased to translate into the terms of plain history, real

Dayton continues by pointing out the irony that, while a vastly different paradigm, premillennialism often emerged in the very centers that had previously been most committed to postmillennialism.

To help explain this transition, Dayton appropriates Paul Hanson's *The Dawn of Apocalyptic*, a monograph on the Jewish prophetic and apocalyptic perspectives. Of course, Hanson's differentiation between these two types of Hebrew literature offers more than just help in the interpretation of the Old Testament; but also pinpoints the issues at stake in *transitions* from a prophetic to an apocalyptic identity.

Dayton summarizes Hanson's claim that a shift took place in Israelite literature from prophetic to apocalyptic types as the realization of the earlier prophetic vision became more problematic in the post-exilic context. As the gap between vision and reality became increasingly greater because of historical circumstances, the message that once belonged to the realm of prophecy began to develop apocalyptic categories. The balance between prophetic vision and political implementation, which seemed more realistic prior to the period of Second Isaiah, disintegrated. Dayton writes, "For Hanson, then, apocalyptic is an effort to maintain the vision in the face of new historical context requiring a more pessimistic analysis of the potential of human instrumentality and a consequent shift of weight to the supra-historical divine sovereignty."[18]

Dayton contends that a parallel phenomenon happened within revivalism prior to the turn of the twentieth century. He writes, "The shift from postmillennial to premillennial eschatology in nineteenth-century America is greatly illumined by this [Hanson's] analysis—indeed it was in many ways a shift from ethical prophetism to ahistorical apocalypticism. Certainly it involved a shift of focus from the prophetic to apocalyptic texts of Scripture."[19] Overly optimistic and perhaps even naive postmillennialist revivalists, facing the impossibility of their vision of a millennium brought into being *via* a divine-human synergy, traded their prophetic eschatology for an apocalyptic one, thus conserving their hope for a soon-coming millennium by simply shifting to a *divinely*-catalyzed inauguration.[20]

---

politics, and human instrumentality due to a pessimistic view of reality growing out of the bleak post-exilic conditions." Ibid., 140.

18. Ibid., 141.

19. Ibid.

20. Dayton writes, "The tension between vision and reality began to disintegrate in

The central point of Dayton's analysis is not, of course, to explain the change from one eschatology to another, but to show how these differences illuminate much of the evangelical *social* attitude after the turn of the century. In the premillennialist mindset, the world was no longer perceived as getting better, but worse. "The approaching end is now signalled [sic] not by upward progress and intimations of the millennium, but by downward decline and the prevalence of evil and sin."[21] Decline, evil, and sin being the new marks of the end, the only hope for millennial peace rested solely upon God's breaking into the downwardly-spiraling history to pull it up into millennial rest by sheer supernatural force. *Only* God's intrusion into history, without the help of a decadent world and church, could inaugurate the thousand years of peace. In this new economy, divine agency was raised so significantly above human instrumentality that it makes the latter virtually, if not completely, nothing.

Such a change in attitude had significant effects upon the earlier revivalist dream of social reform. Dayton states:

> Early revivalists had anticipated the progressive conversion of the world as a way of transformation of all culture as a step on the way to the millennium. As the achievement of this goal appeared more and more unlikely, the revivalists maintained the goal of "world wide evangelism" . . . but scaled down their estimates of the effectiveness of their work. Evangelism became less and less a tool of transforming the culture and more and more a process of calling out a select few . . . The focus was less and less the transformation of culture and more and more the "rescue" of individuals from personal vice. Indeed, the archetypal social ministry of the revivalists was the "rescue mission" in which the goal was to "rescue" or "call out" individuals from the sin and degradation of the culture.[22]

---

the face of internal tensions created by heightened unrealistic expectation and external attack as history took new turns that consistently and cumulatively accentuated the gap between the millennial hope and actual historical experience. The only way to maintain the millennial hope and its imminence was to put the pieces of the eschatological vision into a new configuration. The millennial hope was preserved by moving the return of Christ to before the millennium to become the event that could bridge the growing gap between hope and historical reality." Ibid., 141.

21. Ibid., 143.

22. Ibid., 144. In the next paragraph Dayton continues that this logic was even taken to a more radical social extreme. "Some premillennialists would work out the logic in frightening ways. The tendency of our age is declension, they would argue, and the only hope is to be found in the return of Christ. Things must get worse before they get better;

Dayton's comparison and analysis of Finney and Moody is particularly useful in the interpretation of their respective protégées, Hills and Torrey. Their largely unspoken eschatological differences are as significant as their mentors'. Again, as we have seen in this and other chapters, eschatology in this period is more naturally defined as an overarching vision than as a systematic doctrine. As Dayton points out, differences in eschatological attitude were matched with respective social attitudes. This in turn led Hills and Torrey to the second major difference between them: the founding of, presiding over, and teaching at vastly different types of schools.

In an address for a conference on Methodism and the Fragmentation of American Protestantism, "Dispensationalism and the Emergence of Fundamentalism among American Baptists," Donald W. Dayton outlines the general differences between post and premillennialism. He notes that the difference between the two "is hard to overemphasize . . . The most striking illustration of the profound differences . . . is the fact that postmillennialists in the holiness tradition founded liberal arts colleges (Wheaton, Houghton, Seattle Pacific, etc.) while premillennialists tended to found Bible Colleges (Gordon, Nyack, Moody)."[23] Reflecting upon curriculum differences, he notes, "The Bible school has no place for the study of history, literature, philosophy, science, etc. because these have no real role other than distractions in the the [sic] premillennialist agenda. The urgency of the imminence of the return of Christ requires the minimum of biblical training and the equipping of the student in practical ministries."[24] The postmillennialist university, on the other hand, typically had a very different philosophy of and rationale for more broadly conceived liberal arts education.

This is well illustrated by the schools with which Hills and Torrey were affiliated. While both were college presidents and administrators, Hills founded, presided over, and taught at four-year, liberal arts universities, while Torrey presided over and helped establish two-year Bible colleges.[25] As above, while on the surface the differences seem superfi-

---

thus, any effort at social amelioration is counterproductive. It only delays the return of Christ." Ibid., 144.

23. Dayton, "Dispensationalism and Fundamentalism among Baptists," 11.

24. Ibid., 12.

25. Hills founded and taught at Texas Holiness University, Central Holiness University, Illinois Holiness University and taught at Oklahoma Holiness University

cial, the logic governing curriculum development for the two was widely different. Again, eschatological attitudes can be used as a window into the differences.

A good example of this is seen in the university catalogs that Hills wrote or helped guide. His first catalog, for Texas Holiness University, explicitly states the aim of the school.

> We propose to offer such instruction as may be obtained in any first class modern college, with added training in Theology and Homiletics, giving daily instruction in the Bible and in the work of soul-saving. We shall give special attention to the great doctrine of sanctification, with President Hills' "Holiness and Power" as a text book. We regard the Spiritual Nature of man, as his crowning gift from God, of truly Supreme importance, and we aim to have a great religious school, where a first class secular education can be obtained without sacrificing faith in God and purity of heart.[26]

In 1900, the above statement of purpose was drafted and published, and a curriculum was drawn up to match. Students entering that year would be expected to study not only British, American, Latin, Greek, French, and German literature, but also the lives and periods of many of the great writers. Those working toward the A.B. degree were required to study trigonometry and surveying along with other electives. In the science department, physiology, geography, physics, geology, botany, zoology, chemistry, "and other sciences" were required.[27] Hills also insisted upon a school of music, where numerous single instruments were taught, along with solo and chorus singing, harmony, composition, and music history.[28]

Everywhere he was asked to found a university, chair a department, or fill a faculty position, Hills took this unwavering commitment to liberal arts education. He envisioned an educational atmosphere where Christian young persons could learn a secular trade alongside future

---

and Nazarene University, Pasadena, Calif. Torrey helped rename and presided over Moody Bible Institute and, as a dean, helped establish Biola Bible College.

26. *Texas Holiness University, 1900-1901*, 20.

27. Ibid., 13–14. The preparatory course also included U. S. and general histories, civil government, and algebra. The college course also required of Rhetoric, Evidences of Christianity, Political Economy, Psychology, and Moral Philosophy. Ibid., 16–17.

28. Ibid., 17.

ministers and missionaries also taking Bible, preaching, and moral philosophy classes.

When founding Illinois Holiness University, with a little bit larger budget and faculty than he had in Texas, Hills extended the liberal arts curriculum to include classes on the history of philosophy, ethics, and sociology, with a larger number of elective slots for the college department students to branch out.[29] I.H.U. also offered classes in bookkeeping, shorthand and typewriting, and telegraphy.[30]

Nowhere is Hills' philosophy of higher education more clearly stated than in his 1906 book, *Christian Education and Anglo Israel*.[31] At first glance a rather odd combination of themes, the book is two addresses published together, one on Hills' philosophy of education, the other on his research into the theory that the Anglo-Saxons are the lost ten tribes of Israel.

Hills' address on Christian education was delivered June 5, 1906, between his presidencies at Texas Holiness University and Central Holiness University. In the address, he outlines an educational philosophy intended to guide students into "manhood," a tri-level paradigm including the physical, intellectual and social, and spiritual.

The apostle Paul becomes Hills' key model for education leading to manhood. "He [Paul] tells us that much as he had enjoyed *literature*, and appreciated *philosophy* and admired *law*, and mastered whatever *science* there was in his day, they were all dwarfed into insignificance when compared with the knowledge of Spiritual things . . . Everything else was *nothing* compared with knowing *Christ*."[32]

---

29. *Illinois Holiness University 1909–1910*, 23. Electives could be chosen from quite an extended list including classes with the titles of Hebrew, Spanish, International Law, Church History, Theology, Histology, Oratory, Pedagogy, and History of Civilization. Ibid., 25. Interestingly, Moral Philosophy is not listed anywhere in the catalog, apparently replaced by Systematic Theology.

30. Ibid., 28.

31. Hills, *Christian Education and Anglo Israel*.

32. Hills, *Christian Education and Anglo Israel*, 8. Hills continues, "What is this *manhood*? 1. It is manifestly more than a magnificent physique. . . . 2. Manhood is more also than a *trained intellect*. And God forbid that I should speak a word to disparage that. A trained mind in a trained body is one of the noblest of acquisitions . . . 3. I observe manhood involves the *highest man* and the *whole man*. It therefore includes the *moral* and *spiritual* nature . . . We are three-story beings. The physical nature is the foundation that links us with the earth and the material realm. The *soul* . . . is the intermediate story. It includes the intellect and sensibilities . . . It knows of nature and

One can certainly perceive in Hills' choice of language and curriculum that he had in mind to found schools very much after the model of Oberlin. Indeed, his ideals, values, and leadership style as president of four universities were marked by the same characteristics as what George P. Schmidt calls the "old-time college president,"[33] a significantly older paradigm for university presidency that seems to have been mediated to Hills through Oberlin and to some extent Yale.

Schmidt's portrait of the old-time president is in fact another way of describing the leadership vision of Academic Orthodoxy. James E. Hamilton writes, "The term *academic orthodoxy* is usually applied to the philosophical academicians in most of the older colleges . . . and to

---

of science and art within that; but it knows of nothing beyond. But we have a third person in our trinity of being called in Scripture language the *Spirit*. We here touch that part of our nature that has to do with duty and eternity and God. This faculty is as much above the soul as that is above the body. It brings us into immediate knowledge of moral law, of a personal God, of our filial relation to him as made in his image, and of our responsibility to him. By this faculty we ascend into the realm of prayer, of communion with God, and we make him our portion. This is the top story of man that has a sky-window which opens to the stars and the throne of the eternal God. . . . If the hand should be trained to deftness and cunning, why not train the conscience? If the eye should be trained to accuracy of vision, why not train the eye of the Spirit to see God. Hills, *Christian Education and Anglo Israel*, 9, 11, 15, 16, and 17. Cf. *Herald of Holiness* 8 (October 22, 1919), 3–4.

33. "The most important individual in the early college was the president. He was the leader of a comparatively uncomplicated institution . . . a familiar figure to students and faculty alike . . . He was a teacher, usually taking the philosophical and theological subjects as his field; and in connection with his classroom duties he was the counselor and spiritual guide of all students, collectively and individually . . . The old-time president combined, on a smaller scale to be sure, the present-day offices of the president, the dean of students, the bursar, the chaplain, the department of philosophy, and the office of public relations. And that was not all . . . Fringe activities were expected of him, not covered by the laws . . . President James Manning of Brown . . . was full time pastor of a local church (not an uncommon practice), listened to the complaints of the undergraduates and of their fathers and mothers, cultivated a garden, did the family marketing, and attended the funeral of every baby that died in Providence. Clearly this was not a profession for which one could be trained as one could for law or engineering. It was an art, and was learned by doing . . . The successful president was the man who managed, largely by personal contact, to reconcile the conflicting interests of the various participating groups into that harmonious cooperation without which no college could exist. He created and maintained friendly relations, on different levels, with the students, their parents, the faculty, the trustees, the general public, and the angels who could be tapped for donations." Schmidt, *The Liberal Arts College*, 103, 104, and 105. Interestingly, Schmidt accounts Mark Hopkins of Williams as the last of the "old-time presidents." "Hopkins resigned the presidency in 1872, and when he died in 1887, full of years and honors, the old-time college was a thing of the past." Ibid., 123.

the teachers in the burgeoning new colleges." Quoting E. H. Madden, Hamilton immediately continues, "'The members of the "orthodoxy" generally exhibited the syndrome of minister-philosopher-college president' . . . The academic orthodoxy not only emphasized a non-Calvinistic, freewill, evangelical brand of Christianity; it defended its views within the context of the Scottish realistic philosophy of Thomas Reid and his followers.'"[34]

Sighting other characteristics of Academic Orthodoxy, Hamilton continues by quoting D. H. Meyer, "The American system of higher education in the nineteenth century has been aptly described as 'Protestant Scholasticism' because of its ambitious effort 'to organize all knowledge, including knowledge of the cosmos, of men, and of society, into a consistent and intelligible whole,' establishing a correspondence between secular knowledge and basic Christian principles."[35]

Hills' leadership style, curriculum development, and even the classes he taught all point to the age of his university paradigm. He endeavored to be an old-time college president, with an identity marked by the all-encompassing vision inherent in the postmillennialist worldview and academic orthodoxy. The goal of both was to spread Christianity throughout the world at every level. Hills' vision could easily be characterized as something of an early Oberlinite transplant to the twentieth century.

In general, the dispensationalists' Bible college did not see at all the importance of a liberal arts education as a means to holistic knowledge and gradual societal transformation. They envisioned schools where students could come to study Bible, doctrine, and evangelistic method in a two-year program designed to get practitioners "out there" as quickly as possible. Four-year programs in useful secular trades for society's betterment were simply not valued. Thus, broader programs in various laic trades from a Christian perspective were typically not introduced until later in the twentieth century when the winds of change within fundamentalist schools began to suppress and transform earlier paradigms. Biola, the development of which Torrey helped significantly, is an excellent example of this phenomenon.[36]

---

34. Hamilton, "Academic Orthodoxy," 52.

35. Ibid., 53.

36. While Biola is now a fully accredited university, their website reveals just how recently their status changed. The following schools were listed with the founding dates.

Of course, nineteenth-century millennial views can provide a window into more than just social consciousness in evangelical revivalism and corresponding curricula at universities and Bible colleges. The millennial window also helps explain the reasons behind the matrix of doctrines that were gathered into Hills and Torrey's system. Several doctrines were attracted to and easily wedded with the dispensationalist attitude, themes that fit the basic apocalyptic, supernaturalistic paradigm where the divine-human synergy is reduced to the overpowering activity of God and the passivity of humanity. Perhaps the clearest example is the doctrine of inspiration.

Inspiration and Other Associate Doctrinal Differences

Hills and Torrey's doctrines of biblical inspiration varied greatly. Hills maintained a dynamic theory of inspiration while evangelist L. W. Munhall, in *The Fundamentals*, accuses this theory of being "exceedingly vague and misty . . . The popular and current [dynamic] theory now is that the 'Concept' is inspired. But no one attempts to tell what the 'Concept' is; indeed, I doubt if any one knows."[37] Of course, from the perspective of those who advocated *The Fundamentals*, the vagueness of the dynamic theory of inspiration is that it does not give enough weight to the *details* of the Bible.

It is, of course, of little wonder that dispensationalists were so disposed to doctrines of inerrancy. One way of understanding this development is simply as the extension of their view of an in-sweeping and overpowering Divine applied to a doctrine of the Scriptures. If the simplicity of Earnest Sandeen's twofold (or perhaps even singlefold) definition of fundamentalism is at least partially correct about the roots of the movement, it is not surprising at all that dispensationalists teamed up with inerrancy doctrines of inspiration. The two ideas were perfect bedfellows, embracing the same underlying attitude or worldview where divine influence has inordinate sway, and human participation is at best low.

As a postmillennialist, with a concomitant high view of human participation in the divine-human synergy, Hills rejected mechanical dictation theories of the inspiration. Indeed, taking it a step farther in the

---

Rosemead School of Psychology- 1981, School of Arts and Sciences- 1981, School of Business- 1993, and School of Professional Studies- 1994. http://biola.edu/about.

37. Torrey, *The Fundamentals*.

insistence upon a high view of human participation, Hills also rejected the idea that the biblical texts, received or original, are without mistake.[38]

Another place where Hills and Torrey disagreed is in the doctrine of atonement. Hills' moral government theory differs greatly from Torrey's substitutionary theory. Hills devotes an entire chapter in *Fundamental Christian Theology* to the "Satisfaction" or "Penal Theory," concluding with his objections to it. His final two objections are his strongest. "The satisfaction theory leads direct to that fatal antinomian heresy of a 'finished work' and 'a finished salvation' . . . This theory stands in the way of the highest Christian attainments . . . [leaving adherents] perfectly satisfied with their *fictitious, imaginary, theological* 'STANDING.' Few educated Calvinists seek or enter into the experience of sanctification. Their theology is against it. Now can a theory that naturally produces such fruit be true? We cannot believe it."[39]

Applying an interesting logic, Hills does not reject it because it is less or non-biblical. He rejects it because, at the heart of his soteriology, is a concern that the Christian individual accept personal responsibility not only for salvation, but also for good works and sanctification. His greatest concern with the satisfaction or penal theory, as he calls it, is that it leads to fatal antinomianism, an overly passive view of human responsibility in the divine-human equation.

The discussion could be compounded here with other examples of doctrinal differences that reveal different eschatological attitudes, but these suffice to illustrate an emerging pattern. An eschatologically-centered reading of Hills and Torrey reveals a pattern that differentiates them significantly in underlying attitude, logic, and doctrine. Thus, revivalism's story of the dissolution of the divine-human synergy in the "Great Reversal" is of great significance in understanding not only Hills and Torrey, but also their respective movements. Revivalism's new eschatology, in which the divine agent completely overpowers history and human agency, attracted a series of lesser doctrines with the same low or missing human involvement. A new eschatology weak on the role of human agency in history became the hermeneutical key for a larger system of thought that was developed fully by leaders like R. A. Torrey in the first decades of the twentieth century. Postmillennialists like Hills,

---

38. Hills offers several examples of discrepancies and clear human mistakes in the Bible. Hills, *Fundamental Christian Theology*, vol. 1, 131–35.

39. Hills, *Fundamental Christian Theology*, vol. 2, 86–87.

however, neither shared the attitude nor the associate doctrines orbiting this emerging eschatology. His postmillennial framework rescued him from societal pessimism and concomitant social disengagement, verbal dictation theories of the Bible, and larger antinomianism in all of his doctrines. It put him at odds with the movement with which Torrey is most identified, fundamentalism.

Hills and Fundamentalism

Until very recently, the secondary literature on A. M. Hills has caricatured him as a fundamentalist without recognizing the above doctrinal distinctions. Indeed, were one confined to the secondary literature on A. M. Hills, it might be easy to conclude with his major interpreters that he was a fundamentalist.[40] It is of little help to those who might offer a defense against this accusation that his systematic treatise is named Fundamental *Christian Theology* or that the rhetoric of a few of his later published articles often comes close to the same kind of language and arguments usually attributed to fundamentalism.[41] As with all theologians whose thought is solidified decades prior to the development of a movement, however, Hills is not so easily pigeonholed by the categories of that later movement.

Two factors complicate the question of whether or not Hills rightly belongs to the camp of the fundamentalists. The first and most obvious complication is the difficulty in agreement over definitions of fundamentalism. Several significant treatises have been written in recent decades offering divergent answers to the question of how best to define the movement. To date, no consensus has been reached. The second complicating factor is that, near the end of his life, Hills occasionally used language that is typically considered fundamentalist.

While the historiography of fundamentalism has a much longer history,[42] the first significant and lasting treatise attempting to define the movement was offered by Earnest Sandeen. In his University of

---

40. Bassett, "Fundamentalist Leavening"; Phipps, "Hills, Modernism, and Fundamentalism."

41. Cf. *Herald of Holiness* 1 (November 13, 1912), 6; *H.H.* 8 (August 20, 1919), 3–4; *H.H.* 10 (February 22, 1922), 4–5; *H.H.* 12 (October 17, 1923), 3–4; *H.H.* 15 (August 11, 1926), 5–7; *H.H.* 17 (November 28, 1928), 6–8; *H.H.* 23 (August 18, 1934), 8–9.

42. For an excellent, brief review of the major pre-Sandeen literature on fundamentalism, see Ingersol, "Strange Bedfellows," 124–27.

Chicago dissertation and later published book under the title *The Roots of Fundamentalism: British and American Millenarianism 1800–1930*, Sandeen argues that the movement is best understood within the context of the rise of millenarianism in the nineteenth century. Making a strong argument, Sandeen's strength is that he rightly estimates the power and priority of theology in the movement. Likewise, his central axis of interpretation, underlying dispensationalism, sheds much light on both the choice and shape of the penumbra of doctrines the fundamentalists maintained, and also provides a believable rationale behind their social disengagement.

Insisting that Sandeen's argument can offer a window of interpretation into not only fundamentalism, but also larger turn-of-the-century evangelicalism, Donald W. Dayton has developed a similar eschatologically-centered reading of early twentieth-century American Christianity. In the opening lines of the above-mentioned study on Finney and Moody, Dayton states, "We find it difficult today to grasp the extent to which millennial visions dominated nineteenth-century America. Our lives, at least for most of us, are no longer controlled by the religious currents that once cultivated bewildering variations on the millennial theme. But nineteenth-century America was different."[43]

Dayton echoes a similar sentiment in "Dispensationalism and the Emergence of Fundamentalism among American Baptists." In reference to the impact and importance of the "Great Reversal," he writes, "The significance of this change has been underplayed in both holiness and broader evangelical historiography. The contrast between postmillennial and premillennial perspectives is hard to overemphasize—and permeates the whole theology of the advocate of either position; the difference is not to be categorized as a minor difference in the eschatological timetable."[44]

In Dayton's estimate, not only the differences between these two eschatologies, but the rapid transition in revivalism from one to the other in the late nineteenth century, is the key to unlocking much of the fundamentalist and evangelical mind.

At variance with Sandeen and Dayton is George Marsden, whose 1980 *Fundamentalism and American Culture* emphasizes a spectrum of theological, historical, intellectual, social, and political issues that he

---

43. Dayton, "Millennial Views and Social Reform," 131.
44. Dayton, "Dispensationalism Among Baptists," 11.

argues constituted the fundamentalist movement of the early twentieth century. Several characteristics mark Marsden's definition: theologically, a heightened supernaturalism; socially, an anti-developmental view of history; and intellectually and philosophically, an obsolete Baconian and Common Sense worldview.

Such a perspective certainly has its merits and is useful in explaining some aspects of fundamentalism. Marsden, however, because of the breadth of his classifications, is capable of pulling into his definition movements, denominations, and figures who resist the designation of fundamentalist, causing one to wonder if he has painted with too broad a brush, sweeping in all who are conservative, or at least, *not* liberal. Such a perspective makes the central characteristic of the fundamentalist mindset a social and ideological or theological *conservatism*—a reaction to changing social, philosophical, and scientific paradigms. Where Marsden's perspective is particularly problematic is in the difficulty of pinning "conservative" on every aspect of the movement. It is at least a very problematic adjective to attach to ideas so new to Christian history as premillennialist dispensationalism, the rapture, and inerrant autographs of the Scriptures, to cite only three obvious examples.

The problem with Marsden's underlying assumption is greater than overly broad or slippery adjectives, however, and this becomes clear when he draws upon figures like A. M. Hills to illustrate the holiness roots of fundamentalism. Hills' theology could be construed as frozen in nineteenth-century Baconian science and Common Sense philosophy, systems whose ghosts still linger about the holiness mind. Thus, to this point, it could be said that Hills fits one third of Marsden's definition of a fundamentalist. Where Hills really challenges Marsden, however, is not only in his systematic eschatology, but in his governing postmillennialist attitude that put him in absolute contradiction with fundamentalism's heightened supernaturalism and anti-developmental view of history.

A third definition of fundamentalism is in order at this point, although it must be granted that no major monograph in the broader historiography of the movement recognizes it. This definition is the one located in the secondary literature on A. M. Hills himself. Three published works on the role and usage of the *Scriptures* in the Church of the Nazarene briefly consider Hills among other theologians and offer what could be called the "Nazarene" definition of fundamentalism.

In his article "The Fundamentalist Leavening of the Holiness Movement: The Church of the Nazarene a Case Study 1914–1940," Paul M. Bassett locates the locus of fundamentalist identity solely in a particular usage of Scripture. Believing that Hills maintained a fundamentalist view of Scripture, Bassett names Hills as one of many contributing persons in the "fundamentalizing" of the Church of the Nazarene. In this article, Bassett offers a bit of speculative hearsay that Hills was overlooked for the Nazarene's choice to write their first official denominational systematic theology because he was considered too liberal with respect to the authority and inspiration of Scripture.[45] Bassett comments, "This is indeed quite surprising if it be true, for Hills was clearly a Fundamentalist."[46]

Bassett's implied definition for the movement in this article can be gathered from his words on Hills and the others who "fundamentalized" the Nazarenes. A fundamentalist is one who maintains a mechanical theory of inspiration or whose biblical method lacks the "classical" or "orthodox" hermeneutical key of *testimonium Spiritus sancti*.[47] Thus, for Bassett, what it means to be a fundamentalist revolves simply around the application of a modernist definition of a fact or truth to the Scriptures without regard for the "orthodox" notions of the witness or testimony of the Spirit. Offering a useful approach in one regard, Bassett defines *both* fundamentalism as well as liberalism as modernist, thus regarding both as divergences from "classical" Christianity.

To a much lesser extent, a similar Scripture-centered definition is implied by Michael Lodahl in his short book on the development of the Nazarene article of faith on the Scriptures, *All Things Necessary to Our Salvation*. While he comes to the exact opposite conclusion on Hills— that he was *not* a fundamentalist—Lodahl nevertheless reveals the same Nazarene definition for the movement as a particular biblicism. "Simply stated, the fundamentalist approach was (and is) to read the Bible as a

---

45. Bassett exact comments are, "Conversations with some persons contemporary with the events suggested that Hills was considered too liberal with respect to the authority and inspiration of Scripture." Bassett, "Fundamentalist Leavening," 80. Bassett goes on to state that the person who said this was Mildred Bangs Wynkoop.

46. Ibid.

47. In fairness to Bassett's inadequate definition for fundamentalism, his article was published in 1978, before most of the above monographs were published.

package of objective propositions that simply state the truth about everything they touch on."⁴⁸

Stanley Ingersol's "Strange Bedfellows: The Nazarenes and Fundamentalism" is the only work that explicitly transcends the Nazarene trend of delimiting fundamentalism to a particular biblicism. In this article, Ingersol offers a nearly exhaustive recapitulation of the major and minor monographs defining fundamentalism. To a large extent, his application of the analysis for the Church of the Nazarene defaults to issues of the biblicism of fundamentalism and the Nazarene debates on inerrancy. To his credit, however, Ingersol briefly extends his application to address eschatology as well, stating, "The spread of dispensational premillennialism was a leading factor in the fundamentalist crusade."⁴⁹ Along with A. M. Hills' non-fundamentalist postmillennialism, Ingersol notes Wiley's difficult-to-assess ambivalence toward eschatology and Olive Winchester's amillennialist rejection of premillennialism.⁵⁰ In

---

48. Michael Lodahl, *All Things Necessary*, 30. In fairness to Lodahl, the book is *not* on the subject of fundamentalism, but on the development of the Nazarene's article of faith on the Scriptures. Because it is not Lodahl's intention to define fundamentalism in any extensive way, one cannot assume that his definition is limited to *only* an understanding of Scripture. Indeed, Lodahl notes a greater underlying principle that both Hills and H. Orton Wiley both use in opposition to the "Mechanical Theory" of inspiration. Lodahl writes that Wiley disagrees with it on the grounds that "clearly 'the human element' is null and void." Locating fundamentalism's locus in "conservative Presbyterian, i.e., Calvinist circles . . . the *overriding emphasis* falls upon the idea of God's sovereignty . . . Wiley, a wily Wesleyan-Arminian thinker, wisely detected the problem: 'perhaps the strongest argument against this [mechanical] theory is the fact that it is out of harmony with the known manner in which God works in the human soul' (Wiley 175)." Ibid., 22, italics mine. Of Hills and Wiley's agreement on this subject, Lodahl writes, "There is no doubt that he [Wiley] was in sympathy with Hills' main point: there is an undeniably *human* element that runs throughout the Scriptures, even if one affirms the *divine* inspiration of those humans involved." Ibid., 21. In such recognitions, Lodahl begins to transcend the Nazarene definition of fundamentalism and move toward recognition of "overriding emphases" or underlying philosophies or attitudes that issue forth in a particular doctrine of inspiration. And while risking reading too much into his statements, Lodahl certainly seems to suggest that the overriding emphases in the divine-human relationship at least inform, if not govern, both the fundamentalist and early Nazarene doctrines of inspiration, leading them in different directions and ultimately to different stances. The final word, however, must be that it is *not* Lodahl's intention to define fundamentalism in this book.

49. Ingersol, "Strange Bedfellows," 136. Although Ingersol does not state it explicitly, his usage of views on inerrancy and eschatology implies a leaning toward Earnest Sandeen's definition for fundamentalism.

50. Ibid., 136–37.

these figures, he sees an attempt, at the higher theological level, to steer the Nazarenes away from fundamentalism.

Again, the inherent problem with certain Nazarene definitions is that it overemphasizes fundamentalism's biblicism and overlooks broader scholarship's insistence that the movement must be defined as various combinations of doctrinal, philosophical, social, or political agendas. That is, no monograph on fundamentalism sees the movement so narrowly as *only* a form of biblicism. In broader scholarship, what it means to be a fundamentalist is always more than this.

Beyond the significantly different definitions for fundamentalism that presently exist, another complicating factor in defining Hills is that in a few places, very late in his life, he occasionally used language or concepts that are typically attributed to fundamentalists. Like most evangelicals at the turn of the century, fundamentalist and non-fundamentalist alike, Hills rejected higher criticism, evolution, and various institutions identified as "modern." Of the very small number of his *Herald of Holiness* articles that address these themes, however, most reveal a non-fundamentalist rationale for the use of fundamentalist-like language.

A clear example of this is in his *Herald of Holiness* article entitled "Higher Critics Unscientific Infidels." In the article, Hills attacks higher criticism as being "unscientific, unhistorical, and unscholarly."[51] He continues that archaeological discoveries are regularly thwarting the higher critics' claims and that exhumed documents of other nations are proving the truth of the Bible.

Even as fundamentalistic as this might sound, Hills never intimates that the purpose of the Bible is to provide historical or scientific data or mere fodder for doctrine.

> The New Testament gives us the artless record of the life and words of this Divine Person—the Son of God and the Savior of the world. The value and greatness of the Bible are in this life that it discloses to us. It is upon Jesus that the whole Bible turns. The Book that reveals to us Jesus and His salvation is not to be compared with any other book on earth for preciousness... The Old Testament shows us the way preparing... His coming. The New Testament lifts the veil and bids us "Behold the Lamb of God that taketh away the sin of the world." The worth of the Bible

---

51. Hills, *Herald of Holiness* 1 (November 13, 1912), 6.

is that it helps us to see Him and know Him and build our lives into Him—becoming the church of God, against which the gates of hell shall not prevail.[52]

Another such example is found in his 1923 *Herald of Holiness* article, "A Creedless Christianity Impossible." In logic and language very reminiscent of Hills' 1878 two-sermon series on "creeds,"[53] "Creeds—their Value," and "Creeds and Life," this 1923 article opens with an acerbic line in the sand. "The adherents of Christianity are rapidly dividing into two camps, the creed lovers and the creed haters. In other words there are those who unite in believing something positive, that can be stated in definite words; and also those who do not believe in anything definite, and object to their conglomeration of infidel negations being put in any form of statement."[54]

Hills goes on to give specific names to the latter of these two, although granting that their source is Satan. "With subtle skill he [Satan] sprung evolution and higher criticism of the Bible upon us, and called them 'modern science,' 'advanced scholarship,' 'higher learning.'"[55]

Again, however, as above, while his rhetoric and the denominating of enemies parallels that of the fundamentalists, what Hills defends in the rest of the article is difficult to characterize according to fundamentalist values.

As was and is a common practice in evangelical and even non-evangelical circles then and now, Hills projects his system of ideas onto the earlier creeds of the church, taking it for granted that his nineteenth-century revivalist canon is easily recognizable in "the great historic creeds of Christendom, from the Apostle's creed down to our time."[56] Specifically, he sees six great teachings. Concerning these "great fundamental truths," Hills writes, "On the whole, there has been a very marked and substantial agreement between most of these creeds or symbols. By

---

52. Ibid.

53. In this article, Hills asks, "What is a Creed? It is an open frank, honest, ingenuous statement of what any body of religious people believe in their hearts, profess with tongue and pen, and frankly teach to the world at the time the creed is made." A. M. Hills, "What is a Creed," *Herald of Holiness* 12 (October 17, 1923), 3. Again, as we saw in chapter 4, Hills' use of the word "creed" is best understood as a distillation of nineteenth-century revivalism's core doctrines and ethics.

54. Ibid., 3.

55. Ibid.

56. Ibid.

these doctrinal statements we may know what the Christian thought has been during the ages concerning the great truths of Christianity as understood from a reverent study of the Holy Word."[57]

Hills' six "great fundamental truths" include "faith in a personal God," "the doctrine of the fall of man," "the supernatural birth of Christ," and its sibling doctrine "the God-man Christ-Jesus," "faith in the miracles of Christ, his birth, resurrection, and ascension," and "the atonement, and the cleansing power of the blood of our divine Lord."[58] In this list, Hills reveals the stripe and age of his "fundamental truths." His doctrines arise from the theological canon of mid to late nineteenth-century revivalism.

Other illustrations could be given, but these examples suffice to illustrate that, while on the surface his choice of rhetoric occasionally overlapped with that of the fundamentalists, Hills' contextual qualifications suggest a non-fundamentalist rationale for such language. Thus, while he may have occasionally sounded like a fundamentalist near the end of his life, Hills' worldview and conceptualizations are better categorized as revivalistic. He belonged to a different, earlier paradigm and bore an identity forged and solidified in the mid-nineteenth century, with the addition of the late nineteenth-century Holiness Movement's doctrine of Spirit baptism.

Conclusion: Hills and Torrey's Overlapping Means

Doctrinally, we have seen that Hills is clearly not a fundamentalist. His "fundamental" Christian theology differs greatly from Torrey's fundamentalist Christian theology on the specifics considered vital by the latter. There is, however, a great deal more to Hills' identity than simply the doctrines of his system. For Hills, the revivalists' means were perhaps just as important, and herein lies some of his overlap with fundamentalism.

Donald W. Dayton makes an interesting statement in "Millennial Views and Social Reform" that "it is difficult to see how later revivalists could claim to stand in the succession of both Finney and Moody without sensing the chasm that separated them."[59] In making this statement, it is very likely that Dayton had in mind revivalists like A. M.

---

57. Ibid.
58. Ibid.
59. Dayton, "Millennial Views and Social Reform," 134.

Hills, who thought of himself as in succession to both of these. This is most clearly seen in the naming of his children. A revivalist to the core, Hills named three of his seven children after revivalist leaders. Of the three, two were sons and were named after the two revivalists of Dayton's article. The first, Charles Finney Hills, was born in 1891, while Dwight Moody Hills came into the world in 1897, only a short time before his namesake departed.[60]

Dayton's "difficulty" in understanding how later revivalists, like Hills, could claim to stand in succession to both of these figures perhaps underestimates the power and cohesion of the revivalist identity. Whatever their particular doctrinal peculiarities, all of the revivalists embraced similar revivalistic means, and this was their common denominator. The revivalistic way of religion can be easily seen in the holiness, Keswick, Pentecostal, and fundamentalist movements in the twentieth century. Finney was a revivalist. Moody was a revivalist. Hills, whose revivalist means and methods were at least as important as his doctrines, took this as common enough ground to esteem both Finney and Moody highly, even while mildly criticizing both on the particulars of Spirit baptism and other doctrines.[61]

Here we see Hills' demarcations for his above-mentioned "two camps" framed clearly. While he quibbles with Torrey over the particulars of their respective revivalistic doctrines, Hills still esteems him as in his "camp" because they are both revivalists. Indeed, as is demonstrated in multiple places in his books, Hills is ready to regard any revivalist as "in his camp" whose record indicates marked usefulness to God.[62]

---

60. *Alumnus Report*, 1904, 2.

61. For his criticism of Moody and Finney's doctrines of Spirit baptism see Hills, *Pentecost Rejected*, 65–66; Hills, *Life of Finney*, 218–40; and *Holiness and Power*, 46–54.

62. In *Pentecostal Light*, Hills states, "It was this [divine might] that has made dear black Amanda Smith a benediction to two continents, and started Jennie Smith out as a most successful railroad evangelist, and mad Annie Fothergill an evangelist in England. It was this that enabled Robinson Watson, a lay evangelist of England, to secure ten thousand trophies of grace in four years, and helped James Caughey to see twenty-one thousand six hundred sinners repenting, and ten thousand Christians at altars, claiming a sanctifying Saviour [sic] in six years. It was this that gave to Phoebe Palmer her twenty-five thousand souls, and to Maggie Van Cott her seventy-five thousand, and to A. B. Earle his one hundred and fifty-seven thousand, and made Andrew Murray, and F. B. Meyer, and Torrey, and Chapman, and Mills, and Moody so wondrously used of God. It is this that has made Smith, and Pickett, and Thompson, and Carradine, and Godbey . . . such heroes of faith and power, and enabled Bishop Taylor and General

A contrastive picture of Hills and Torrey offers an interesting window into the relationship between the holiness and fundamentalist movements, a relationship of doctrinal differences, but practical similarities. As we have seen, the doctrinal differences between Hills and Torrey are profound enough to put the two, their schools, and later their movements on significantly divergent trajectories. Indeed, as Dayton intimates in "Millennial Views and Social Reform," their underlying eschatological attitudes alone are as different from each other as are any two of H. Richard Niebuhr's fivefold categories. Their underlying revivalist way of religion, however, being so similar, made lay and ministerial crossover and inter-leavening very likely.

According to a doctrinal definition, Hills is not a fundamentalist. Indeed, according to this definition, Bassett's charge that Hills was one of several major fundamentalizing forces in the Church of the Nazarene is not only basically, but completely, wrong. Far from being a contributing fundamentalizer, Hills is arguably the most important early twentieth-century figure in steering Nazarene institutions on a path away from fundamentalism. Even though Hills' postmillennialism was never appreciated and even somewhat suppressed in the Holiness Movement, its more optimistic DNA was written into the identity of the lay, pastoral, and missionary leaders that earned four-year degrees at one of his universities. Indeed, Hills' very philosophy of liberal arts education set a precedent that would eventually allow—indeed, even require—his schools to embrace philosophies and scientific paradigms that both he and the fundamentalists rejected. His steadfast commitment to eradicationism against Keswick drove a wedge not only between him and R. A. Torrey, but also to some extent between the holiness and fundamentalist movements when later the lines between them were being clarified. Further, Hills' commitment to revivalist means had at least some effect

---

Booth and his wife Catherine to belt the world with gospel radiance." Hills, *Pentecostal Light*, 47–48. Even after his holiness maturation and subsequent rejection of Keswick, Hills writes in *The Secret of Spiritual Power*, "It would be difficult to name one conspicuously great soul winner during the last two hundred years who was not by the baptism with the Holy Spirit equipped for his work. Such men as Edwards, Wesley, and Whitefield, Fletcher, Finney, Caughey, A. B. Earle, Moody, Bishops Matthew Simpson, W. M. Taylor, and the Booths, Phoebe Palmer and Maggie Van Cott, are illustrations of the enduement of Pentecostal power. A hundred others only less famous might easily be named who graduated from the Pentecostal chamber into usefulness and fame. It is not at all an exaggeration or overstatement to say that they were made by the baptism with the Holy Ghost." Hills, *Secret of Spiritual Power*, 54–55.

at keeping Nazarenes from the political militancy that characterized some fundamentalists.

Again, however, this is not to say that Hills did not share characteristics with fundamentalism. Fundamentalism was, at least as represented by figures like R. A. Torrey, a movement with revivalist means and institutions. In Hills' "two camp" way of thinking, other revivalist movements could be counted on as bedfellows, even if doctrinally they were, as Ingersol intimates, "strange bedfellows."

HILLS AND THE PENTECOSTALS

Having said that Hills overlaps (although somewhat uneasily) with figures like Moody, Torrey, and Meyer because they were revivalists is not to say, however, that every revivalist of the early twentieth century was a welcome or even uneasy ally. There was one group of revivalists for which Hills had nothing but disparaging words.

A. M. Hills was not a man to pull a punch in a disagreement. As we saw above, he took issue with everyone, even friends and mentors, when they differed with him in their definitions of Spirit baptism. Believing sanctification to be the key to his revivalist aspirations and system, Hills thought it vital to proclaim the message clearly and correctly. Because Hills felt that Torrey and the Keswick movement lived lives that were "better than their theory about the work of the Spirit,"[63] and that they were still clearly very much in line with his larger revivalistic concerns, they received only a mild rebuke.

Another revivalist movement of the early twentieth century, however, received stronger criticism from Hills for not only its differing views on Spirit baptism, but on other accounts as well. The movement took "Pentecostalism" as a name for itself, although Hills and many in the Holiness Movement were thoroughly irritated by what they perceived to be the hijacking of a designation and identity that belonged rightfully to them. Believing those in the Holiness Movement to be the *true* pentecostals, Hills refused them their own self-designation and simply called them "the tongues movement."

It should be stated clearly that Hills never offered a single word of affirmation for the tongues movement. They differed with him on too

---

63. Hills, *Pentecost Rejected*, 63.

many key issues for him to say anything praiseworthy about them. Not only did they take his beloved Spirit baptism and twist it so that many Christians no longer sought after holiness, but epistemologically, they also smacked of mysticism. Thus, unlike Torrey, who flouted only one aspect of Hills' revivalist canon, the tongues movement was deserving of a more significant tongue-lashing. Most of Hills' words on this movement are written in a pamphlet descriptively entitled *The Tongues Movement*.

In *The Tongues Movement*, Hills publishes his three major arguments with Pentecostalism. First, its emphases endanger the movement of God in a revivalistic way. Of this danger, we hear Hills' strongest warnings in the closing paragraph of the pamphlet. He encourages his readers to "most studiously avoid and thoroughly let alone" the tongues movement.[64] Why? The issues revolve completely around the perceived danger to revival and revivalism. Of Pentecostalism, Hills states, "It has ruined Christian workers . . . It has stopped revivals, and brought deep spirituality into disrepute, and deterred the Churches from seeking the much-needed baptism with the Holy Spirit for holiness and power . . . It has been strangely destitute of the convicting and converting and sanctifying power that may be properly expected of a genuine movement inspired by the Holy Spirit."[65] Thus, because it undermines his conception of the true movement of God in revival, Hills concludes that the tongues movement should avoided entirely.

The second major argument Hills has against Pentecostalism is also seen in the above concluding remarks—its emphasis upon tongues deters Christians from seeking holiness and power in Spirit baptism. We have already seen that in Hills' holiness-oriented mind, it is thoroughly unsound to relate the experience of Spirit baptism with anything but inward cleansing and power for witnessing. Early in the pamphlet, Hills attacks the idea of *glossolalia* as the evidence of the Spirit's indwelling.

> It [tongues] *was not an essential evidence of the baptism with the Holy Spirit*. It was not mentioned by John Baptist [sic] when he foretold that Jesus should baptise [sic] with the Holy Spirit and fire. The Holy Spirit came upon Jesus, but He never spoke with tongues. In Acts viii. 12–17 we have a complete account of the Samaritan converts receiving the Holy Spirit but no mentions of

64. Hills, *The Tongues Movement*, 15.
65. Ibid., 14.

their speaking with tongues. It is well to further bear in mind that in this book of Acts the Holy Spirit is mentioned fifty-seven times, while speaking in tongues is mentioned in only five verses.[66]

Hills' third major argument against the early Pentecostals is that they were also too mystical. In order to drive holiness folk away from this movement Hills retells several very negative stories as proof that "there is an abundance of evidence that this movement is of the devil by the deception it has wrought. The Holy Spirit does not deceive people. But the victims of this lying delusion are numberless."[67]

One such story of delusion is of a poor Christian couple, Mr. and Mrs. Garr, who were caught up in the movement. When they spoke in tongues, for some reason they thought there were speaking an Asian dialect. They applied for the mission field and were sent, but when they arrived, they could not find their language in any one of the hundreds of dialects in India or China.

Hills tells another story of a different couple, Mr. and Mrs. Mackintosh, who went to China expecting the Holy Ghost to give them the language, but it was reported that they always used an interpreter.

Of these two stories, Hills concludes, "The Holy Ghost does not thus deceive people and counterfeit a gift, and send His deluded victims half round the world to cover them with shame and chagrin, and break their hearts with disappointment. The devil delights to deceive and ruin people; 'he is a deceiver and liar from the beginning,' and this work must be from him."[68]

Adding to this, Hills produces several more very negative stories as evidence that the tongues movement's mysticism is greatly detrimental to not only the spiritual, but also the psychological makeup of persons.

> *This "tongues" delusion has proved to be the highway to the rankest and wildest fanaticism.* Couple the eight precepts or principles just mentioned and constantly taught "with sleepless nights, prolonged fastings, overwrought nerves, anxious straining after manifestations, an unnatural intoxication of excitement and enthusiasm, long and uncontrolled meetings, and immediate acceptance of every manifestation from God, and the feeling that there must be manifestations, and it is not to be wondered

66. Ibid., 3.
67. Ibid., 8.
68. Ibid.

at that the enemy had come in as an angel of light, and flooded the movement with his manifestations." If such things did not produce a perfect field for the development and spread of *fanaticism* we do not know what could.[69]

Hills offers nine more stories to help illustrate the attitude he is advocating for the Holiness Movement to take toward Pentecostalism. While each of the stories is vivid enough to frighten many holiness persons, Hills ends with the following story.

Hills' final story goes that there was a "well-known Christian lady" in Germany who was deluded in her search for a "so-called baptism of fire," which she received, but which was later revealed to be demon possession. When she was finally delivered, she sent a letter to another friend whose demons, after much prevailing prayer, were compelled to confess, through the friend's lips, their own wicked schemes and devices. The story continues:

> It was as though, in opposition to their own will, the demons were driven to make them [the confessions] by an irresistible power . . . The following are a few of the confessions forced from these demons by God, in answer to prevailing prayer:—"I have perverted everything in order to mislead men . . . I have feigned to be the Holy Spirit in order to seduce many. Oh, how I have deceived this soul, and other souls! They longed for truth, and I gave them lies . . . I have lied to them and have deceived them . . . I have not yet told everything about the mischief I did even before the tongues-movement. We know what would happen if the Church were to be endued with power from on high. But we have spoiled this by means of the tongues-movement. Now the Church has ceased to long for power . . . The tongues people have subscribed to it that I am from above; they acknowledge me to be the Pentecostal Spirit and they have worshiped me . . . As baptism of the Spirit I entered into the Church; I came to her piously with the Word of God. I will have worship . . . I am a God—a god of hell . . . If I am vanquished, all the other tongues-demons will be vanquished too . . . The blow would be too terrible for the whole tongues-movement throughout the world. In it we have too good an instrument for seducing all believers. It is by God's permission, he has used her for the exposure of the tongues-spirit. I would never have done it. But God has used her mouth against

---

69. Ibid., 9.

> my will, and I was compelled to unmask . . . We must kill her, then you cannot publish the tongues-deceit."[70]

Needless to say, whether or not this story is true or its usage appropriate, it would certainly have frightened most holiness readers; and this *is* Hills intention. He writes:

> But why tell these unvarnished facts? Simply that God's people, in seeking for God's best, may know the possibilities of danger, and may be forearmed . . . Nobody can read this awful narrative of the tongues-movement . . . without (if moved by the evidence) being painfully impressed with the fact that this modern movement of tongues is a Satanic counterfeit of Pentecost that has come from the bottomless pit. In no particular does it measure up to a spiritual movement that really comes from God, and is led by the Holy Ghost.[71]

Hills does not reserve any harsher criticism of a Christian movement or a theologian anywhere in his works. Indeed, it would be difficult to find a more caustic critique of Unitarianism, higher criticism, liberalism, Darwinism, or even atheism in any of Hills' writings.

In his systematic theology, Hills again criticizes Pentecostalism, although this time indirectly, addressing various forms of mysticism in general. "Mystics are those who claim to be under the immediate guidance of God or His Spirit . . . In a still wider use of the word, any system of thought, whether in philosophy or religion, which ascribes more importance to the feelings than to the intellect, is mystical."[72]

Hills' basic problem with mysticism is its epistemology. He sums up his position, quoting from J. D. Morell's *History of Modern Philosophy*.

> "Reason is no longer viewed as the great organ of truth. Its decisions are regarded as well-nigh worthless, while the inward impulses are held up as the true and infallible source of human knowledge. The fundamental process, therefore, of all Mysticism is to reverse the true order of nature and give the precedence to the emotional instead of the intellectual element of the human mind" . . . This differs essentially from the Scriptural doctrine of divine illumination as held by all evangelical Christians. The Scriptures teach that the Holy Spirit takes truth already made

---

70. Ibid., 14.
71. Ibid., 12.
72. Hills, *Fundamental Christian Theology*, vol. 1, 14.

known in the Bible, and makes it real to our minds by quickening in us a spiritual discernment of its meaning. The Mystics, on the other hand, claim a revelation of truth quite apart from the Bible, and the use of any means of grace, and, indeed, by an utter neglect of them.[73]

Thus, Hills explicitly disagreed with the Pentecostals on three different issues: their overall threat to true revival, their *glossolalia*-centered understanding of Spirit baptism, and their mystical epistemology. These three issues alone would have been sufficient to bring on Hills' sharpest criticisms. These differences were not, however, the only issues dividing holiness folk and Pentecostals. While disagreements over shared and differing doctrinal categories would have been enough to drive them apart, overlapping geography and constituencies complicated the feuds even more.

Other Complicating Factors

We have already seen the explicit doctrinal problems Hills had with Pentecostalism. Not only was their mysticism completely unacceptable, but their doctrinal language was too close to his, while their definitions were too far away. Just like with Torrey, however, there were other underlying, unspoken differences and issues that drove Hills and the tongues people into dispute. Not only did they occupy the same biblical texts and doctrinal language as their holiness counterparts, but Pentecostals also occupied the same geographical space. To put it simply, the major centers of the Holiness Movement and early Pentecostalism were literally right on top of each other.

This is, of course, no mere coincidence. Indeed the doctrinal and geographical territories over which these two movements warred in the first decades of the twentieth century illustrate the interrelationship between the two and reveal the holiness roots of Pentecostalism. It is significant to the interpretation of their interrelationship that Azusa Street is within a few blocks of where Phineas F. Bresee's Glory Barn sat. It is likewise significant that the Chicago area was home to at least the three different versions of revivalistic Christianity that are the core of this chapter; Keswick, several holiness conventions, and Pentecostalism.

---

73. Ibid., 14–15.

In the years immediately prior to and after the turn of the century, those who would eventually identify themselves as holiness, Pentecostal, or Pentecostal-holiness adherents crossed the then semi-permeable boundary between churches, conventions, and movements rather freely, keeping the lines fuzzy. It is very likely that, to the outside observer, the "holy rollers" of one church or movement in Los Angeles, Chicago, and even England were indistinguishable from those of another. Out of the same pool of nineteenth-century revivalism sprung multiple twentieth-century holiness and Pentecostal denominations.

The implication of all this is, of course, that Hills was not only contending to keep Pentecost, so to speak, in the holiness camps, but he was also fighting to keep holiness people in as well. Indeed, his pamphlet *The Tongues Movement* would hardly have been necessary to write were it not for regular lay crossover. The implication is fairly obvious; many of the holiness and the "tongues" people *were*, at least for a few years of the twentieth century, the *same* people.

Summary

Hills' relationship with Pentecostalism is much less complicated than his relationship with fundamentalism, although with both he follows the same line of reasoning. As we saw above, the farther a movement was from his canon of doctrines and means, the less likely Hills was to accept it. Since his position was only slightly at variance with Hills', Torrey received only a mild correction. Pentecostalism, however, was much farther away in Hills' estimate. Not only were they at variance with his doctrine of Spirit baptism, but their mysticism, Hills was convinced, led many down paths of deception. When combined with the fact that they often drew followers from the Holiness Movement's ranks, these differences were sufficient to call out Hills' strongest rhetoric. The Pentecostals were simultaneously too similar and too dissimilar for him to esteem them as anything but "counterfeiters."[74] As such, the tongues

---

74. The "counterfeit" accusation was and is a common way to vilify another movement which stands close enough to one's own position to "steal" from one's lay constituency. The charge employs the notion that the devil is skilled at slipping his deceptions and lies in so close to the truth that the unsuspecting cannot recognize the difference. That is, when he cannot completely destroy something directly, the devil produces a counterfeit, an incredibly believable fake that, in the long run, is worthless. As we saw in chapter 2, Hills developed his own variation on this concept. Of an encounter with a "three-blessings heretic," he comments, "It is a well known trick of Satan, when he

movement was anathematized by Hills. So even with all that they held in common in revivalist doctrine, language, and praxis, Hills' logic and canon led him to only an antithetical relationship with them.

HILLS' CONTROVERSY WITH THE CONGREGATIONAL CHURCH

Having considered in chapter 5 the first of two lingering and difficult questions in the interpretation of A. M. Hills, the second will now be addressed—why did A. M. Hills, who for almost seventeen years in the Holiness Movement advocated a "stay-inner" position, seemingly suddenly "come-out" of the Congregational Churches of America and join the Pentecostal Church of the Nazarene?[75]

On one level, the answer is not as difficult or complex as the previous question. To put it simply, Hills' curt autobiographical telling of when and how he joined the Nazarenes offers too few words of explanation for a decision that was actually decades in the making. When, in the spring of 1912, he told Phineas Bresee that the Congregational Church was on its last probation, Hills was referring to a relationship break that began as far back as the 1870s. Not surprisingly, the issues that were the most central to his decision were those concerning his revivalist identity, doctrine, and means.

Hills was obviously neither a *holiness* "stay-inner" nor "come-outer" before 1895. Of course, such designations were not peculiar to holiness folk, but the only way in which Hills used it before 1895 was in wishes that certain kinds of "liberal" pastors would "come-out" of the Congregational Church. Still, it was not a common way of articulating Christian identity for Hills until after his sanctification experience.

It is clear from Hills' writings and endeavors in the first fifteen years after 1895 that he identified with the "stay-inners." This group of holiness folk felt their truest identity was to leaven the whole lump of

---

cannot suppress holiness, to sidetrack it, or switch it off into some foolish excess of unscriptural absurdity. Remember the Devil is not <u>dead</u> because we are striving to be holy, and it is only good things that are counterfeited." Hills, "Autobiography," 148 (94).

75. In his 1988 Drew University dissertation, Kenneth O. Brown offers an eschatologically-oriented answer to this question. Brown argues that, in general, the come-outers were premillennialists, while the stay-inners were postmillennialists. While such an analysis has its merits, another explanation is clearly required for A. M. Hills. Cf. Brown, "Leadership in National Holiness Association."

Christianity by remaining in their respective home denominations. At the camp meetings, they could gather together as a unified body to fan the identity into a hot flame. But the every day life and service of the holiness person took place in her or his hometown, local church, and mother denomination.

This vision was thus interdenominational. The Holiness Movement remained a *movement*, with the natural benefits of fluidity to spill over the boundaries of denominationalism *via* incarnational emissaries, so to speak. At the heart of his early holiness identity, Hills was one such emissary in the Congregational Church.

There were, however, many forces working against the stay-inners. These forces are well illustrated in various ways throughout Hills' writings. His biography of Bresee, for instance, illustrates the class tensions that took place when much of the constituency of Methodism rose in social standing and began to view revivalism, holiness preaching, and the more emotional expressions of both as fit only for the lower classes.

There were pragmatic, ecclesiastical tensions. Many perceived the Holiness Movement as inherently dissentious in nature and feared that such divisiveness would split denominations.

There were tensions within the mainstream denominations as the relationships to their own revivalist pasts and its doctrines and means were gradually replaced by less radical ideas and measures. The transition within Congregationalism from revivalist to non-revivalist means and doctrines in the mid to late nineteenth century is the key to understanding why Hills eventually left the church of which he had been a part for sixty-four years.

Hills' Controversy with Washington Gladden

A telling window into why Hills left the Congregational Church after nearly seventeen years of staunch "stay-in-ism" can be seen in the brief story in his "Autobiography" of his meeting with Washington Gladden. Indeed, much more Congregational history in the latter half of the nineteenth century is between the lines of this story than is at first obvious. Much controversy underlies Hills' account that only rises to the surface when Hills and Gladden's respective autobiographies are juxtaposed. Together, their autobiographies are a revealing microcosm of the inner tensions that were brewing in late nineteenth-century Congregationalism.

Ironically, the areas of Hills and Gladden's agreement are so numerous that, from a superficial reading of most of their texts, one could easily think they were part of the same movement. Both were adamant, life-long opponents of the Calvinist "orthodoxy" of the Synod of Dort.[76] Both were strong advocates of ministry to and among the poor. Neither was afraid of political means to secure their ends. On modern research and the re-translation of the Bible, the two agreed fully. For instance, as we will see below, neither Hills nor Gladden approved of the older English translations of the Bible.

With as many similarities, were it not for three pages in Hills' autobiography, the casual reader of Hills and Gladden might imagine them to have been friends and colleagues. From Hills' comments in "Autobiography," however, nothing could be farther from the truth.

As was recounted in chapter 2, Hills and several other Congregationalist ministers had been invited to an interview and potential installation of a new pastor at Stubenville, Ohio.[77] Gladden was also invited and, as he was the most prominent and the oldest minister present, he was unanimously elected moderator of the interview and installation.

Hills' recollection continues that he was incensed to be the only pastor out of several concerned with whether or not the interviewee had been "bitten" by the higher criticism "viper." Gladden's silence during the interview eventually led Hills to a somewhat presumptuous questioning of the candidate himself, even though he was the junior minister present. In a 1922 article for the *Herald of Holiness*, Hills recalls that he asked about the historicity of the Bible's major characters, the deity of Jesus, the atonement through Christ, the necessity of conversion by faith, and whether or not eternal punishment awaits the wicked who knowingly and willfully reject Christ.[78] Of course, while the moderator's general silence was bothersome enough, what seems to have troubled Hills the most was that no other elder on the board was concerned at the candidate's answers, which were unacceptable to Hills.

---

76. Gladden, *Recollections*, 224–25; Hills, *Fundamental Christian Theology*, vol. 2, 137–64.

77. While he offers no specific date for this encounter, Hills mentions that it was near the end of his pastorate in Allegheny. Thus, a safe assumption is that the story probably either took place in 1888 or 1889.

78. Hills, *Herald of Holiness* 10 (February 22, 1922), 5.

Hills' interpretation of this story, as well as his larger reflections on its relationship to the growing tensions within the Congregational Church, is scant enough in "Autobiography" to be disappointing. Indeed, he does not even say what his questions were in the meeting and, for some reason, is reticent in "Autobiography" to discuss his disintegrating relationship with the Congregational Church.

While Hills' commentary is too brief, however, Washington Gladden's version fills in some of the gaps. In his autobiography, *Recollections*, Gladden speaks of the tensions within Congregationalism and the very issues that were driving him and Hills to variant forms of religion. Gladden, of course, does not anywhere mention A. M. Hills. Apparently while the meeting was burned into Hills' memory for the rest of his life, it was not historic enough for Gladden to recall, or at least not important enough for him to retell. Nevertheless, in the eighteenth chapter of *Recollections*, "Heresy Hunting," he spins the narrative of his personal adoption of certain "heresies" and the tensions and eventual victory he experienced in the Congregational Church to his way of thinking.

The chapter begins with a brief mention of the European and American scholars who were meeting in London "for the revision of the received version of the Bible . . . This was, in itself, to many, a disturbing suggestion. Revision implied change, and change, whether of word or phrase, in the language of the Bible, could be nothing less than sacrilege."[79] Gladden, however, undaunted by the fear of change, continues the story in the warmth and color one quickly comes to expect from his style in *Recollections*. "Gradually, however, the light that was shining all about us found its way through our shutters."[80] The work of Theodore Parker, he suggests, slowly became less stigmatized, and soon a gradual paradigm shift took place in biblical theology. "In newspapers and magazines, and in an occasional heretical book, statements of fact appeared which arrested the attention of thoughtful men. There were even Biblical commentaries which ventured to call attention to interpolated verses and doubtful passages. It began to be evident to some that the doctrine of inerrancy had been overworked; that there was need of the application of critical study to the sacred Scriptures."[81]

79. Gladden, *Recollections*, 259.
80. Ibid., 260.
81. Ibid, 260. Gladden continues that it was about 1875 that he was sitting with

Gladden's yarn continues that in the early 1870s a copy of the New Testament in the received version was published with footnotes indicating variations with the three oldest and best manuscripts, the Vatican, the Alexandrian, and the Sinaitic Bibles. Applying the textual-criticism rule that the older manuscript is to be preferred over the younger one, certain verses needed re-translating. "This edition of the New Testament put within the reach of all intelligent readers the means of judging to what extent our English version needed revision, and made it plain that the task undertaken by the men at work in the Jerusalem Chamber was one of serious importance."[82]

It is immediately after this phrase that Gladden takes what many in the Congregational Church, including Hills, would have considered to be an enormous jump in application. Gladden immediately concludes, "Such a concession, however reluctantly it might be made, involved considerable relaxation of the rigidity of theological dogmatism, and opened the way for the examination of many traditional beliefs."[83]

It was in this application that Hills and many Congregationalists had the problem. Well aware of the textual superiority of the Revised Version over the King James, Hills never argued against the newer translation. In fact, in his *Homiletics and Pastoral Theology*, Hills' *first* of four words of advice to preachers on the selection of the text is:

> I. *That all who fill the pulpit should use the Revised Version of the Scriptures.* Every scholar knows that the old version though written in the finest English, oftentimes was not accurate in translation. The critical study of the manuscripts and the new ones found during the last century and a half, have made it clear that there were, here and there, mistakes in the King James Version, which warranted a new revised and more accurate translation. God raised up the scholars to make it, and we have it and ought

---

"a score of intelligent Congregational clergymen, when the question arose whether it would be judicious to tell the people of our congregations that 1 John v, 7—a verse not found in the Revised Version—was an interpolation; and not one of the twenty agreed with me in thinking that the fact could be safely stated. They all admitted that the verse was spurious, but feared the effect of letting the people know a truth so disturbing." Ibid., 260–61. It was about this same time, Gladden writes, that from the pulpit, he pointed out that the thirty-seventh verse of Acts chapter 8 was not in the original manuscript. For this he received "an indignant letter calling [his] attention to the fate reserved for those who 'take away from the words of the book of this prophecy.'" Ibid., 261.

82. Ibid., 261.
83. Ibid., 261–62.

to use it . . . To preach from some *texts* according to the wording of the Old Version might subject the preacher to ridicule as an ignoramus, which is, to say the least, unfortunate![84]

While certainly much less polished and palatable than Gladden's words, such statements on the part of Hills were a deliberate challenge to preachers to accept and benefit from the newer textual scholarship. On this issue, Hills and Gladden saw eye to eye. Of course, Hill's appeal to his audience was based to a much larger extent on the pithiness of his rhetoric, a characteristic often held in high esteem among revivalists.

Beyond the mere wrappings of rhetoric, however, the two differed more significantly in what conclusions should be taken as self-evident from the evidence. Gladden and many others' judgment that "considerable relaxation of the rigidity of theological dogmatism" was the natural course to take first manifested itself in Congregationalist doctrine through a challenge to the doctrine of eternal punishment. Long held and used in revivalistic preaching, the idea of hell was not to be lost easily.

Interestingly, Gladden illustrates the tensions in Congregationalism in the same way Hills does, in the context of pastoral interview and installation. Gladden tells of a Mr. Merriam, who was to be interviewed in 1877 for the pastorate of the Congregational Church in Indian Orchard, Missouri, a suburb of Springfield. While "a man of a most unselfish and consecrated temper," when asked his views on the eternal destiny of sinners, Merriam stated that he believed "that those who were incorrigible might suffer extinction."[85] When Merriam would not revise his statements, the board, of which Gladden was a part, refused his installation.

Very soon thereafter, the two on the board, Gladden and another, who had voted positively for Merriam's installation, were called to give account for their votes. Gladden offered his defense in a series of sermons on the Kingdom of God. In *Recollections*, he relates the core of his sermons.

> The man who believes in Christ, who has the spirit of Christ in him, who shows in his life the fruits of that spirit, who, denying himself and taking up his cross, is following Christ in toilsome but loving labor for the salvation of men—he is my brother, and nothing shall hinder me from offering him the right hand of fel-

---

84. Hills, *Homiletics and Pastoral Theology*, 38. Italics Hills'.

85. Gladden, *Recollections*, 262.

lowship. I do not care what name they call him by, whether he is Churchman or Quaker, Universalist or Roman Catholic, he who is united to my Master shall not be divided from me . . . I will take great care always lest I exalt the letter above the spirit, the dogma above the life.[86]

Gladden continues *Recollections* with the story of yet another council meeting for the installation of a pastor. He writes that it was only a few weeks after the Indian Orchard council vote that another council at North Adams was convened for the installation of the Rev. Theodore T. Munger. Gladden points out that Munger was known to hold liberal views on many questions.

On one or two points which Mr. Merriam had not touched he diverged from the traditional statements, and on the subject of future punishment he was even more emphatic in his rejection of the orthodox view than Mr. Merriam had been. He was somewhat sharply criticised, [sic] but he defended himself, and when the discussion was ended, the council voted to proceed with his installation. It was pleasant to be in the majority again, and to carry back to Springfield the testimony that there were other views of Congregational fellowship than those which had prevailed at Indian Orchard.[87]

Taking place when Hills was still in his twenties and not yet four-years experienced in pastoral ministry, these two councils sent the Congregational Church into a frenzy. Reflecting on this, Gladden states: "Everywhere the ecclesiastical bees were buzzing. What were the conditions of fellowship? How much must one believe to be a Congregational minister in good standing? . . . There was no national Congregational creed, and no ecclesiastical body which had the power to frame or impose such a creed upon the denomination; the only creeds were those of local churches, and these were by no means uniform."[88]

Of greater importance in the larger history of Congregationalism, the latter of these two councils set a precedent into motion that allowed less "orthodox" views to become more acceptable. Of course, it also set into motion a decades-long debate concerning what Congregationalists believed.

86. Ibid., 263–64.
87. Ibid., 265.
88. Ibid., 265–66.

Reactions against the obvious implications of this ordination took several forms. Most argued that there was a *"consensus of doctrine, which was sufficiently understood by Congregationalists; and that those who did not, ex animo, accept that consensus of doctrine had no right to remain in the Congregational ministry."*[89] The only problem was that Congregationalist polity was not centralized enough to have a governing body for impeachment. For this reason, many wrote to and were published in the *Congregational Quarterly* that every person "knows whether he is an orthodox Congregationalist or not; if he knows that he is not, he is bound to take himself out of fellowship; and if he fails to do so, he is acting a dishonorable and unmanly part."[90]

Gladden, not one to remain silent, (despite Hills' opinion of him), wrote an article in the next *Congregational Quarterly* that he resented being told he was not acting a manly part. "I am here in the Congregational denomination; I suppose that I have a right to be here, and here I propose to stay . . . I do not care to be in a ministry in which I have not equal rights with every other minister."[91] Gladden goes on to point out that, in the previous issue, the editor claimed that the moral theory of the atonement was of unorthodox character, to which Gladden responded that it was a part of his orthodoxy. He closes by stating, "I happen to know that I am not alone in my opinions, nor in my determination to stand by them. There are quite a number of us who have no wish for controversy, but who do believe to some extent in the manly art of self-defense, and we shall not be posted as sneaks in the 'Congregational Quarterly' without mildly protesting."[92]

Gladden writes that, to his own surprise, letters and post cards "came pouring in for a week or two with the heartiest approval of this declaration of independence. Yet those who were standing for the new measure of liberty in the denomination were still in a small minority, and many ways were found to make them quite uncomfortable."[93]

Such stories and statements from *Recollections*, coupled with Hills' 1888 story, reveal just how quickly the Congregationalist majority shifted from Hills' to Gladden's position. While in 1877 Gladden admits that he

---

89. Ibid., 266.
90. Ibid.
91. Ibid., 267.
92. Ibid.
93. Ibid., 267–68.

was in the minority, the tables were turned within at least eleven years. The speed with which these, and many other, doctrinal changes took place happened fast enough for many Congregationalists to be taken by surprise. This is perhaps well illustrated by Marion L. Starkey's colorful and often pithy writing of Congregationalist history in this period when he quotes an unnamed women confiding in her pastor, "I miss hell."[94]

This is not to say that the theme of hell disappeared completely or without advocates of the older revivalism raising a stir. The battles continued against the new social scientific interpretation of religion and the Bible for some time. Gladden continues his story that even though the Congregational Church had no body vested with authority to bring charges or to remove credentials, much pressure was still applied against him. He writes, "There is always a denominational 'machine,' more or less political in its methods, by which ecclesiastical affairs are managed, and those who incur the displeasure of this machine are apt to find their paths to promotion obstructed, and their opportunities of service limited."[95]

That machine took the form of the Vermont State Convention of Congregationalists, which following the lead of the *Congregational Quarterly*, "passed a resolution declaring that men who rejected 'any substantial part' of the doctrines 'commonly called evangelical' ought to take themselves out of the Congregational fellowship."[96]

Again Gladden picked up the pen and defended his right to stay within the fellowship. From his perspective, the fellowship was too dear and necessary to him to abandon on matters in which he thought the majority was wrong. Writing of himself in the third person, he states, "Fidelity to his Master and love for his brethren constrain him to continue in the fellowship."[97]

Of course, many disagreed with him that one could claim fidelity to the Master while drinking from the well of higher criticism. Indeed, Hills' strongest contention with higher criticism is over the issues of Christology. Always the first to spot a slippery slope, Hills could not understand why anyone would even read the writings of the higher critics. In his slippery-slope logic, reading such writings would naturally lead

94. Starkey, *The Congregational Way*, 291.
95. Gladden, *Recollections*, 268.
96. Ibid.
97. Ibid., 270.

to accepting those writings, which deny the ground of human salvation, the death and resurrection of Jesus Christ, deity in the flesh. Concerned that higher criticism naturally tends to the denial of every necessary aspect of Christian confession, Hills followed the lead of Thomas Reid toward a more faith-engendering religion.

On the surface, the issues at stake in this story seem fairly straightforward. Two theologians are disagreeing over theology. Allowing only this, however, does not give a sufficiently all-inclusive picture to understand the variety of forces that were driving wedges into Congregationalism in the nineteenth century. As we saw in Hills' controversies with fundamentalism and Pentecostalism, there were other complicating factors in Hills' relationship with the Congregational Church.

While located between the lines of their respective autobiographical accounts and, therefore more difficult to see, there were the tensions between the increasingly marginalized revivalist camp within Congregationalism and those advocating new means for religious and societal transformation. Congregationalism eventually experienced the phenomenon of the split consciousness that takes place within a denomination or movement that has been heavily influenced by revivalism. After a few decades of the radicalizations that revivalist means and doctrines often bring, some within the movement or denomination seek less psychologically-exacting forms of religion.

This is especially true in denominations and movements that are decades removed from their original revivalistic outpourings. Over two or three generations, cross-trends begin to war as the children or grandchildren of revivalism embrace what could be characterized as more temperate, traditional, or sophisticated expressions of worship and begin to put into practice methods that produce the kind of disciples that they themselves have become. These cross those who, whether consciously or not, intuit a sense of loss as revivalistic religious experience, doctrines, and methods are sometimes suddenly, but more often than not gradually, replaced. Nowhere are the tensions of this split consciousness better illustrated than in the two figures of A. M. Hills and Washington Gladden.

The Congregational Church by the mid to late nineteenth century could be characterized as a "burned-over" denomination. By the time of Oberlin's cooling and Hills' entrance into ministry, revivalism had been its staple fare in most places for decades. After the dynasties of

Jonathan Edwards and George Whitefield and then Finney and Mahan, Congregationalism was perhaps primed for religious change by the 1870s when the revival-hungry A. M. Hills entered the ministry. Having been converted and raised in revivalistic churches and trained at revivalistic Oberlin and revivalist-friendly Yale, Hills was hardly in a position to sympathize with Washington Gladden, whose childhood experiences with revivalism had been psychologically and spiritually debilitating enough for him to completely reject it.

The "hell" issue provides an interesting example of the layers of cross-trajectories that are represented in Hills and Gladden. On the surface, one might question whether or not the disagreements were simply exegetical or theological. A more flat-footed approach would simply assume that Hills thought the proclamation of hell was biblically precedented while Gladden did not. Their respective personal stories, however, reveal layers of complication to this "doctrinal" question.

Gladden's experience of revivalism as a child can be starkly contrasted with that of Hills. In *Recollections*, Gladden writes of the sermons of his youth that "hardly ever touched life in the remotest way."[98] The religion of his boyhood produced only fear and spiritual uncertainty. He specifically recalls the preaching of Jacob Knapp, who spun terrifying pictures of the torments and tormentors of hell.[99] These descriptions,

98. Ibid., 33. "While . . . I had as large an experience of church-going in my boyhood as most boys can recall, I cannot lay my hand on my heart and say that the church-going helped me to solve my religious problems. In fact, it made those problems more and more tangled and troublesome. I wanted to find my way into the peace of God, in the assurance of his friendship, and that I could not do . . . So I kept trying, for years, to gain that assurance of the favor of God of which I heard people talking, and which, I felt sure, some of them must possess. I listened, in prayer meeting and revival meeting, to what they said about it; I noted with the greatest care the steps that must be taken, and I tried to do just what I was told to do. I was to 'give myself away,' in a serious and complete self-dedication . . . But I understood that when I had done it, properly, I should have an immediate knowledge of the fact that it had been done properly; some evidence in my consciousness that could not be mistaken; that a light would break in, or a burden roll off, or that some other emotional or ecstatic experience would supervene; and when nothing of the kind occurred, the inevitable conclusion was that my effort had been fruitless; that I had failed to commend myself to the favor of God, and was still under his wrath and curse." Ibid., 34, 35, and 36.

99. "The preaching, in all the churches, when it was not controversial, was almost wholly evangelistic. The conversion of sinners was supposed to be the preacher's main business. Respecting the eternal punishment of those who die impenitent, and the impossibility of repentance beyond the grave, there was no difference of opinion among evangelical Christians, and the immense importance of saving men from this fate over-

while driving some into the arms of the Lord for mercy, only angered the very young Gladden. He was just a boy when he heard Knapp, but the memory penetrated his mind for the rest of his life.

Such preaching was not by any means unusual in Congregational churches of the early and mid-nineteenth century. A necessary part of Calvinist evangelistic preaching, the terrors of the wrath of God functioned to drive the sinner into the arms of the forgiving God. Under the best of circumstances, of course, this style was and is used with the aim of producing spiritual *release* from the bondage of guilt and fear. From Gladden's accounts, it seems highly unlikely that many of the evangelists he heard as a boy successfully navigated the careful balance between wrath and grace.

Of course, the radical revivalistic atmosphere in which Gladden grew up was haunted not only by the more dysfunctional side of Calvinist preaching, but also by many end-times prophets of doom. Gladden's church invited their share of "Millerites," which served only to scare him further.[100] Thus, among the Knapp-type evangelists, the Millerites, and other negative forces, one is forced to agree with Congregationalist historian J. William T. Youngs that "Gladden was raised in a spiritual atmosphere that tormented his youth."[101]

These pangs were only heightened by the very premature death of his father, Solomon, and the vivid memories Gladden associated with him. During his son's infancy, Solomon Gladden, who was raised a

---

shadowing all other interests... The motive of fear was the leading motive, but the bliss of the heavenly life was also vividly portrayed. That hell was a veritable lake of fire and brimstone was hardly questioned by any one... I was accustomed to hear, in my boyhood, the famous Jacob Knapp, one of the most popular evangelists of the central states; and I shall never forget some of his descriptions of the burning pit, with the sinners trying to crawl up its sides out of the flames, while the devils, with pitchforks, stood by to fling them back again. It was intended, of course, to frighten sinners; probably it had that effect on many, but I wonder whether it was, on the whole, even then, as telling as it was supposed to be. For myself, though a small boy, I distinctly remember that it made me angry." Ibid., 58–59.

100. "The expectation of the destruction of the world by fire was another nightmare. The Millerite horror was hanging over us in my earliest days; I remember well a lecture, in the Baptist church, when I was only seven years old, in which the lecturer, with figures drawn from the prophecy of Daniel, proved with chalk upon a blackboard that the world was going to be burned up in 1843... There was a blazing comet, too, in the sky that winter... I shall not be blamed for hiding my head under the coverlet, from the terrible portent." Ibid., 59–60.

101. Youngs, *The Congregationalists*, 165.

Congregationalist, went to the Methodist church because there were no Congregational churches in Southampton, and the staunch Calvinism of the Presbyterians in the area was too strong for him. One of the last and most vivid memories he had of his father, Gladden recalls a service at the Methodist church where a stirring evangelist had been preaching, and the frenzy that frequently followed such preaching began to manifest itself. "Men and women were prostrate on the floor, groaning and screaming frantically; some were trying to pray; some were shouting 'Glory!' the excitement and confusion were indescribable. I sat on a low seat near my father and looked into his face; he stood perfectly silent; there were tears in his eyes, but the expression on his countenance was one of intense pain."[102] It was not long after this, in 1841, that his father died of "an attack of some enteric malady."[103]

Gladden was five years old when his father died, and, although it is said that "childish sorrows are short-lived," he grieved the loss for a very long time. "This man had so wound himself into the life of this child that they could not be torn apart without lasting suffering."[104]

History and bad memories like these put an interesting context around Gladden's adulthood choice of doctrines and methods. With such a radical and painful early life, it is little wonder that he had no use for revivalism's means and creeds. Eventually finding spiritual peace by rejecting much of the religion of his childhood, he began to embrace a religion of friendship with Father God and his fellow humanity. Of course, simpler, rapture-less friendship with God, while much more functional for his own spiritual development than the revivalism of his childhood, neither emphasized the essential estrangement of humanity and God, nor a personal new birth as its remedy.[105]

Paralleling this personal transition, mid-nineteenth-century philosophies of justice were dissolving the revivalist notion of eternal punishment.[106] Likewise, new scientific research was fretting away the

---

102. Gladden, *Recollections*, 10. While Gladden does not offer a year for this event, the immediate context suggests that he was probably five years old.

103. Ibid., 11.

104. Ibid., 12.

105. Youngs states that Gladden's new theology was a far cry from that of his Puritan ancestors.

106. In Cameron (ed.), *Universalism and the Doctrine of Hell*, David J. Powys offers the four stages in the dissipation of the doctrine of hell in the nineteenth century. First, new philosophical themes in the nineteenth century led to questions concerning

cosmologies and anthropologies with which the revivalists had worked for decades. Gladden, seizing upon and developing these new ideas, moved himself and as much of Congregationalism as he could away from the revivalistic religion of his childhood.

Hills had no way of seeing that the engines that would eventually lift Congregationalism completely out of revivalism were already well in motion by the 1870s, the first years of his ministry. As big a fight as he and others offered, Congregationalism lacked a centralized polity that could do anything to stop or even slow or redirect this trend.

It should be noted clearly that Hills and Gladden *were* moving along trajectories that would eventually land them in opposing positions in what Jean Miller Schmidt calls the "two-party system" in American Protestantism.[107] From Hills' perspective, however, the issues dividing these two were not, as Schmidt argues, the difference between public and private expressions of piety. Both Hills and Gladden promoted social and personal pieties, but disagreed on the exact parameters and shape of both.

Thus, while he rejected Gladden and much of his social gospel, Hills' rationale for doing so had nothing to do with a divorce of individualistic and social pieties. Hills' contention with Gladden was that he was proclaiming social and individual pieties with a contemptuous regard for revivalist means and doctrines.[108] In order to see more clearly,

---

the duration of divine punishment. Quality was next to be modified. Third were the questions of purpose. New transformational penal philosophies began to be applied heavenward. Powys states, "Penal practices and philosophies which had come to be regarded as unenlightened in the human arena could hardly be ascribed to God." Powys continues by questioning, if the impenitent is beyond reform, then what purpose does his eternal punishment serve? The final category to undergo reconsideration was finality. "The other challenges had had the potential to effect modification, but this challenge had the capacity not merely to modify but to totally dislodge the traditional view." Cameron (ed.), *Universalism and Hell*, 118–22.

107. Schmidt, *Souls or Social Order*. In this work, Schmidt attempts to explain why American Protestantism seems to be split into two parts. As the title implies, she sees one side working largely for the saving of individual souls while the other side works to reform the structures of society.

108. In his biography *Washington Gladden: Prophet of the Social Gospel*, Jacob Henry Dorn presents Gladden as more open to revivalism than Gladden's own words in *Recollections* suggest. Dorn writes, "Gladden, it is important to recognize, was not opposed to evangelism or even to the work of professional evangelists . . . Throughout his career he rather consistently supported such evangelists, or revivalists." Of course, Dorn continues by naming a very small list of revivalists with whom Gladden was willing to

however, that Hills' issues with Gladden are not simply the early twentieth century, "conservative" evangelical dislike of the social gospel, another illustration is in order—Hills' relationship with Horace Bushnell.

The issues at stake for Hills can be seen clearly in his words of affirmation for Bushnell. In two places in his pastoral sermons Hills feels enough resonance with Bushnell's religion to quote him positively. In 1885, Hills wrote "Individualism in the Church," an important enough sermon for him that he re-preached it twelve times by his records and reprinted portions of it in *Dying to Live*. In the sermon, Hills' quote of Bushnell takes up nearly three pages with the introductory phrase, "As Dr. Bushnell has wisely written . . ."[109] Of course, use of the adverb "wisely" is only a shadow of the adjective Hills offers Bushnell in his 1881 sermon series to young people. In one of the sermons in this series, Hills quotes Bushnell, prefixing the quote with the words, "The saintly Horace Bushnell wrote . . ."[110]

One is easily struck by the apparent contradiction Hills illustrates by quoting the "wise" and "saintly" Bushnell in his early sermons, while blasting his colleague, Washington Gladden.[111] For Hills, of course, there

---

work. The first listed evangelist is Dwight Moody, whose "candor and gentleness and [whose] central theme of the love of God" Gladden admired. The second listed evangelist is B. Fay Mills, "one of the first and perhaps the only professional revivalist ever to break with the emphasis upon individual reform and to preach primarily a doctrine of social responsibility and social action." Dorn's third listed evangelist is Lyman Abbott. Of course, Dorn quotes a letter from Abbott to Gladden stating that he preached on the topics that would involve "'an appeal to the will, a definite acceptance of Christ, and a definite choice of the Christian life,'" but that would be in the context of the Social Gospel and liberal theology." After listing a very narrow band of evangelists with whom Gladden would work, Dorn admits, "Despite this record of support, Gladden always had reservations about revivalism . . . He supported them [Moody and J. Wilbur Chapman] in spite of some of their views . . . Moreover, Gladden always felt that the popular fascination with revivals led to the neglect of other means of evangelism. In *The Christian Pastor* (1898) Gladden . . . contended that revivalism had a disastrous effect on more gradualistic, and what should be more normal, methods of winning and nurturing souls." Dorn next continues by retelling the story of Gladden's feud with Billy Sunday. Dorn, *Washington Gladden*, 379, 80, 81, and 82. Thus, in order to take Dorn's words that Gladden was not "opposed to evangelism or even to the work of professional evangelists" at face-value, one would have to add a strong qualification. Gladden worked with professional evangelists whose doctrines and means stood significantly in continuity with his own.

109. Hills, "Individualism in the Church," 6, 6–8.

110. Hills, "To Young People, 'Amusements,'" 10.

111. For some of the larger story of the close relationship between Gladden and

is no contradiction. As we have seen with every other figure and movement in this chapter, for Hills, the distinctions center completely around the degree to which others flout his revivalist doctrines or means.

It was Hills' habit much of the time to carry a bound ledger of blank pages everywhere he went, filling it with sermon illustrations and stories as he encountered them. In one such ledger of hundreds of stories and illustrations Hills scribes an interesting anecdote about Horace Bushnell and revivalism. The story goes: "There was a revival in Yale College many years ago, and Horace Bushnell stood in the way. He was one of the most popular professors in the College, and hundreds were waiting to see what he would do. He went to his room to think over it. A voice said to him: 'Horace Bushnell, what do you believe?' 'Well, I believe in the eternal difference between right and wrong.' 'Then take your stand on the side of right.' He accepted X, and over 600 followed him over into the kingdom of God."[112]

Another example Hills offers of Bushnell's openness to revivalism is in *The Life of Charles G. Finney*. Hills writes:

> In the early winter of 1851–2, Mr. Finney was invited to Hartford, Conn. There was at the time a lack of unity between Dr. Hawes and Dr. Bushnell, the two leading Congregational pastors, on questions of theology. Dr. Hawes did not think Dr. Bushnell sound on the doctrine of the atonement. Finney was laboring in a third Congregational Church. The two brethren attended the meetings of Finney, and saw that God was manifestly present, and they agreed to lay aside their differences so as not to be a stumbling-block in the way of the salvation of men. From that time there was a good degree of cordiality, and the work spread through the city.[113]

We see in Hills' contrasting opinions of Gladden and Bushnell the issues at stake for him. Hills is not ill-disposed to the social gospel in and of itself as many later evangelicals would be.[114] His rejection or acceptance of the social gospel is determined entirely by the individual proponent's rejection or acceptance of revivalism. Bushnell, who at

---

Bushnell see Youngs, *The Congregationalists*, 170–71.

112. Hills, "Ledger," 51.

113. Hills, *Life of Finney*, 163.

114. It is likely that his postmillennialist attitude saved him from a more flat-footed, fundamentalist rejection of the social gospel.

least Hills *believed* stood in continuity with revivalism, was read and generally accepted by him. Gladden, who was moving himself and Congregationalism away from revivalism as fast as he could, was likely never read and certainly thoroughly dismissed by Hills.

Of course, the differences between Hills and Gladden were brought to an acute pitch when, in December 1895, Hills was baptized with the Holy Spirit and began a serious relationship with *holiness* revivalism. This adaption engaged Hills with the poor and marginalized to an even larger degree and put him on a different social trajectory than Gladden.

Of course, illustrated in both Hills and Gladden's ministries is a deep, compassionate concern for the empowerment of the poor. Both were major advocates of socially-relevant gospels. Yet, both approached the task differently and worked for different kinds of disciples and heavenly kingdoms.

The essential difference between Gladden and Hills is the means and the end of ministry to and among the poor. Gladden, moving out of what, by the end of the nineteenth century, had become socially-peripheral revivalism, embraced the changing scientific, sociological, and philosophical currents in order to secure a more mainstream, and to some extent political, ministry. From this position, he helped accomplish some significant social and political changes.[115]

Hills, on the other hand, was working for a teetotaling millennium through the Christianization of Christianity and the conversion of the majority of persons in the world. His theology smacked of the radical themes of perfectionism and millennialism and held fast to other themes like hell, all of which were already losing credibility and functionality in mainstream thought. Thus, while both were ministering to the poor in the same denomination, and while both were unafraid of political measures to secure reform, Hills and Gladden were in fact worlds apart and following increasingly divergent religious and social trajectories.

To put it succinctly, the basic difference between their respective ministries to and among the poor was in their personal trajectories. Gladden was moving from the social periphery, with its methods and ideas, to the centers of society and politics; Hills was moving farther into the revivalist and holiness movements and, therefore, deeper into an older identity that was becoming more and more socially marginalized. Again, the cross-currents within Congregationalism placed Hills

---

115. Cf. Youngs, *The Congregationalists*, 168–80.

in an awkward position—he was plunging deeper into revivalism after 1895 just as his denomination was climbing out of it. Those like Hills whose religious identities and ministries were grounded in revivalist doctrines and means found themselves gradually pushed within their own denomination to the periphery. A diminishing number of pulpits were open to them. Fewer Christians were willing to mourn at the altar in the hope of transformation as such outwardly visible expressions were replaced by less conspicuously demanding forms.[116]

It is ironic, therefore, that just when Congregationalism was the least likely in decades to accept revivalism, Hills was embracing an even more radical form of it. In 1895, he added what Congregationalists might consider to be the most peculiar of all revivalist themes to his repertoire, a Methodist doctrine of cleansing by the pentecostal baptism of the Holy Spirit.

Of course, even in 1895, Hills, who was then serving as an evangelist for the Congregational Church, still deeply embraced the positive hope of the holiness stay-inners. Indeed, he nurtured this hope for seventeen years, working to Christianize Christianity in his beloved Congregational Church. Then, suddenly it seems from his autobiographical account, Hills made a significant switch of identity and joined the Pentecostal Church of the Nazarene. The reason behind this had mostly to do with changes within Congregationalism.

By the end of the first two decades of the twentieth century, Congregationalism had moved past the doctrines and means of revivalism enough that Hills considered his church entirely unsalvageable. Youngs offers a picture of the kind of secularized religion that Gladden and Bushnell's theology produced in twentieth-century Congregationalism. He writes:

> Arthur Cushman McGiffert, Jr. . . . suggested the atmosphere that pervaded most Congregational households during the early twentieth century, when he described his own background. At the seminary he was the first faculty member who had been raised in a home which "took theological liberalism for granted." The family held weekly prayers and said grace at meals . . . but he had been "largely ignorant" of orthodox Christian thought until he entered seminary, where he studied the traditional theology

---

116. This seems to be the very issue underlying Hills' writing of the 1885 sermon "Individualism in the Church."

> "much as he studied Buddhism or Hinduism, as an almost novel form of theological interpretation"... As an example of the extremes to which religious rationalism had gone, McGiffert noted that "non-theistic humanists" could be found on the faculties of many seminaries. They were men who in reaction against "a popularly misconceived orthodoxy, to which they were exposed in their youth, had swung the full arc of the theological pendulum away"... Many had been raised in a liberal theological tradition that tended to ignore sin and conversion.[117]

Perceiving a complete loss of the religion of his youth and early ministry in only thirty years time, Hills eventually came out of Congregationalism for two simple reasons. First, Congregationalism, by the second decade of the twentieth century had virtually no place left for revivalists, (much less *holiness* revivalists). Second, Congregationalist polity left Hills and those in his or similar camps powerless to affect change.

In *Fundamental Christian Theology*, one can hear a hint of residual frustration between the lines as Hills systematizes a polity that for at least the first fifty-five years of his life he did not embrace. In his chapter on "The Church and its Sacraments," Hills echoes the *Congregational Quarterly* from decades prior. He writes:

> It is the duty of a church or denomination to silence any teacher or preacher within its pale who proclaims doctrines contrary to the accepted standards. If a preacher or theological professor changes his views and comes to accept doctrines contrary to those of his church, let him withdraw, like an honest man, and join himself to those of a like faith with his own. To stay in a church and disrupt it by sowing infidelity to its articles of faith, or to draw a salary from trust-funds contributed by godly men to propagate the Gospel of faith in a Divine Redeemer, and then to teach a Christless infidelity, is to be another Judas Iscariot and a wolf in sheep's clothing. We have seen colleges and churches and a theological seminary blotted out by such conduct... Every minister is commanded by God to "contend earnestly for the faith once delivered unto the saints," not to destroy it. Whoever has fallen low enough to seek to destroy it, should step down and out of the ministry. If he does not, he should be put out of it. This is no violation of Christian liberty, or any right of man.[118]

---

117. Youngs, *The Congregationalists*, 185–86.
118. Hills, *Fundamental Christian Theology*, vol. 2, 292.

In these words, one can clearly hear the second reason Hills gave up his stay-inner identity. When, in Hills' estimate, most of the long-treasured revivalist doctrines and means began to be distorted in Congregationalism, and the polity of his church was powerless to excise the heretics, Hills adopted a new polity that was more centralized and powerful. The Pentecostal Church of the Nazarene, which had recently been formed by many others experiencing similar ecclesiastical frustrations,[119] seemed Hills' only choice.

Thus, while Hills is disappointingly silent in "Autobiography" on the reasons he came out, a careful reading between the lines of his systematic ecclesiology and of Congregationalist history suggests that he switched affiliation because he wanted to be part of a movement that affirmed revivalism. Since it was impossible for him to make any difference in his church by political means, when his platform as a revivalist preacher was all but taken from him, Hills despaired at his inability to affect change. He thus did what so many others with the holiness-revivalist stamp in that generation did—he left his church to join the revivalist Pentecostal Church of the Nazarene.

SUMMARY

Chapters 4 and 5 defined the revivalist canon of doctrine and means against which Hills measured every theologian and movement. This chapter has shown how Hills applied this canon in critique of the Keswick, fundamentalist, and Pentecostal movements and the Congregational Churches of America. In each case, we have seen that Hills' friendship or ferocity toward other theologians and movements related directly to his perception of the other's distance from his vision of revivalist Christianity. Adamant that his revivalist doctrines and means were the clearest representation of Christianity and the only path to global conversion and reform, Hills tirelessly practiced his religion and worked against those who disparaged it.

---

119. It was not untypical at all for early Nazarenes to find themselves in the company of come-outers who came out for issues of church government and polity. The founder of the Pentecostal Church of the Nazarene, Phineas F. Bresee, came out of the Methodist Episcopal Church as much for organizational reasons as for doctrinal.

7

Conclusion

WHILE THE MAJORITY OF this study has aimed at understanding A. M. Hills better, the implications of this study are in fact applicable far beyond the mere interpretation of the man alone. Since he was one of the key leaders who helped engender the splintering of revivalism and American Protestantism at the turn of the twentieth century, Hills' life and accomplishments, doctrines and means, and especially battles and alliances reveal at least one of the main issues that was at stake in the divisions. Indeed, as it is arguable that Hills was *the* key leader of one of the revivalist splinter groups—the Eradicationist-Holiness Movement—it is fair to say that understanding the mindset and rationale underlying his small role in the fracturing of Protestantism is necessary to understand part of the whole.

HILLS AND THE "TWO-PARTY SYSTEM" OF AMERICAN PROTESTANTISM

In the above mentioned 1923 *Herald of Holiness* article, "A Creedless Christianity Impossible," A. M. Hills makes an interesting assertion concerning the dividing of American Protestantism after the turn of the century. To quote the article again: "The adherents of Christianity are rapidly dividing into *two camps*, the creed lovers and the creed haters. In other words there are those who unite in believing something positive, that can be stated in definite words; and also those who do not believe in anything definite, and object to their conglomeration of infidel negations being put in any form of statement."[1]

A considerably earlier proto-statement of what Jean Miller Schmidt would later call the "two-party" system in American Protestantism,[2] Hills' differentiation in context of his whole life and works offers a critique of Schmidt's explanation of what split turn-of-the-century Christianity.

In chapter 6, we saw that the autobiographies of A. M. Hills and Washington Gladden together offer a microcosmic picture of the split in early twentieth-century Protestantism into two parties. While both originally came from the same denomination and were raised under relatively similar religious conditions, from the point of their college education forward, they moved along vastly different trajectories that eventually landed them in opposite sides of the Protestant split. Gladden helped establish and develop the Social Gospel movement, while Hills remained an evangelistic revivalist all his life.

What *neither* of the two exemplifies, however, is a separation of the social and personal spheres. Indeed, it is not possible to suggest that either, at any point in their careers, separated their private from their public pieties. This fact, of course, challenges Schmidt's placement of the relative dividing line between the two parties, separating soul-winners from societal transformers. As we saw in chapter 6, what put Hills and Gladden on differing trajectories was something altogether different— their attitudes toward the revivalistic religion of their early years.

As was demonstrated in the previous chapter, when he spoke of the "creed lovers" and the "creed haters," Hills' context is his defense of the *revivalist* creed and its corresponding means. While on the surface the use of the word "creed" seems to suggest that his issues are merely doctrinal, Hills' objection to those of the other camp is actually far more than just that their ideas do not match up with his. As we saw exemplified in Hills' contention with Gladden and the Congregational Churches of America, the other camp's rejection of Hills' creed was actually much more than this—it was a wholesale rejection of the vision, doctrine, and means inherent the revivalistic religion.

What Hills offers the discussion concerning the two parties, therefore, is his conviction that the line between the two fell along acceptance and rejection of nineteenth-century revivalism. Thus, were Hills used

1. Hills, "Creedless Christianity Impossible," 3. Italics mine.
2. Schmidt, *Souls or Social Order*.

as a hermeneutical lens through which to explain the two-party system, one would have to conclude that the line does not fall between those merely interested in saving souls and others working to bring about transformed structures to society. At least from his perspective, Hills reveals that the line is best described as separating a different two groups: those who embraced revivalistic means and doctrines for the transformation of individuals and society according to the revivalists' vision and those who rejected the dominance of nineteenth-century revivalism to embrace various other methods and ideas for the transformation of souls and the social order according to the visions of new movements.

A clear example of this is seen in *Fundamental Christian Theology*. In his chapter "Higher Criticism Continued," Hills differentiates between those who reverence the Bible and those who "take our Bible, written by holy men 'as they were moved by the Holy Ghost,' and hand back to us a purely human 'scrap-book of anonymous compilations' with which the Holy Spirit had nothing whatever to do." Continuing on about "them," Hills quotes an unnamed source, "'Modern thinkers reject the strictly miraculous everywhere. Hence they reject the authority of the Scriptures. The incarnation is totally unintelligible . . . With the incarnation will also disappear the doctrine of the Trinity and the Atonement.'"[3]

Hills immediately continues by defining "them" even more specifically. He next quotes two unnamed professors at unnamed schools. They write: "Whiskey brings temporary insanity, and so does a revival of religion. This is simply a form of drunkenness, no more worthy of respect than the drunkard in the ditch." "Such language," says another, "is too mild, religious revivalism is a social bane more dangerous to society than drunkenness. As a sot, man falls below the brute; as a revivalist, he sinks lower than the sot."[4] Contrasting this position on revivalism, Hills simply responds, "Think of Wesley, Finney and Moody!"[5] In these phrases, we see clearly Hills' differentiation between "us" and "them." In alliance with Hills are Wesley, Finney, and Moody, four men who perhaps have little more in common than the fact that they were all leaders of revivals. Against this alliance, Hills pits two unnamed professors, whose opinions of religious revival and revivalism could not have been lower.

3. Hills, *Fundamental Christian Theology*, vol. 1, 172.
4. Ibid., 173.
5. Ibid.

In defense of a Hills-centered critique of Schmidt's thesis, we have already seen where the natural lines of alliances fell in the first decades of the twentieth century. As uneasy as the "strange bedfellows" may have felt or still feel allying themselves with one another, the underlying revivalist identities of the Holiness, Keswick, and fundamentalist movements were often enough for them to consider the others in the same camp, even if disagreeing on the exact particulars of doctrine.

The ease with which the laity in these movements crossed (and indeed still cross) back and forth further illustrates the reality of alliance between revivalists, even pulling the Pentecostals into Hills' camp. As was stated in the previous chapter, there were no clear lines between the revivalist movements emerging out of late nineteenth and even early twentieth-century revivalism. Revivalists who were fundamentalists, Keswickians, Pentecostals, and Holiness advocates crossed the semipermeable boundaries of these movements without a passport, so to speak. Maintaining at least partially overlapping revivalist creeds and very similar means, members of these movements related to each other more like neighboring colors in the spectrum than islands in a chain. Indeed, the only place Hills drew an absolute line was where he felt revivalism was rejected or counterfeited.[6]

Our analysis of Hills, likewise, calls into question the somewhat populist assumption that American Christianity is divided into "conservatives" and "liberals." While even Hills' own language, on the surface, seems to lean toward such over-simplistic designations, a more comprehensive analysis of his thought in its context reveals the underlying motive for his rhetoric. Hills was a revivalist, whose entire system of doctrines and means was built theologically on a conception of the fall of humanity and its restoration through the resurrected God-man. This restoration, Hills was convinced, is most naturally appropriated individually through new birth and strengthened by sanctification. Many of these ideas, however, were often thoroughly denied by emerging anti-revivalist theologians and movements.

The perspective that even a comprehensive analysis of A. M. Hills offers is, of course, a limited one. As a study of only one interstitial figure in a much larger story, this book does not touch on every aspect of early

---

6. Even in drawing the line to keep the Pentecostal "counterfeiters" out, however, holiness, Pentecostal, Pentecostal-holiness, and present-day Charismatic folk still regularly cross the border, so to speak.

twentieth-century American Christianity. Obviously, Schmidt's definitions will continue to stand as a partial way of understanding certain facets of the split of American Protestantism. Nevertheless, this analysis of A. M. Hills, when used as a hermeneutical lens through which to interpret the same, offers the scholarly discussion a line that stands between the revivalists and the *anti*-revivalists. From Hills' perspective, when American Christianity split at the turn of the twentieth century, on the one side were all those whose underlying identities were permeated with revivalism. On the other were those who were *rejecting* revivalism and its means and doctrines. With Hills were those who allied themselves with revivalism's methods and ideas; against him were those whose means and doctrines opposed the revivalist worldview. A unique perspective, it is perhaps only possible to acquire from A. M. Hills' interstitial vantage point.

Bibliography

"A History of the Holiness Movement in Great Britain." Connect World-Wide; available from http://connectworld-wide.com/chc/hiles/.htm
Barnard, John. *From Evangelicalism to Progressivism at Oberlin College, 1866–1917.* Columbus, OH: Ohio State University Press, 1969.
Bassett, Paul Merritt. "The Fundamentalist Leavening of the Holiness Movement, 1914–1940 The Church of the Nazarene: A Case Study." *Wesleyan Theological Journal* 13.1 (1978) 65–91.
———. "The Interplay of Christology and Ecclesiology in the Theology of the Holiness Movement." *Wesleyan Theological Journal* 16.2 (1981) 79–94.
———. "Study in the Theology of the Early Holiness Movement." *Methodist History* (April 1975) 61–87.
Bozeman, Theodore Dwight. *Protestants in the Age of Science: The Baconian Ideal and Ante-bellum American Religious Thought.* Chapel Hill, NC: University of North Carolina Press, 1977.
Brown, Kenneth O. "Leadership in the National Holiness Association with Special Reference to Eschatology, 1867–1919." Ph.D. diss., Drew University, 1988.
Cameron, Nigel M. de S., ed. *Universalism and the Doctrine of Hell.* Grand Rapids: Baker, 1991.
Catalogue of Illinois Holiness University. Olivet Nazarene University Archives, Olivet Nazarene University, Bourbonnais, IL.
Catalogue of the Officers and Students in Yale College, 1871–72. New Haven, CT: Tuttle, Morehouse, and Taylor, 1871.
Catalogue of the Officers and Students in Yale College, 1872–73. New Haven, CT: Tuttle, Morehouse, and Taylor, 1872.
Catalogue of the Officers and Students in Yale College, 1873–74. New Haven, CT: Tuttle, Morehouse, and Taylor, 1873.
Cochran, William. *Simplicity of Moral Actions.* Alethea in Heart Ministries; available from http://truthinheart.com/EarlyOberlinCD/CD/Philosophy/SMA1.htm; Internet.
Corbett, C. T. *Pioneer Builders.* Kansas City, MO: Nazarene, 1979.
Cowles, Henry. "The Millennium." Alethea in Heart Ministries; available from http://truthinheart.com/EarlyOberlinCD/CD/Cowles//Rev/Millenium.html; Internet.
Cowles, Henry. "The Millennium.—No. 1, Introductory." *The Oberlin Evangelist* III.4 (17 February 1841) 28.

Dayton, Donald W. "Dispensationalism and the Emergence of Fundamentalism among American Baptists." Keynote address presented a conference on Methodism and the Fragmentation of American Protestantism, 29 September 1995.

———. "Millennial View and Social Reform in Nineteenth-Century America." In *The Coming Kingdom: Essays in American Millennialism and Eschatology*, edited by M. Darrol Bryant and Donald W. Dayton, 131–47. Barrytown, NY: International Foundation, 1983.

———. *The Theological Roots of Pentecostalism*. Metuchen, NJ: Scarecrow, 1987.

Dorn, Jacob Henry. *Washington Gladden: Prophet of the Social Gospel*. Columbus, OH: Ohio State University Press, 1966.

Fairchild, James H. *Elements of Theology*. Oberlin, OH: Goodrich, 1892.

———. *Moral Philosophy; or the Science of Obligation*. New York: Sheldon, 1869.

Finney, Charles. *Finney's Systematic Theology*. Reprint. Minneapolis, MN: Bethany House, 1994.

———. *Lectures on Systematic Theology*. Alethea in Heart Ministries; available from http://truthinheart.com/EarlyOberlinCD/CD/Finney/Theology/stcon.htm; Internet.

———. *Revival Lectures*. Reprint. Grand Rapids: Revell, 1993.

First Catalog of Texas Holiness University, Greenville, Texas for Years 1900–1901. Fred Floyd Archives, Southern Nazarene University, Bethany, OK.

Fisher, George Park. *History of the Christian Church*. New York: Scribner, 1887.

———. *The History of Christian Doctrine*. New York: Scribner, 1896.

———. *Manual of Christian Evidences*. Meadville, PA: Flood and Vincent, 1892.

———. *The Reformation*. New York: Scribner, 1906.

Fletcher, Robert S. *A History of Oberlin College; from its Foundation through the Civil War*. New York: Arno, 1971.

Forrest Gump. Directed by Robert Zemeckis. 1994; Hollywood, CA: Paramount Pictures.

Gladden, Washington. *Recollections*. Boston: Mifflin, 1909.

Gresham, L. Paul. *Waves against Gibraltar*. Bethany, OK: Southern Nazarene University Press, 1992.

Hamilton, James E. "Academic Orthodoxy and the Arminianizing of American Theology." *Wesleyan Theological Journal* 9.1, (1974) 52–59.

Harris, Samuel. *The Self Revelation of God*. New York: Scribner, 1887.

Hills, A. M. "A. M. Hills." In *Pentecostal Messengers*, 33–42. Cincinnati: Revivalist Office, 1898.

———. "Autobiography, 1932 (?)." The Nazarene Archives, Kansas City, MO.

———. *Backsliders and Worldly Christians*. Salem, OH: Schmul, 2004.

———. "Christ Gracious." The Nazarene Archives, Kansas City, MO.

———. *Christian Education and Anglo-Israel: Two Addresses*. Chicago: Christian Witness, 1906.

———. *The Cleansing Baptism*. Manchester, UK: Star Hall, 1910.

———. "The Coefficients of Soul Safety." Olivet Nazarene University Archives, Olivet Nazarene University, Bourbonnais, IL.

———. "Commentary on the Book of Romans." The Nazarene Archives, Kansas City, MO.

———. "Commentary on the Gospel of John." The Nazarene Archives, Kansas City, MO.

———. "A Creedless Christianity Impossible." *Herald of Holiness* 12 (October 17, 1923) 3–4.

———. "Creeds and Life." Olivet Nazarene University Archives, Olivet Nazarene University, Bourbonnais, IL.

———. "Creeds–their Value." The Nazarene Archives, Kansas City, MO.

———. *Dying to Live*. Cincinnati: God's Revivalist Office, 1905.

———. *Eradication of Carnality: Why We Teach It*. Kansas City, MO: Nazarene, 192_.

———. *The Establishing Grace*. Kansas City, MO: Nazarene, 1937.

———. *Food for Lambs. Or, Leading Children to Christ*. Grand Rapids: Alethea in Heart Ministries, 2002.

———. "Friendship with Christ." The Nazarene Archives, Kansas City, MO.

———. *Fundamental Christian Theology*. Pasadena, CA: Kinne, 1931.

———. *Fundamental Christian Theology: Abridged Edition*. Pasadena, CA: Kinne, 1932.

———. "God will Judge the World," *The Portage County Democrat* (7 April 1875).

———. "God's Question Answered." Olivet Nazarene University Archives, Olivet Nazarene University, Bourbonnais, IL.

———. *A Hero of Life and Faith: Or, Life of Rev. Martin Wells Knapp*. Cincinnati: Knapp, 1902.

———. "Higher Critics, Unscientific Infidels." *Herald of Holiness* 1 (November 13, 1912) 6.

———. *Holiness*. Cincinnati: Office of God's Revivalist, 1905.

———. *Holiness and Power for the Church and the Ministry*. Cincinnati: Office of God's Revivalist, 1897.

———. *Holiness and Power for the Church and the Ministry*. Manchester, UK: Star Hall, 1913.

———. *Holiness in the Book of Romans*. Kansas City, MO: Beacon Hill, 1950.

———. *Holiness: Not a Modern Fad Run by Cranks*. In *Sparks from Seven Hammers*, 73–90. Salem, OH: Schmul, 2004.

———. *Homiletics and Pastoral Theology*. Kansas City, MO: Nazarene, 1929.

———. "Individualism in the Church—A Want in Modern Life." Olivet Nazarene University Archives, Olivet Nazarene University, Bourbonnais, IL.

———. "Lectures to Young People. VI. 'Amusements.'" The Nazarene Archives, Kansas City, MO.

———. "Ledger." Olivet Nazarene University Archives, Olivet Nazarene University, Bourbonnais, IL.

———. *Life and Labors of Mrs. Mary A. Woodbridge*. Ravenna, OH: Woodbridge, 1895.

———. *Life of Charles G. Finney*. Cincinnati: Office of "God's Revivalist," 1902.

———. "No. 2- Resisting the Devil and Drawing Nigh to God," The Nazarene Archives, Kansas City, MO.

———. *Phineas Bresee, D.D.: A Life Sketch*. Kansas City, MO: Nazarene, 1930.

———. *Pentecostal Light*. Cincinnati: God's Revivalist Office, 1898.

———. *Pentecost Rejected; And the Effect on the Church*. Cincinnati: God's Revivalist Office, 1902.

———. "The Responsibilities and Relations of Life." The Nazarene Archives, Kansas City, MO.

———. *Romans and Sanctification*. Manchester, UK: Star Hall, 1910.

———. *Sanctification: What it is and How Obtained*. Nashville: Pentecostal Mission, 19_.

———. *Satan's Devices*. Manchester, UK: Star Hall, n.d.
———. *Scriptural Holiness and Keswick Teaching Compared*. Manchester, UK: Star Hall, 1912.
———. *The Secret of Spiritual Power*. Kansas City, MO.: Beacon Hill Press, 1952.
———. "Sermons to Young People: No. 1: Books and Readings." The Nazarene Archives, Kansas City, MO.
———. "The Solemn Alternative." Olivet Nazarene University Archives, Olivet Nazarene University, Bourbonnais, IL.
———. "Temperance Address." The Nazarene Archives, Kansas City, MO.
———. *The Tobacco Vice*. Cincinnati: Revivalist Office, 1904.
———. *The Tongues Movement*. Manchester, UK: Star Hall, 1910.
———. "Total Abstinence." *The Portage County Democrat*, 28 April 1875.
———. "To Young People—Lessons from the Life of Lot." The Nazarene Archives, Kansas City, MO.
———. "Turning Back." The Nazarene Archives, Kansas City, MO.
———. *The Uttermost Salvation*. Kansas City, MO: Nazarene, 1927.
———. *The Whosoever Gospel*. Cincinnati: Knapp, 1899.
———. "What is Man?" *Pentecostal Advocate* 15.11 (March 14, 1912).
———. "What it is to be a Christian?" The Nazarene Archives, Kansas City, MO.
———. "Who was it that was Progressing Backwards?" *Herald of Holiness* 10 (February 22, 1922) 4–5.
Hunter, F. M. *Women Preachers*. With an introduction by A. M. Hills. Dallas: Berachah, 1905.
The Illinois Holiness University 1909–1910. Olivet Nazarene University Archives, Olivet Nazarene University, Bourbonnais, IL.
Ingersol, Stanley. "Strange Bedfellows: The Nazarenes and Fundamentalism." *Wesleyan Theological Journal* 40 (Fall, 2005) 123–41.
Jernigan, C. B. *Pentecostal Advocate* 15.11 (March 14, 1912).
Keen, S. A. *Faith Papers*. Chicago: The Christian Witness, 1919.
Ketcheson, W. G. *Gems of Truth*. With a preface by A. M. Hills. Berne, IN: Published by the Author, n.d.
Lodahl, Michael. *All Things Necessary to our Salvation*. San Diego: Point Loma, 2004.
Mahan, Asa. *Autobiography: Intellectual, Moral, and Spiritual*. Alethea in Heart Ministries; available from http://truthinheart.com/EarlyOberlinCD/CD/Mahan/Auto.htm; Internet.
———. *Doctrine of the Will*. St. Fenwich, MI: Alethea in Heart Ministries, 2003.
Marsden, George. *Fundamentalism and American Culture*. Oxford: Oxford University Press, 1980.
McClendon, James. W. *Biography as Theology: How Life Stories can make Today's Theology*. Philadelphia: Trinity, 1990.
McWilliams, H. E. "Rev. A. M. Hills, D.D. LL.D.: A Life Sketch, 1936." The Nazarene Archives, Kansas City, MO.
Metz, Rudolf. *A Hundred Years of British Philosophy*. London: Allen & Unwin, 1950.
Miller, Perry. *The Life of the Mind in America*. New York: Harcourt, Brace & World, 1965.
Mozart, Wolfgang Amadeus. *Don Giovanni*.
Palmer, Phoebe. *Four Years in the Old World*. New York: Foster & Palmer, 1866.
———. *The Gift of Power Received by Faith*. New York: Palmer, 1868.
———. *The Promise of the Father*. Salem, OH: Schmul, 1981.

Peters, John Leland. *Christian Perfection and American Methodism*. Grand Rapids: Asbury, 1985.
Phipps, Paul T. "A. M. Hills, Modernism, and the Rise of Fundamentalism or A. M. Hills and the Modernist-Fundamentalist Controversy." Research Essay, The Nazarene Archives, Kansas City, MO.
Porter, Noah. *The Elements of Intellectual Science*. New York: Scribner, 1886.
———. *Human Intellect: With an Introduction Upon Psychology and the Soul*. New York: Scribner, 1868.
Quanstrom, Mark R. *A Century of Holiness Theology: The Doctrine of Entire Sanctification in the Church of the Nazarene 1905–2004*. Kansas City, MO: Beacon Hill, 2004.
Sandeen, Earnest. *The Roots of Fundamentalism: British and American Millennarianism, 1800–1930*. Chicago: University of Chicago Press, 1970.
Schmidt, George P. *The Liberal Arts College: A Chapter in American Cultural History*. New Brunswick, NJ: Rutgers University Press, 1957.
Schmidt, Jean Miller. *Souls or the Social Order: The Two-Party System in American Protestantism*. Brooklyn, NY: Carlson, 1991.
Starkey, Marion L. *The Congregational Way*. Garden City, NY: Doubleday, 1966.
Sweeney, Douglas A. *Nathaniel Taylor, New Haven Theology, and the Legacy of Jonathan Edwards*. Oxford: Oxford University Press, 2003.
Torrey, R. A. *The Baptism with the Holy Spirit*. New York: Revell, 1895.
———. *The Fundamentals*. Available from http://www.xmission.com/~fidelis/; Internet.
Waller, Gary L. "The Historical and Theological Contribution of A. M. Hills to the Doctrine of Christian Perfection within the Church of the Nazarene." D.Min. thesis, San Francisco Theological Seminary, 1989.
Warfield, B. B. *Studies in Perfectionism*. Phillipsburg, NJ: Presbyterian and Reformed, 1958.
Youngs, J. William T. *The Congregationalists*. New York: Greenwood, 1990.

Index

Academic Orthodoxy, 16, 19, 34, 43, 58–62, 67, 74, 77, 82, 212–13
Alleghany, Pennsylvania, 23–27, 235
American Civil War, 14, 169, 186, 206
Anglo-Israel, the doctrine of, 57, 260
amusements, 17, 121–29, 134, 141, 149, 247
antinomianism, 94, 215–16
anti-slavery reform, 99, 100
altar, 36, 49, 112, 137, 224, 250
Arminianism, 16, 33, 59, 85, 86, 117, 220
Arnold, D. S., 35
Asbury College, 33–34, 171,
Asbury, Francis, 38
Asuza Street, 231

Bacon, Francis, 58–62, 82, 218,
baptism with the Holy Spirit. *See* Spirit baptism
Baptist Church, 9, 10, 53, 209, 217, 227, 244,
Barnard, John, 29
Bassett, Paul Merritt, 2, 3, 18, 216, 219, 225
Beecher, Lyman, 54,
Bethany College Church, 47,
Bethany Nazarene Rescue House, 47
billiards, 128, 134

Biola, 210, 213, 214
bondage of the will, 69, 85–88, 90
Booth, William and Catherine, 225
Bosworth, E. J., 29
Bowdoin College, 20, 58,
Brand, James, 29
Bresee, Phineas F., 47, 51, 182, 231, 233, 234, 252
Broadway Tabernacle, 24
Brown, Kenneth O., 233
"burned-over," 242
Bushnell, Horace, 151, 247–48, 250
Butler, G. S., 30

Calvinism, 33, 54, 68, 85–86, 89, 117, 245
Calvinist decrees, 33, 68–69, 85, 110, 117
Canaan, 182
card playing, 23, 32, 134, 180,
carnal Christian, 56, 161, 162, 164, 184, 185, 187, 192, 194, 195, 196, 202
causality, 85, 95
cause and effect. *See* causality
Central Holiness University, 40, 41, 43, 209, 211
Chapman, J. B., 3, 50, 51, 199
Chesbrough, Aaron, 11
Chesbrough, Alonzo, 12

265

Chesbrough, Julie Ann. *See* Hills, Julie Ann
Chesbrough, Merritt, 12
Christian Millennium, 17, 37, 62–66, 79, 97, 99, 103–7, 113, 144, 160, 173, 175, 181, 204–8, 249
Church of the Nazarene. *See* Pentecostal Church of the Nazarene
Church of the Redeemer, 24
circuit rider, 178
Civil War. *See* American Civil War
Clarke, Adam, 37, 38, 183
Cochran, William, 84
coefficients of safety, 132, 134–35
come-outer, 40, 233, 252
Committee of Seventeen, 23
Common Sense. *See* Scottish Common Sense Realism
Congregational Church, 4, 5, 7, 8, 9, 10, 12, 21, 23, 25, 27, 28, 29, 30, 32, 47, 48, 53, 107, 108, 112, 141, 156, 157, 160, 161, 170, 172, 173, 175, 201, 233–52
Congregational Churches of America. *See* Congregational Church
Congregationalism. *See* Congregational Church
Congregational Quarterly, 240, 241, 251
consciousness, 69, 72, 73, 74, 80, 81, 109, 152, 214, 242, 243
consecration, 29, 66, 89, 162, 163, 165, 169, 178, 238
conservatism, 218, 220, 247
"counterfeiters," 35, 36, 46, 228, 230, 232, 233, 256
Cowles, Henry, 4, 14, 54, 58, 62–67
Cowman, Charles E., 41

creeds, 107, 108, 140–44, 153, 176, 222, 239, 245, 253, 254, 256
Crossley, Ella D., 41, 42, 45, 46, 49
Crossley, Francis, 41
Currier, A. N., 29

dancing, 23, 32, 125, 126–28, 134, 180
Dayton, Donald W. 102, 186, 206, 207, 208, 209, 217, 223, 224, 225,
decrees. *See* Calvinist decrees
divine sanctions. *See* moral sanctions
doctrine of the will. *See* will, doctrine of the
demonstrated truths. *See* truths of demonstration
dispensationalism, 204, 205, 209, 213, 214, 217, 218, 220
double cure, 184, 189
Dowagiac, Michigan, 9, 12
Dunham, E. S., 32, 172
Dwight, Timothy, 21, 54, 83

Earle, A. B., 188, 224, 225
education reform, 99, 121, 131–32
Edwards, Jonathan, 13, 54, 86, 112, 225, 243
Ellis, John, 15
Elida, New Mexico, 44
epistemology, 5, 32, 58, 60, 80, 82, 158, 161, 171, 172, 175–83, 227, 230, 231
Eradicationism, 5, 36, 37, 38, 189–97, 201–4, 253
eschatology, 17, 44, 50, 57, 62, 63, 74, 102–16, 123, 124, 132, 135, 144, 145, 146, 147, 150, 151, 155, 159, 172–75, 181, 204–18, 220, 225
Estabrook, Joseph, 27

eternity principle, 114–16

Fairchild, James, H., 4, 14, 16, 31, 54, 58, 74, 76, 77–79, 80, 84, 89–92
faith, 25, 110, 117, 118, 136, 144, 149, 163, 167, 168, 169, 186, 188, 210, 233, 242, 251
Finney, Charles G., 4, 7, 12, 13, 14, 15, 16, 17, 18, 29, 31, 39, 53, 54, 55, 56, 58, 60, 62, 64, 67, 74, 75–77, 80, 84–89, 92, 93–98, 99, 100, 104, 106, 107, 108, 109, 110, 112, 115, 136, 137, 144, 156, 159, 160, 174, 182, 188, 193, 197, 198, 199, 206, 209, 217, 223, 224, 225, 243, 248, 255
first truths, 75–77, 95, 109
Fisher, George P., 21, 54,
Fletcher, John, 38, 41
Ford, Altha Alamanda. *See* Hills, Altha Alamanda
Ford, Henry, 6
Fowler, C. J., 33, 40
Four Days with God, 42, 46
Fox, George, 38
Francke, August Hermann, 38
Free Methodist Church, 8, 12, 169, 170
free will, 87, 90
Freischkorn, Hulda Jane. *See* Hills, Hulda Jane
full salvation, 43, 51, 167, 168, 187, 204
Fundamentalist Movement, 2, 3, 5, 11, 18, 193, 200, 204, 205, 209, 213, 214–26, 232, 248, 252, 256
future judgment, 102, 108–13, 117, 135, 141, 142, 145, 176
future reward, 88, 102, 108, 109, 110, 141, 142

Gladden, Washington, 25, 234–45, 245, 246, 247, 248, 249, 250, 254
global reform, 83, 135, 159
Glory Barn, 231
glossolalia. *See* tongues
Godbey, W. B., 177, 178, 224
Gordon, A. J., 37
Great Reversal, 215, 217
Greenville, Texas, 34
Gump, Forrest, 1, 2, 5

hamartiology, 183–84
Hanson, Paul, 206–7
Harris, Reader, 42
Harris, Samuel, 20, 54, 57
Harvard Seminary, 19, 55, 58, 59
Hatch, Mary A., 41, 42, 45, 46, 49
heathen classics. *See also* education reform
heaven, 56, 89, 94, 108, 110, 112, 116, 118, 153, 161, 163
hell, 89, 108, 110, 111, 112, 116, 121, 126, 129, 130, 131, 154, 194, 222, 229, 238, 241, 243–46, 249
Hendricks, A. O., 50
Herald of Holiness, 25, 39, 48, 50, 127, 212, 216, 221, 222, 235, 253
higher criticism, 25, 48, 221, 222, 230, 235, 241, 242, 255
Hills, Altha Alamanda, 21, 24
Hills, Amos B., 8,
Hills, Anna Althea, 23
Hills, Charles Finney, 224
Hills, Dwight Moody, 27, 224
Hills, Henry Cleveland, 8
Hills, Henry Merritt, 23
Hills, Hezekiah, 7–9, 53
Hills, Hulda Jane, 24, 51
Hills, James Aaron, 26, 43, 44, 199
Hills, Julie Ann, 8, 9, 10, 11, 12, 26,
Hills, Mary Woodbridge, 27

Hills, Nellie Ford, 23
Hills, William, 7
Holiness Movement, 3, 6, 32, 36, 37, 39, 42, 44, 57, 103, 104, 154, 156, 157, 158, 159, 161, 163, 164, 167, 170, 173, 181, 182, 183, 186, 201, 202, 203, 219, 223, 225, 226, 229, 231, 232, 233, 234, 249, 253
Holy Spirit baptism. *See* Spirit baptism
Huff, Will, 34, 40, 50
Hugo, Victor, 129

infidel education. *See* education reform
Ingersol, Stanley, 2, 3, 216, 220, 226
Inskip, John, 158
inerrancy, 214, 218, 220, 236
inspiration, the doctrine of, 25, 56, 73, 109, 130, 140, 142, 143, 178, 205, 214, 219, 220
intemperance, 23, 100, 104, 105, 114, 128, 129–30, 145
Iowa Holiness Association, 40

Jernigan, Charles B., 47,
Jordan River, 187
judgment. *See* future judgment

Keen, S. A., 31, 167, 168
Keswick Movement, 5, 36, 37, 45, 46, 182, 183, 184, 186, 187, 189, 194, 201–4, 224, 225, 226, 231, 252, 256,
Kilbourne, Ben, 41
King James Version of the Bible, 237
Kinne, C. J., 51
Knapp, Jacob, 243, 244
Knapp, Martin Wells, 32, 33, 39, 172,

laws of nature, 60, 61, 76, 83, 87, 95, 96,
laws of religion, 61, 66, 83, 88, 94, 95, 96, 98, 136,
liberal arts education, 35, 41, 209, 211, 212, 213, 225
liberalism, 3, 218, 219, 230, 233, 239, 247, 250, 251, 256
Lodahl, Michael, 2, 3, 219, 220
Lord, E. J., 48
Lowery, Asbury, 186

Madame Guyon, 38
Mahan, Asa, 4, 14, 16, 18, 22, 31, 58, 59, 67–74, 99, 115, 155, 159, 188, 243
Manchester, England, 41, 42,
"manhood," 211. *See also* "whole man"
Marsden, George, 2, 3, 18, 193, 217, 218
Masons, 24–25,
McClendon, James W., 119
McClintock, John, 38
Mead, Hiram, 22, 56,
means, 4, 5, 6, 55, 57, 60, 64, 65, 85, 88, 89, 93–98, 103, 117, 135, 145–54, 155, 156, 159, 160, 171, 173, 180, 182, 200, 205, 223–26, 232, 233, 234, 242, 245, 246, 247, 248, 250, 252, 253, 254, 255, 256, 257
means of grace, 93, 103, 122, 139, 205, 231
Mesch, Jr., Fred, 43, 46, 48
Methodist Church, 3, 8, 9, 10, 24, 30, 32, 38, 40, 53, 85, 87, 92, 94, 156, 158, 167, 169, 170, 172, 204, 209, 234, 245,
Methodist Episcopal Church, 252

Methodist Episcopal Church, South, 38
Meyer, F. B., 31, 37, 168, 224
millennial prediction, 106, 174
millennium. *See* Christian millennium
Millerites, 244
money, Christian use of, 124–26
Monroe, T. E., 12, 13, 21, 55, 92
moral government, doctrine of, 17, 74, 84–89, 92, 108, 110, 111, 215
moral sanctions, 77, 84, 88, 89, 108, 109, 110, 111, 112, 113, 143
Mount Vernon, Ohio, 12
Moody, Dwight, 13, 24, 30, 31, 42, 159, 178, 206, 209, 217, 223, 224, 225, 226, 247, 255
Moody Bible Institute, 36, 190, 192, 202, 209, 210
Mozart, Wolfgang Amadeus, 126
Murray, Andrew, 163, 164, 224

National Camp Meeting Association for the Promotion of Holiness, 33, 158, 182, 189
natural theology, 20, 75–79
Nazarene University, 48, 210
New Divinity, 85

Oberlin College, 4, 7, 8, 12, 13, 14–19, 20, 21, 22, 23, 25, 26, 27, 28, 29, 30, 31, 32, 33, 34, 35, 39, 47, 52–58, 59, 60, 62, 66, 67, 71, 74, 76, 77, 79, 81, 82, 83, 84, 89, 90, 91, 92, 93, 99, 100, 103, 104, 107, 116, 117, 122, 131, 134, 137, 156, 158, 160, 161, 162, 182, 198, 212, 213, 242, 243
Oberlin Perfectionism, 18, 84, 92, 156, 160
Olivet College Church, 26,

Oklahoma Holiness College/University, 45, 46–48, 209
orders. *See* secret orders
Oskaloosa, Iowa, 40, 41

Palmer, Phoebe, 158, 194, 224, 225
Panic of 1893, the, 28
pan-millennialism, 173
Pasadena College/University, 50–51, 210
Pentecost, 36, 37, 162, 173, 174, 175, 186, 187, 188, 190, 191, 192, 193, 195, 196, 197, 202, 203, 230, 232
Pentecostal Church of Scotland, 42
Pentecostal Church of the Nazarene, 3, 43, 44, 47, 49, 147, 156, 182, 233, 250, 252
Pentecostalism, 46, 182, 201, 226–33, 242, 256, *See also* Tongues Movement
Peter, the apostle, 39, 187, 196, 197
Phipps, Paul T., 216
Pierson, A. T., 30, 31, 159, 205
Plan of Union, the, 7
playing cards. *See* card playing
poor, ministry to, 21, 28, 41, 146, 147, 178, 235, 249
Porter, Noah, 4, 20, 54, 58, 59, 74, 80–82,
power. *See* spiritual power
postmillennialism, 17, 44, 50, 51, 58, 59, 60, 62–67, 71, 82, 98, 102, 103–8, 113, 115, 132, 135, 145, 146, 154, 160, 171, 172, 173, 182, 204, 204–14, 215, 216, 217, 218, 220, 225, 233, 248
prayer, 15, 32, 97, 105, 106, 107, 116, 117, 121, 133, 135, 136, 144–54, 166, 176, 180, 196, 229

premillennialism, 44, 50, 51, 102, 104, 146, 158, 173, 204–14, 217, 218, 120, 233
Presbyterian Church, 7, 53, 220, 245
Presler, L. C., 30
prohibition, 104, 105, 146, 154
Puritans, 7, 245

Quakers, 239
Quanstrom, Mark R., 2, 186, 188
quietism, 87, 94

Ravenna, Ohio, 21, 22–23, 118, 146, 148, 159
Rees, Seth Cook, 50
Reform. *See* anti-slavery reform, sabbath reform, etc
regeneration, 180, 184, 185, 186, 189, 196
Reid, Thomas, 16, 60, 61, 75, 78, 80, 81, 82, 213, 242
Revised Version of the Bible, 237
Robinson, "Uncle" Buddy, 34, 39, 40
Rochester, New York, 7, 53

Sabbath reform, 114
saloons, 105, 128
sanctification, 3, 5, 18, 19, 24, 30, 32, 33, 34, 36, 38, 43, 48, 101, 156–97, 202, 204, 210, 215, 226, 233, 256
sanctions. *See* moral sanctions
Sandeen, Earnest, 214, 216, 217, 220
Schmidt, Jean Miller, 246, 254, 256, 257
Scottish Common Sense Realism, 16, 19, 20, 58, 59, 60, 71, 74–77, 78, 80–82, 94, 176, 179, 201, 218
second blessing, 38, 185, 186, 191
secret orders, 24

self-evident truths. *See also* first truths
Sharpe, George, 42, 46, 49
simil justus et peccator, 89
Simpson, A. B., 177
Shipherd, John J., 26
simplicity of moral action, 84, 89–92, 161, 162, 164, 166
slippery slope, 17, 107, 116–35, 180, 181, 241
Smith, Amanda, 158, 163, 178, 224
Smith, Hannah Whitall, 158
Smith, Judson, 14, 15, 54
Social Gospel Movement, 25, 246, 247, 248, 254
social reform, 17, 23, 102, 104, 115, 116, 124, 154, 205, 206, 208, 217, 223, 225
soteriology, 5, 37, 74, 102, 163, 164, 167, 169, 171, 181, 183, 184, 187, 190, 197, 215
Southwestern Holiness College, 44–45
Spencer, Platt Rogers, 100
Spener, Philipp Jakob, 48
Spirit baptism, 5, 18, 19, 21, 30–33, 36, 37, 38, 100, 112, 157, 159, 167, 168, 170, 171, 172, 173, 174, 175, 179, 181, 182, 183, 185, 186, 187, 188, 189, 190, 191, 192, 193, 194, 195, 196, 197, 201, 202, 203, 223, 224, 225, 226, 227, 229, 231, 232, 250
Springfield, Missouri, 28, 158, 238, 239
"stamp," 8, 9, 12, 15, 92, 93, 198, 199, 252
Star Hall, 41–42, 45–46, 48–49, 147,
stay-inner, 40, 156, 233, 234, 250, 252
Steele, Daniel, 158, 186

stewardship. *See* money, Christian use of, and time, Christian use of
"Suppressionists," 36, 37, 204. *See also* Keswick
Synod of Dort, 235

Tappan, Lewis, 99
Tayler, Nathaniel, 53, 85, 91,
Taylor, William M., 24
Taylor University, 41
temperance, 23, 28, 99, 104, 105, 106, 107, 108, 116, 121, 128, 130, 145, 146, 153, 154,
Tenny, Henry M., 29
Texas Holiness University, 34, 40, 43, 171, 209, 210, 211
theater, 23, 32, 125–26, 134, 180
third blessing of fire "heresy," 35
time, Christian use of, 99, 123, 124, 126
tobacco, 39, 134, 161, 180
Todd, John E., 24
tongues, 45, 46, 226, 227, 228, 229, 230, 231
Tongues Movement, 45, 46, 226–33
Torrey, R. A., 18, 19, 21, 36, 37, 140, 192, 193, 194, 201–4, 205, 209, 210, 213, 214, 215, 216, 223, 224, 225, 226, 227, 231, 232
truths of demonstration, 75, 77, 87, 109
true Christians, 116, 121, 165, 166
"two-party" system in American Protestantism, 246, 253, 254, 255

Unitarianism, 33, 179, 180, 230
unity of moral action. *See* simplicity of moral action,
universal reformer, 99–100, 116, 136, 160

Varley, Henry, 31, 167, 168

Walker, E. F., 50
Warfield, B. B., 84, 92
Warren, Olive, 7
W.C.T.U. *See* Woman's Christian Temperance Union,
Weld, Theodore, 99
Wesley, John, 26, 38, 158, 188, 225, 255
Wesleyan Methodist Church, 169
Whitefield, George, 112, 225, 243
"whole man," 35, 37, 48, 211
Wiley, H. Orton, 50, 220
will, doctrine of the, 58, 59, 67–74, 82
Williams, R. T., 93, 198
Wilmore, Kentucky, 33
Woman's Christian Temperance Union, 22, 104, 105, 107, 121, 146, 153, 154
Wood, J. A., 186
Woodbridge, Mary A., 22, 29, 146, 157

Yale Seminary, 4, 19–21, 22, 24, 32, 34, 52–58, 59, 60, 62, 67, 81, 82, 83, 100, 201, 203, 212, 243, 248

www.ingramcontent.com/pod-product-compliance
Lightning Source LLC
Chambersburg PA
CBHW071244230426
43668CB00011B/1580